STROLLS THROUGH ITALY

Volume 3

Ferdinand Gregorovius

Fides Legals Publishing

CONTENTS

THE ISLAND OF ELBA. (1852).

* * *

I n the summer, the Tuscan state steamer 'Giglio' travels to Elba once a week to transport government dispatches and passengers. The journey from Livorno takes roughly five hours because the ship stops in Piombino for a bit.

Still, the view of the verdant plain that falls to the sea and is limited inland by the mountains around Volterra cheers one along the lonely Maremma coast. A few towers at the landing spots, a few small harbours, a few industrial buildings, and a few farmhouses dispersed here and there disturb the uniform strip of the Maremme, lush with myrtle groves, where there is a rich wild boar hunting in the thicket.

This coast was rich in Etruscan cities, powerful for their culture, from Volterra to Cere and as far as Vejo in the Roman Campagna. One goes via the old Cecina, which still bears the same name and is located near the coast. Further south was the famed Vetulonia, afterwards Populonium, one of the Etruscans' most powerful cities, which ruled over all the neighbouring islands. It was destroyed during the civil war between Marius and Sulla, and by the time of Strabo, all that remained of its splendour was an old tower, a temple, and a few wall fragments. Its ruins can be seen on the point of a little peninsula extending out from the coast, which has been left wild by plum shrubs and heather. Here is a little fortress. The port of Piombino is reached after sailing around the Populonium peninsula.

This small village of barely 1,200 people was originally the estate of the House of Appiani, and in 1805 of Count Felice Baciocchi, Duke of Lucca and Piombino and Elisa Bonaparte's husband. Extinguished by the House of Appiani in 1631, the principality fell to Spain, then to Ugo Buoncompagni-

Ludovisi in 1681, whose descendants reclaimed control in 1815, under Tuscany's rule. The town's tiny alleys, with their yellow dwellings, the regal castle above, and the black walls and a tower exposed to the winds on a wave-beaten rock in the harbour, appear lonely down into the sea. The view from the city is fit for a sovereign; a full archipelago unfolds before the eyes, and exquisite islands appear on the sea's surface: Giglio, Cervoli, Palmarola, Elba, and Corsica. Elba rises its tall mountains precisely opposite and barely half an hour away, with the towered islands of Cervoli and Palmarola in front of it.

The closer we come to Elba, the more majestic its rocks look; there are no villages to be found, except for a small harbour on the left. The cliffs are steep and bleakly majestic. A very ancient grey structure, dubbed by the inhabitants 'Jupiter's Tower,' stands majestically on the summit of a mountain, a marker cherished by the sailor who raises his bow to Napoleon's island. The ship is now approaching a rocky outcropping, which comes as quite a surprise. For the great and beautiful gulf of Porto-Ferraio, a magnificent shallow bay enclosed like an amphitheatre by high mountains, the slopes of which are covered as far as the sea by gardens, groves, villas, farms, chapels among the cypresses, tall aloha plants, and mulberry trees with their verdant shadows, is revealed all at once. To the right, the gulf is bordered by a peninsula with a very small isthmus, which contains the town and port of Porto-Ferraio, the ancient Argo, later La Cosmopoli, the splendid monument of the fortunate Cosimo I, the house of Medici, and Napoleon's prison.

I set foot in the city with the sensation of entering an ideal domain of history. The great, bold lines of the gulf have a joyous feel to them; the city on the peninsula, so beautifully Tuscan, exudes rustic simplicity and out-of-this-world well-being.

The streets are crowded, yet noticeable at a glance; the

little squares and aromatic gardens that line the heights undoubtedly entice you to stay. The entire town is bathed in a light-yellow backdrop colour that contrasts well with the green of the trees and the deep blue of the sea. A good place to stay for ousted rulers who want to write their memoirs.

The turrets and bastions of the three forts, Stella, Falcone, and Castell'Inglese, are also not intimidating. At their feet sits Cosimo de' Medici's circular port, flanked by gorgeous quays. After reading the highly hopeful text, one enters the city through the trumpet, the gorgeous gateway to the centre:

TEMPLA MOENIA DOMOS
ARCES PORTUM COSMUS MED. FLORENTINORUM DIE XII
A FUNDAMENTIS EREXIT A. D. MDXLVIII.

Everything was created here by that lucky Cosimo, temples, houses, walls, castles, and the harbour; he left nothing to Napoleon but castles in the air of a new empire.

The ship comes at the stairs from which he once sailed with his guard for France, a scenario that the imagination immediately recreates; after all, how many times have we not seen this image in the entire world? "Napoleon's embarkation on the island of Elba', as the gaze rises towards the splendid city, looking for the exiled emperor's residence.

"Don't you see the brilliant yellow cottage beneath Fort Stella up there? It appears to be right here on the harbour, where the sentry stands before the sentry box.

"What a Tuileries mansion for a pygmy king! It looks like a garden pavilion'.

That is the Emperor's Palace, which now serves as the Governor's house.

A boat takes us to the quay, where some of the townspeople have gathered to browse; here, there is no hustle and bustle of Livorno, where one is unsure of one's life among the boatmen and porters; here, everything is quiet, humble, and happy. From the door, one enters through a small street, where the fish and herb market is, into the 'piazza d'armi,' a long and narrow square, at the end of which is the town's main church. The most serene Sunday peace reigns here, a truly idyllic disposition and comfort of life. The neat little houses are adorned with flowers, and the few needs of the inhabitants are met by the small shops, the café and the modest hotel 'The Golden Bee', in which I take room with my travelling companions. A modest dining room, a couple of simple and quiet diners, a discreet island wine, a frugal lunch and a loyal and unpretentious hotelier, that's the first impression.

We can't relax until we've climbed to Napoleon's residence, which is located between Forts Stella and Falcone, on the rock, high up, overlooking the gulf from the front and the sea towards Piombino from the back, offering a beautiful view, but surely this view of Italy's beautiful coasts is too exciting.

The building consists of a flat central body with four windows on the façade and two small side wings that are significantly lower; one enters the interior through these as the central building has no door. A wall encloses the small garden, in which Napoleon took his morning and evening walks. Lemon trees, flowers, a couple of marble busts in the greenery, this is all the richness of the imperial garden on Elba, which Napoleon created, adorning it with acacias. It seemed very characteristic to me to find cannons planted there. As the garden belongs to the enclosure of Fort Stella, it also serves as a trench and the cannons were undoubtedly planted among the flowers in Napoleon's time and must have been the Emperor's favourite plants, as they gave him the most agreeable scent of all the roses and orange blossoms. One can therefore imagine the Emperor wandering here in his cannon garden, pausing by a howitzer, making plans and pondering decisions, investigating the sea, where the coast of Italy is embraced by the eye, peering further out over the continent, the stalls of his glory, reminding him of his deeds, reproaching him for his inactivity, and continually ticking at his soul, saying 'Caesar, you sleep'.

But we must confess that the figure of Napoleon on Elba does not impress us very much.

The heroic strength of a single man who fights against the world and stubbornly defies fate is always worthy of admiration, but it leaves one cold when it no longer serves the ideas and moral aims of history, but only his own petty selfishness. History had pushed Napoleon aside; by rebelling from Elba, he appeared as a man who no longer had anything to do in the world and who was relieved to be free; his struggle was as titanic as one man's struggle against the order of the world must have been; he broke it down like a reed being crushed by a moving wheel. Such is the tragic impression of Elba and the Hundred Days.

Napoleon is a radically different image on St Helena, where he conjures a tragic grief, like the hero of a tragedy dying, his soul purged and reconciled by desire.

Strange; in this Tyrrhenian Sea, there is another rocky island, Capri, which will always bear an immortal name in history, for the exile of an emperor; there, an emperor violently exiled on the small island, who yearns to return to world history, seized with unbearable anguish, never satiated with domination and heroic deeds; here, an emperor violently exiled on the small island, who yearns to return to world history, seized with unbearable anguish, never satiated with domination and heroic deeds; here, an emperor, who uncontestedly possesses the world, guiding it with a nod of his eyes, and who, with a half-ironic, half-fearful smile, voluntarily exiles himself to the small rock to live like a hermit.

In truth, Napoleon's exile to the island of Elba was a childish naivety of Europe's greatest politicians in 1814, which one might be tempted to explain as a romantic whim. Therefore, I suddenly received the impression of the unique significance of Napoleon's exile on the island of Elba, when as far as the iron mines of Rio I told myself then that the high diplomacy of 1814 had thought very poetically of exiling the God of battles to this iron island. From its inexhaustible ore deposits, people have been making weapons for more than 20 centuries, and Rome, to whom Porsenna, king of the Etruscans who first forged the ore on Elba, had once dictated that iron should only be used in the future for agricultural tools, then conquered the world with iron from this island.

Could it be believed that the ruler of half of Europe, who was used to playing with royal crowns, could suddenly transform into a retired officer who plants cabbages on an idyllic island, breeds birds, has a couple of grenadiers under his command, like a toy, in memory of times past, and goes hunting on Sundays with his neighbours? Was one thinking of Diocletian, Tiberius, and Charles V? Tired rulers, they lay down their tiara, because it seems heavy to them, after they have had their fill; but even the heaviest crown has never seemed heavy on the head of a man who has snatched it from fortune, as a son of the revolution. Such men can only cease to dominate by being overwhelmed in the struggle, by fate itself. A strange idea, then, to place the Corsican lion on this island, between France and Italy, at the very spot where his passion for domination burned brightest.

However, there is a deeper significance to Napoleon's exile. The fatality that hangs over great men is often cruel irony; it takes it upon itself to repel its victims at the outset and to strike them down afterwards, when they tempt the gods of Fortune for a second time. If Napoleon climbed one of those great mountains of Marciana, from their summit he could see Corsica before him, with its towns, its forests and its mountains, and a thousand places that reminded him of his youth. The sight must have been painful for him. And so he found himself thrown back to the land from which he had come as a young man, as an ignorant son of fortune, with an uncertain yearning for great deeds.

This was unbearable. He had to break the fatal ring, but he could not free himself from the pain of his fate, which did not prevent him from returning to France in the adventurer's garb, in which he had once again crossed the world from Corsica.

When Marshals Macdonald and Ney told Napoleon that he should choose Elba or another place, say Corsica, as his sovereign, he shouted: 'No, no. I want nothing to do with Corsica'. It takes little psychology to read his soul here - the island of Elba! Who knows the island of Elba? Find me an officer who knows Elba! Show me the maps of Elba! Elba it is! And an idea came to him. His sister Elisa of Tuscany was the one who had suggested Elba, because it was very close to Tuscany; and so he went to take possession of this small island: and this was the result of the many battles that had shaken the world.

On 20 April 1814 he took leave of his guards. Forgive me for recalling old and familiar things. It is also good to remember the figure of an extraordinary man, especially in his fall. Such a spectacle elevates the soul to a wiser contemplation of life and its eternal order. When small men fall from the heights of the great, where they are placed not by their own strength but by the weakness of the times, there is a terrible end, not a tragic one. The fall of Napoleon, on the other hand, is perhaps the greatest tragedy in world history.

What did this man say when he took leave of his guard, his instrument of war? His words are a mixture of inaccuracy and truth, of politics and sentimentality! The whole farewell scene is characteristic because it is entirely theatrical. In general, there is always more theatrical pomp and golden stage brocade around the figure of Napoleon than around those of Alexander and Pompey. Be faithful to the new king that France has chosen," he said to the weeping guards, "do not abandon our dear fatherland, which has been unhappy for too long. Do not weep for my fate; I shall always be happy knowing that you are. I could have died, nothing was easier for me; but I want to follow the path of honour without stopping. I must write down what we have done. I cannot embrace you all, but I will embrace your General. Come, General... (he takes General Petit in his arms). Bring me the eagle... (he kisses the eagle). Beloved eagle! May these kisses descend to the hearts of all good men... Farewell, my children... my vows will always follow you... Keep my memory".

On the 27th of April, he arrived in Fréjus, poorly disguised, in order to escape the assassination planned by Provence, by travelling in the opposite direction along the road of his own fortune. The road he had taken triumphantly on his return from Egypt, he now crossed in haste, disguised as a postillion and a footman.

In the harbour, a French and an English ship were waiting. He went with the English one. On May 5, he arrived in Porto Ferraio; seven years later, he would die on the same day on a remote island in the sea, the name of which he had never heard.

It was 6 p.m. on a lovely midday day. Elba's subjects had all gathered on the quay. Poor men in goat's wool coats and Phrygian caps waited for the great monarch, who had conquered the world and given kingdoms and crowns as other sovereigns give rings and decorations, and awaited him as their sovereign, as the prince of Elba. A pastoral dirge was played by a brass band. Napoleon was having a rough night on the ship. How he must have felt trapped in this small chasm surrounded by rocks that seemed to imprison him!

When he arrived on the shore, he was greeted by the French commander Dalesme, who had been in command up until that point. 'General, I have sacrificed my rights to the needs of my country, reserving for myself the possession and sovereignty of the island of Elba; let the inhabitants know that I have chosen their island for my sojourn, tell them that they will always be the object of my liveliest interest,' he had written to him.

Elba, the target of his undivided attention from now on! A single oyster shell in place of the entire globe!

The mayor and elders of Porto-Ferraio presented themselves with the city keys. They were received by the Emperor. It was the same scene he had seen so many times before in Berlin, Vienna, Dresden, Milan, Madrid, and Moscow—only the characters had changed and were now... the town's elders and the mayor of Porto-Ferraio, who is old and stammers.

Napoleon went to stay at the Governor's home, which is the imperial palace with the modest cannon garden and flower gardens I mentioned before. He got right to work on restoring the house. I discovered a lovely dining room as well as 10 or 12 other rooms, small and huge, that are presently occupied by the commander of the city and fortress. Copper paintings portraying scenes from Egypt hang in Napoleon's bedroom, while his work table remains in the study. This was thus the Emperor's Tuileries Palace, a small symbol of his power, and his Court stood in relation to it. Count Bertrand was Grand Marshal of the Palace; Count Cambronne, General of Artillery Drouot, and others comprised the Court, which numbered 35 ranks and was well represented.

In actuality, the holiday on Elba resembled that of a Roman emperor, who foregoes the ceremony of the huge court of the loud capital in favour of seeking air and repose at Anzio or Baia with a few faithful and a few attendants. No, the air of Elba was perhaps more oppressive to Napoleon's senses than the air of St. Helena, where he set foot resignedly.

As a juggler, he was left with 700 men on foot and around 80 men on horseback. One could image that small cottage filled with veterans, almost like castaways washed ashore on an island and camped on the shore. Whoever heard the voices of these rugged men, French, Czechs, Italians, and Poles, heard the most wonderful things and saw visions of half the world pass before him: the pyramids, Russia's awful ice, the Alps, Leipzig, Marengo, the Austerlitz sun, Eylau, and names like Ney, oh, Ney! That saddens-Marmont, Bernadotte-that tears the aged heart of veterans-Murat, the false, the brilliant Murat! What became of Murat? Oh, he's still king over in Italy! One can assist him with a ship that sails for two or three days. "Patience!" exclaims the Italian. -"The Emperor lives!" exclaims the Frenchman. "Still, nothing is lost," the Pole says. - Sometimes exercises are performed; the Emperor has not forgotten his trade. Cannons are fired, but they just rumble in the air, and their song is terrible.

A achievement is to be accomplished. The Emperor of Elba wanted to get to know his new empire right away, so he travelled around the island on horseback with the English ambassador, Niel Campbell. He is supposed to have taken him and a guard of armed men with him because he was afraid he would be assassinated. He was especially apprehensive of the commander of Corsica, Brulart, who had earlier been chief of the Chouans and a friend of George Cadoudal and now commanded in Corsica against Napoleon's wishes. Within a few days, the Emperor had convinced himself that his empire was not large enough; therefore, he devised a plan to create roads, water conduits, and other improvements. He wished to embellish Elba in the same way that Tiberius had beautified Capri. After all, the restless spirit needed to do something with his leisure.

Napoleon, who constructs roads through the rocks on the island of Elba, is a contemplative man, making figures and lines in the sand; he is old Frederick, sitting on the pipe after the lost war, digging ahead of him with his stick.

His eyes was drawn to the Palmarola rock. He dispatched forty guards to take that small island, to which no one objected because it was uninhabited. The old guards built a tower, and thus the kingdom grew.

Napoleon also captured Pianosa, a little desolate island where Augustus had exiled his nephew Agrippa Postumius, who was murdered shortly thereafter by Tiberius. A fort guarded the island's perimeter. Perhaps he was influenced by that ancient imperial name, or by the fate of Agrippa, which was, unhappily, so close to his own.

He constructed warehouses, docks, horse stables, a water conduit, a lazaret, and the same tiny theatre at Porto-Ferraio where he had his stage as he did in Paris. He built a villa in the countryside for himself. A road he created on the right side of the gulf goes to this Elba Versailles. There he went or rode with delight, often conversing to peasants he met on the route, pushing their fruit-laden donkeys in front of him.

The valley where Villa S. Martino is located and where Scipione Nasica is reputed to have once had a palace is breathtaking. It is nestled in the midst of the gorgeous mountains that rise up on the side of Corsica. A stream meanders through the lush bottom, rich flora on both sides, many cottages scattered in the green, and a blessed profusion of vines filled with grapes as far as the eye can see, as if one were in the happy countryside of Naples. He who is content in his heart can undoubtedly live happily there. Roses blossom all year; the atmosphere is moderate and the air aromatic; and on the side of the valley that opens up to Portoferraio, the gulf and sea gleam brilliantly.

Prince Demidoff presently owns the villa. It was turned into a Napoleonic museum by this Russian Croesus. It became spectacular, with porticoes with marble columns and captivating apartments where the Emperor's splendours were portrayed in murals on the walls. Napoleon, who had planted orange trees on the villa's terrace, was satisfied to have the dining room painted in Egyptian style; it appears that the memory of Egypt was the most cherished of his life, representing to him the epic and romantic poetry of his youth. Demidoff has now gathered all available artefacts from Napoleonic history and will display them in the chambers of St. Martin's. A still living Napoleonic relic, in whose possession the prince has been, he will not be allowed to exhibit in this villa because, according to legend, he would not have preserved it well; I refer to his first wife, Matilda Bonaparte, daughter of the former king Jerome, a Westphalia relic.

The villa employees told me that once the relics are all in place, the prince would have a steamer come every Friday from Livorno to Portoferraio at his own expense to carry all visitors who want to appreciate the magnificent artefacts. No one is to enter for the time being, and this is stated on a board. As a result, I was unable to enter the villa.

When I returned to Portoferraio, the beautiful moonlight consoled me and told me many things. In the moonlight, one can better view ruins and reflect on memories of many kinds; the allure of an uncertain light goes so well with all that is temporary and fleeting!

Is it possible to adore Napoleon? Can a human spirit be moved to tears a thousand years from now in any of the theatres of his deeds? I have my doubts; I do not believe it.
Timoleon is a beautiful historical name that sounds partly like Napoleon's name. When I thought of him again when touring

the theatre in Syracuse, the remembrance of this ancient man struck me greatly. How terrified Napoleon would have been in the presence of this Greek, who, like the tyrant Dionysius, would have banished him to Corinth, scorning him brutally. Other times, different grandeur; in his youth, Napoleon was enthralled by Plutarch's heroes; when he became emperor, he vehemently disputed Tacitus and wrote a panegyric to Tiberius.

He has been compared to Prometheus in chains so many times that the image is tired; nonetheless, it fits this banished hero so perfectly that he was able to break the chains of Elba until force and brutality forced him back in diamond shackles to the rock of St. Helena. What titans' struggles followed! Blücher and Wellington had to overcome this talent, which had been unleashed as force and brutality on the demigod. The hussar general Blücher was used by fate to bring down Napoleon, or to put it another way, to beat him, for what could a good man like Blücher have done except beat him strenuously? This is a scathing mocking. Nature thus employs the most powerful powers when forming or developing something, and the most humble when accomplishing or destroying.

Weeks in Elba may have seemed like years to Napoleon. He frequently complains to Campbell that his wife and child have been snatched away from him, denying him a favour afforded to even the most miserable of human exiles.

During the summer, his mother visited. Letizia Ramolino's journey to find her son! His mother's foolish heart had also fallen from the heights of prosperity, but it had not broken; Josephine's more noble heart broke at Malmaison, 30 days after Napoleon's first collapse. Even her sister, Pauline Borghese, once the new Helena of the world, the lovely etéra at whose feet crowned sovereigns laid, was forgotten in the solitude of Elba.

Many people arrived and mysteriously left. The seven ports on the island had never been busier. 900 Italians and 600 Englishmen came to meet the guy from Elba during the nine months, including numerous officers in Italian, French, and English uniforms, now from Marseilles, now from Corsica, now from Genoa and Livorno, now from Naples, Civitavecchia, and Piombino. Napoleon entertained himself joyfully and wittily with all of them, and they all informed him of events in his nation and on the continent.

A foreign lady with a child visited Portoferraio one day. The emperor received her privately and lodged her in the country; but after a few days, she mysteriously returned to Italy with the kid. Many rumours flew, and only a few people knew who the stranger was; she had not been able to avoid the stare of curiosity. One may readily envision Napoleon on Elba finding himself in the position of an interesting guy, staying in a tiny provincial town, being watched by all eyes and discussed in all tongues. That foreign lady was a Polish countess, Napoleon's daughter, the result of an hour's pleasure in chilly Poland. I don't know what happened to the child after that, but I believe I can say that in December 1852, this child appeared before Queen Victoria of England as France's official ambassador, to inform her that the surface of the world, despite Elba and St Helena, had become Bonapartist again, as 8 million Frenchmen had enthusiastically elected Louis Bonaparte, the only surviving son of the former King of Holland, Emperor of France.

It's all a dream. Like an individual, the history of the world has its dreams of old lovers and old occurrences. It dreamed of Napoleon in the year 1852.

Meanwhile, the Emperor was being chastised by aunts and comrades, as they say. It was widely reported throughout Italy that a certain Miss Vantini had won his heart, that he had received her at romantic hours, both in the villa and in his palace, and that she was already carrying a second little Napoleon in her womb, which she proudly boasted about. This young lady was the daughter of an Elba landowner, a former mayor of Portoferraio; he, on the other hand, was the brother-in-law of a Mr Cornelio Filippi from Livorno. This Mr. Filippi's sister, on the other hand, was a true Messalina, the professed lover of the Englishman Grant, a Livorno merchant, and Grant, in turn, was an ardent adversary of Napoleon and manutengolo of the spy Giunti, and so on. Even in Elba, there was a history of scandals.

However, funds were quickly running out. Napoleon's annual salary was only 400,000 lire. Despite its agreement, France did not pay the annual income of 2,500,000 lire stipulated under the Fontainebleau Agreement. The Emperor complained, and Lord Castlereagh interceded for him; but the French government delayed and did not pay, perhaps because the exile intended to use his money for a coup d'état; at most, a raid on Italy was expected; but the possibility of a landing in France did not occur to anyone.

Here on Elba, close to France and Italy, the two countries had to propose themselves as viable repair sites to the fallen emperor's imagination. How indecisive he must have walked in this garden, in this study, and in that villa, his hands crossed on his back, weighing the scales of choice, here France and there Italy, here the renewal of a known path, the restoration of a kingdom that had belonged to him, there a new path, an entirely new monarchy to be established.

Allow us to pause for a time, because this is a perplexing point in Napoleon's history, a point of tremendous seduction, when one wants to build a criterion, like all the possible outcomes of a great character. While Napoleon was on Elba, it is supposed that the apparition of an incalculable future flashed over Italy for a split second.

What would have happened if this man had abruptly abandoned his desire for France, if he, an Italian, had appeared in Italy in a new guise, that is to say, as the orderer and unifier of these beautiful countries, in the world city of Rome, on Capitol Hill, as the Roman emperor of the Latin peninsula?

There is no doubt that such a group was considered, but it is impossible to say how far Napoleon's relations with the agents of the Italic Union, who had their headquarters in Turin, progressed, despite what has been uncovered. That concept of a constitutional empire in Rome, to be led by Napoleon, seems as amazing today as it did in 1814. Napoleon was to be Roman Emperor, the monarchs of Sardinia and Naples were to be compensated financially, and the major towns, such as Milan, Venice, Florence, and Naples, were to be elevated to vice-rulers in order to placate their patriotism and become seats of the national parliament. The Pope was considered a ghost to be extinguished. This was the Italian plan, and a war could be enough to carry it out. Murat, who was still King of Naples at the time, could have been involved in a war with France; if Napoleon had emerged at the point of conflict, he would definitely have beaten the two armies and completed the unification of Italy, forcing the Bourbons of France to recognise him.

But enough of these fantasies. When Napoleon lent his ear to them, he kept Italy on edge, and his landing on the peninsula would have shook everything. If France had offered him no prospects, he would have surely headed to Italy; nevertheless, what his agents in Italy informed him of clearly demonstrated that he only needed to land to see the Bourbon restoration melt away like mist.

Meanwhile, in the castle on the island, people lived simply and carefree; Pauline, the soul of society, threw the occasional party. However, in order to save money, the house train was curtailed, a few construction projects were halted, and even an artillery park was sold. The emperor was completely inundated with papers, newspapers, and reports. His modest study looked exactly like the one in the Tuileries; the guy was still Napoleon, ruminating in the back of his mind about huge schemes, battle plans, and ideas that would shock the world.

So he stood in the small chamber of his house in Portoferraio, on the roof of which flew the humble banner of Elba, white and amaranth with imperial bees, while high diplomacy convened in Vienna. All of Europe's powers are gathered around the green table, moving a thousand pens and tongues; the entire world is a protocol and a field of diplomatic strife, all for the sake of the little guy from Elba. He is silent and forgotten, alone in the cavern like a magician conjuring up unseen spirits, sending them out and receiving them back; those engulfed in the clamour of victory celebrations and disputes. So the months went by. Suddenly, the little iron man in Elba rose from his seat: the Congress had ended, the princes and diplomats had been divided, and the world had become a roaring war zone once more.

Napoleon was kept aware of all that was going on in France and Vienna; in the start of 1815, discontent threatened to bring the allies to war with each other. Austria, France, and England agreed to a secret treaty against Russia and Prussia. France also asked that the Bourbons be restored in Naples. Murat's kingdom was shaky, so he naturally presented himself as an ally to Napoleon in his campaign for Italian unity, at the head of which he was to be placed.

Napoleon had already heard the horrible news about St Helena. His soul was kidnapped by the party. He became increasingly reclusive, and he avoided conversing with Campbell. He only saw him on rare occasions, when the Englishman returned from Livorno, where he occasionally went. A French warship then cruised about the island spying on Napoleon, who was rumoured to be preparing a landing in Italy; instead,

Campbell's English corvette sailed continuously up and down between Elba, Genoa, Civitavecchia, and Livorno. As ruler of the island, Napoleon owned warships, i.e. four bastions; they frequently sailed, manoeuvring on the sea, under the new banner of Elba, which was also respected by the barbarians; they frequently delivered gifts to the captains of the Elban bastions, claiming to be paying the Moscow debt. The Emperor sent the ships out regularly to conceal his intentions, and he kept them so well hidden that only Bertrand and Drouot were privy to the secret and knew it only 24 hours before departure. Nothing was conveyed to the women; in adjacent Corsica, only Colonna, Paoli's buddy and Napoleon's confidante, was aware.

Napoleon's decision to depart, to emerge from that dreary loneliness, to fight new wars like giants, must have been a horrible shock to his psyche, similar to Caesar's when he crossed the Rubicon. It was certainly one of those frantic stretches that, depending on the outcome, qualify as either daringly courageous and magnificent, or silly and risky. Such scenes, in which a resolute man goes to meet his fate with a lost body, captivate our attention, and if the accomplishment is successful, the daring itself appears to double the hero's greatness. Napoleon, like Fernando Cortez, looks to us, and in truth, he went to the conquest of France and the struggle against the forces of the European nations with a few more troops than the daring great Spaniard had when it came to taming the Indian savages. Certainly, two of his main armies were already in France: the allure of his name and the hatred for the Restoration.

It was a Saturday, February 26th; Pauline was giving a ball; the guards and other troops, 800 men, were marching in marching gear on the Piazza d'Arme; seven ships were ready for departure into port; the Emperor appeared restless; the little man was pacing up and down, at the window, looking out at the sky and the gulf, which was moving with the bellowing waves. The order to embark was finally given to the guards! It is Alea jacta.

Napoleon went off the dock and boarded the boat about eight o'clock in the evening.

'The sad, eternal law of fate disposes for all things, that when they have reached their pinnacle, they fall back to the bottom sooner than they have risen,' a voice calls out behind the powerful man as he takes to the sea for the second time to tempt the gods. Seneca, the ancient bird of misfortune, has a special right to throw this maxim after Napoleon, because he saw the great ones of the earth, the Emperor Tiberius, the Emperor Caligula, the Emperor Claudius, and Caesar Germanicus, come to a terrible end, because he was in exile for eight years in Corsica and studied wisdom and knew nature by deep experience, and so he could foretell the end of things Napoleonic as well. Napoleon sailed away, unnoticed by the English corvette stationed in Livorno. The sea was choppy. It was hoped that they would have passed Capraja before sunrise, but the wind died and by daylight they were still within sight of the island; it wasn't until around 4 o'clock in the evening that they arrived in Livorno and saw two frigates and then a French warship, the Zephir, approaching them. The crews wanted to board the ship, but Napoleon told them to stay below deck. When the Zephir asked what was new on Elba, Napoleon responded with a trumpet, "The Emperor is perfectly well." As a result, he pleasantly avoided danger.

He had already written two proclamations to the French army and people before embarking, but because they could not be interpreted, he threw them overboard and dictated two more. All those who could write created copies; on board, one could see those who wrote on the trumpets, the grenadiers' colbacs, and the counters. It was a strange sight that transpired on the Inconstant, which was Napoleon's ship and fortune.

Here are the two declarations.

On March 1, 1815, from the Gulf of San Juan.

Napoleon, by the grace of God and the constitution of the Empire, Emperor of France.

DIRECTIVES TO THE ARMY:
"Soldiers! We were not defeated. Men in our midst have betrayed our honour, their nation, their prince, and their benefactor. Will those who have been seen travelling over Europe for the past 25 years, stirring up our adversaries, who have spent their life fighting against us in enemy ranks, cursing our lovely France, be able to boast of chaining and conquering our eagles, they who could never sustain their gaze? Will we put up with them reaping the products of our wonderful labours, seizing our honour and possessions? That they deny our celebrity? If their tyranny remained, everything would be lost, including the memory of our memorable fights. What rage they displayed in disfiguring them and attempting to poison that which had astounded the world! And if any defenders of our glory survive, they are among the very adversaries we fought on the battlefields. Soldiers! I heard your voice in my exile, and now I'm here, having surmounted all hurdles and dangers.

"Your General, elected to the throne by the people and elevated on your shields, is restored to you. Come and join him. Tear up the colours that the nation has forbidden and that have gathered all of France's enemies for the past twenty-five years. Raise the tricolour cockade you wore during our glory days. We must forget that we were the masters of the peoples, but we must not allow anyone to interfere with our activities. Who could claim to be our ruler? Who would wield power? Return the eagles that you took to Ulm, Austerlitz, Jena, Eylau, Wagram, Friedland, Tudela, Eekmühl, Essling, Smolensk, Moskva, Lützen, Wurschen, and Montmirail. Do you believe that this little bunch of haughty Frenchmen can stand the sight of them? They will return to where they came from, where they will govern for the next nineteen years if they so desire.

"Your goods, rank, and glory, as well as the riches, rank, and glory of your children, have no stronger opponents than these foreign-imposed ideas. They are your adversaries, since the remembrance of so many great deeds that honoured the French people when they fought against them to escape their oppression is their own condemnation.

"Veterans of the armies of the Sambre and Meuse, the Rhine, Italy, Egypt, the East, and the Grand Army are humiliated; their honoured scars are mocked; their achievements would be crimes, and the valiant would be rebels if, as opponents of the people claim, legitimate sovereigns were among the enemy armies.

"Those who have served them against their country and against us deserve the honours and accolades.

"Soldiers! Come, form a line beneath your leader's flags; his life is yours; his rights are those of the people and yours; his interest, honour, and glory are your interest, honour, and glory. Victory will march to the charge, and the eagle will fly from tower to tower to the towers of Notre-Dame. Then you will be able to proudly display your scars; then you will be able to brag about what you have accomplished, and you will be the liberators of your homeland.

"In your old age, surrounded by your fellow citizens who will listen intently, you will tell them of your great deeds; you will be able to say with pride: I, too, was part of that great Army that entered twice into the walls of Vienna, Poma, Berlin, Madrid, and Moscow, that liberated Paris from the infamy that treachery and the presence of the enemy had imprinted on it." Honor to these valiant men, and honour to the fatherland! ...

eternal humiliation to the guilty French, in whatever state fortune may have placed them, who fought for twenty-five years to rend the fatherland's heart apart.

signed: Napoleon'.

To the French People.

"Frenchmen! The capitulation of the Duke of Castiglione handed Lyon over to our enemies without any attempt at defence. The army, the command of which I had entrusted to him, was in a position to beat the Austrian army corps opposed to him, due to the number of its battalions and the heroism and love of country of the troops that composed it, thus passing behind the left flank of the enemy army that threatened Paris."

The victories of Champ-Aubert, of Montmirail, of Château Tierry, of Bauchamps, of Monterom, of Craonne, of Rheims, of Arcis-sur-Aube and of Saint-Dizier, the uprising of the good peasants in Lorraine, in Champagne, in Alsace in Franche-Comté and Burgundy, and the position I occupied behind the enemy armies, so as to cut off their stores, reserve parks, communications and thus take away everything they needed, had placed them in a desperate condition. The French had never been on the verge of being more powerful, and the finest part of the enemy armies was irretrievably lost; it had found its burial in those deserted regions, which it had so cruelly stripped, when the betrayal of the Duke of Ragusa handed over the capital to the enemies and produced the dissolution of the army.

"The unforeseen behaviour of these two generals, who betrayed their country, their prince and their benefactor all at once, changed the fortunes of the war; the enemy's condition was such that, at the end of the combat that took place in front of Paris, they were out of ammunition, having been separated from their reserve fleet.

"In these sudden and grave circumstances my heart was torn, but my soul remained unshaken; I then took counsel only from the good of my country; I relegated myself to my rocks in the middle of the sea; but my life was and should still be useful to you. I did not allow the large number of citizens who wanted to accompany me, to share my fate; I thought their presence was useful in France; I led with me only a small handful of brave men, necessary for my defence.

"Elevated to the throne by your election, everything outside of you is illegal. For the past 25 years, France has had new interests, new institutions and a new glory, which can only be guaranteed by a national government and a dynasty, born under these circumstances. A prince who would reign over you, who would be placed on my throne by the force of those weapons that have devastated our country, would rely in vain on the principles of feudal law; he would only guarantee the privileges of a small number of individuals, enemies of the people, who for 25 years have always condemned them in all our national assemblies. Your peace at home and your prestige abroad would be lost forever.

"Frenchmen! In my exile I have heard your laments and your desires; you have claimed this government at your vows, which alone is legitimate; you have blamed my long inertia and proposed to sacrifice my peace for the good of the fatherland.

"I have crossed the seas amid dangers of all kinds. I am here to take back among you my rights, which are also yours. I will disregard everything that has been done, written or said by some since the occupation of Paris; this will have no bearing on the relevant services they rendered for the time being, for it is events of this nature that are to be found in human organisation.

"Frenchmen! There is no nation that, however small, would

not have had the right to escape the shame of obeying a prince who was imposed by a momentarily victorious enemy. When Charles VII returned to Paris and overthrew the ephemeral throne of Henry VI, he recognised that he was in possession of the throne through the valour of his valiant troops and not through the prince-regent of England.

"Thus I also acknowledge and will acknowledge to you alone and to the valiant men of the army their due honour.

Signed: Napoleon'.

These are the declarations he issued from the Elbe Sea. For the last time, the military spirit of those times, when the people became an army and the sovereign, a general, confronts us in its barbarity through these records. Who can read these expressions of military glory and fighting of the heroic of the army and always and eternally of the army without being irritated?

The fleet of seven transports arrived in the Gulf of San Juan at 3 p.m. on March 1st, and Napoleon set foot on French territory at 5 p.m. The fleet took refuge in an olive orchard.

How Napoleon resembled his Côrsa homeland's romantic heroes here. For, although adopting an adventurer's demeanour, he was fundamentally côrso. In the same way, the most renowned warriors of his motherland attempted to reclaim it from exile.

In 1408, Vincentello d'Istria landed on that island with a couple of Spaniards and Côrsi to take it from the Genoese. He was captured and beheaded after a magnificent battle.

Giampaolo led an assault into Corsica in 1490, with four Corsicans and six Spaniards serving as his army. He perished in exile after a gallant war.

Renuccio della Rocca emerged from his exile in Corsica three times, the first with 18 men, the second with 20, and the third with eight friends. Each time, he fearlessly invaded the country, issuing exile edicts and proclamations while banking on the backing of his friends. After several spectacular engagements, he was murdered in the Alps in 1511.

Sampiero, the most heroic of the Côrsians, landed in his country with 37 Côrsians and Frenchmen in 1564. He was murdered in the mountains in 1567, following a heroic battle with Genoese armies.

The Côrsian Napoleon Bonaparte went to fight against France and the royal army with 500 French guards, 200 Côrsian hunters, and 100 Polish lancers who had no horses but carried saddles themselves. He was demoted to the island of St Helena after a magnificent battle.

Joachim Murat landed from Corsica to Naples in October 1815 with a handful of Corsicans to seize a kingdom. After his courageous landing, he was shot.

The Corsican Louis Bonaparte landed in Strasbourg with a couple of troops to conquer a nation of 35 million people. After his failed attempt, he surprised France once more in Boulogne. History owes it to recognise these certainly daring expeditions as historical precedents for a man who went on to become Emperor of France not long after. As a result, no one should be deemed joyful before his or her death.

Things will fall soon, warns old Seneca. Swift was Napoleon's flight across Waterloo from the Gulf of St. Juan to St. Helena. He was at Cérénon on the 2nd of March, Barême on the 3rd, Digne on the 4th, Gap on the 5th, Lyon on the 7th, Chalons on the 14th, and Paris on the 20th at 9 p.m. On June 1, he was already politically beaten. He was killed at Waterloo on June 18th. On the 21st of June, he returned to Paris, and on the 22nd, he said, "Ma vie political est terminée, et je proclame mon fils sous le titre de Napoléon II empereur des Français!"

He boarded the Bellerophon on July 15 and the

Northumberland on August 7. He arrived at St Helena on October 16.

Afterwards - and this is the last picture of the story of that wonderful year, he lay on the distant African rock, on his deathbed, pale and mute, clothed in the turquoise mantle of Marengo, with the marble bust of his son, the King of Rome, at his feet; his close friends Bertrand and Antommarchi, as well as his attendants, were on their knees, weeping. At that same moment, the sun sinks into the water. The priest who performed the Emperor's dying rituals lifts his arms and declares: Sic transit gloria mundi!

At St. Helena, Napoleon reviewed his works and who he was, and wrote as a colossal epigraph, "I have closed the abyss of anarchy, ordered chaos; I have quieted revolution, ennobled peoples, and moderated monarchs." I have promoted every competition, rewarded every merit, and expanded the boundaries of glory. All of this was still something.- So, from where could one attack me if the historian couldn't defend me? Maybe in my intentions? He can undoubtedly clear me of the charge in this regard. My tyranny? However, it will be accepted that dictatorship was required. Will he say I was an impediment to his freedom? He will demonstrate that the gates were still guarded by arbitrariness, chaos, and the utmost disarray. Will I be chastised for my excessive enthusiasm for war? He will demonstrate that I was always attached. That I desired global monarchy? He will demonstrate that it was merely a random collection of circumstances, as well as our opponents, that led me to it step by step. Finally, will he accuse me of being ambitious? Yes, much of this will be found in me, but the highest and most beautiful impulse that a man has possibly ever had is that of finally regulating and inaugurating the empire of reason, the exercise and total pleasure of all human capacities (ingenuity). And the historian may be bound to lament the fact that such an aim was not realised and fulfilled'.

This was Napoleon's perspective on his own mission on St. Helena. And thus, like every other messiah before him, he was tasked by history with carrying the world like an atlas for a while and renewing Hercules' labours for the sake of progress. And even if we despise human nature because it is transformed more by Napoleon's soldierly despotism than by Solon's and Timoleon's civil laws; if we openly accuse this great man of having forgotten his mission and of dying because of his selfishness and thirst for domination, we remain full of awe and reverence before his figure, and we glorify the great impetus that came from him to the life of peoples and to general progress.

As a result, I've given the Emperor what is rightfully his, and I'd want to offer the people of Elba what is rightfully theirs. They are a peaceful population of 20,000, with entirely Tuscan habits and language and no national traits. The island is too small (a little more than 7 square miles in size) and too close to the mainland to have developed its own popular spirit. There is no evidence of Côrsian customs on this island so near to Corsica, and there have only been occurrences of vengeance in ancient times; there is no evidence of them today. The Corsican bandit only seeks sanctuary in Elba when he is desperate and cannot stay. Hospitality is a feature shared by both islanders.

Portoferraio (the iron port), the Longone fortress and marina, Marciana with the marina, Poggio, Campo, Capoliveri, Pila, Sampiero, Rio with the marina, and Sant'Ilario are the towns on Elba.

Because the villages are made of natural stone, they have a dark and dismal aspect, similar to those in Corsica. Because of the barbarians, they too stand on high ground and are fortified with towers. Marinas have been formed where there is a near proximity to the water. The countryside in the valley that spans from the mountains of Marciana, to the right of the huge gulf, to Porto Longone is very fruitful and beautiful: it crosses the island for the majority of its length and provides a spectacular contrast to the untamed majesty of the mountains. These reach their peak above Marciana, with Cavanna reaching as high as Vesuvius. The island dips down towards the Italian coast. Elba appears as a single rocky mountain with a magnificent double pyramid shape from the Corsican shore, because it is the rocks of Marciana that face Corsica; from the Italian coast, however, one can see the lower part stretching towards Piombino, where the island's greatest treasures are to be found: iron and fruit.

Marciana's mountains are abundant in granite and marble, as well as alabaster, crystal, and other stones. Marciana has the best chestnuts; olives are scarce and of poor quality, and wood is scarce elsewhere. Lemons grow everywhere, but Campo lemons are especially prized. Wine is also abundant; the best is made in Capoliveri, where an aleatico rivals that of Tuscany. Maize grows abundantly in the huge valley. Thus, nothing is lacking for the inhabitants to live in this appealing and mild land, because the earth has also provided them with infinite quantities of iron from Rio, as well as salt and seafood from the sea. Sardines and tuna, which are abundant around Portoferraio, were previously caught by the Etruscans and Romans. Fish and iron were available to all the peoples that greedily roamed the waters of Elba in antiquity, particularly the Côrsians, Phoenicians, Carthaginians, Tyrrhenians, and Romans. In antiquity, the island was known as Aethalia, then Iloa, and finally Ilva in the Middle Ages, from which the modern-day Elba derives.

A decent carriage route connects Portoferraio to Longone via the valley above Capoliveri, then across the island to the opposite side of the sea. It travels around the gulf to S. Giovanni, a little fishing village from whence boats depart for

Portoferraio. We boarded one of these boats and sailed across the gulf to S. Giovanni at the speed of an arrow. There, we ascended a rise littered with the ruins of Roman structures before descending into the valley on the other side of the gulf.

On the marina, there is a villa owned by a Demidoff employee; I don't recall seeing a more peaceful location elsewhere. The charming small house is surrounded by a flower garden and orange trees, in the midst of vineyard hills, and looks out over the magnificent gulf and Portoferraio, which lies in front of it and has a wonderfully seductive image from here. Going down into the valley is like going through a garden, in a rich and pleasant countryside where you would gladly stay. There are verdant plains, green mountains, floral forests, and the shimmering sea here and there.

A downpour compelled us to seek cover in a peasant cottage in the heart of the Capoliveri valley. Many peasants, both men and women, were busy preparing figs to be dried. They offered us bread, grapes, and new wine, and because we didn't like must, an elderly gentleman went to get a large earthenware container and poured us red wine from it; it was a wonderful local Aleatico.

We resumed our voyage to Porto Longone in glorious sunshine (it was September) and arrived at this small harbour at midday. Elba's second town is located in a narrow bay surrounded by steep rocks, from which the stronghold rises impressively. There are a handful of streets on the shore that the waves pass through, reaching as far as the houses. A tremendous silence and abandon reigns here; a few ships softly rock on the water; sailors and fishermen repair capsized boats while singing a monotonous melody. Flower pots adorn the windows and balconies everywhere; further on, little buildings, like those on the island of Procida, are lost among the luxuriant gardens. Porto Longone's soil is more southerly than Portoferraio's. There, the aloè grows in beauty and plenty, as an entire avenue of aloè plants leads over a rise to the port of Longone on both sides of the carriage road. Their floral plants were in full bloom, resembling gigantic candelabra. I had never seen so many aloes together before, not even in the southernmost areas of Corsica; such a sight I had only seen in Sicily, where a row of these plants, arbitrarily organised by nature, led to the shrine of Segesta. Palm trees can also be found here.

The stronghold of Longone, which can be accessed by descending a modest route, is located on a massive granite plateau and appears very old, with its walls and crenellated turrets. It was built by the Spanish during the reigns of Philip IV and V. This little Elba was divided under three distinct dominions at the same time; then, while the island belonged to the Prince of Piombino, he ceded Portoferraio to Cosimo in 1537; the King of the Two Sicilies, on the other hand, owned Porto Longone. Then, in 1736, all of Elba, including Piombino, passed to the Kingdom of Naples, and then to the Kingdom of Etruria in 1801, before being amalgamated to France in 1805.

The Spaniards resided in Porto Longone for a long time, thus their memory lives on, and the 'Don' is still used in the apostrophy.

Because of its location, the stronghold is undoubtedly resistant. It encircles the city proper, a desolate scene of devastation and neglect. Napoleon ordered the destruction of a substantial portion of the works in 1815. When the French fought the Spanish here during the reign of Louis XIV, the fortification had to withstand many attacks. An officer of the Tuscan garrison, whose family we spent a pleasant day with, showed us what was noteworthy.

He was the director of the punishment firm, from which he recruited repentant soldiers for a military school. We met a small group of Tuscan veterans at the fort, some of them had known Germany since Napoleonic times and talked about the beauty of its regions as well as the neatness of its dwellings.

Everything our host showed us, from his company's interior architecture and organisation to its administration and penal code, was a true model of military address; everything had its rule and every object its allocated position, even the iron of the feet and the fatal nerve.

Napoleon also had a so-called palace in Longone, a little cottage into which he dropped whenever he rode his horse from his capital. The vicinity of this fortress suited him perfectly. As Valery describes Elba, he used to eat outside, under the mountain, on a seat carved out of the rock (called a canapé) where he had planted mulberry trees in a semicircle. With a telescope, he saw passing ships and the Italian shores.

Fort Fucardo is located opposite the Gulf of Longone and has a lighthouse for ships entering the harbour. It is surrounded by magnificent coasts and the steepest mountains on the landward side, which in certain rocks are reminiscent of Capri, but without the southern warmth in the tone of the colours. The hermitage of Monserrato, founded by the Spanish, is located amid these lovely and deserted areas, near to the road that leads to Rio's mines.

To go to Rio, we had to cross the rocks with our host. The route winds through desolate areas, across plains, and past springs. One of these springs is named after the corsair who raided and sacked Porto Longone in 1544, not the German ruler. His name lives on on several Mediterranean islands, perhaps on all of them, as there isn't one that hasn't been visited by this most daring of all pirates.

As we descended to Rio, we travelled through various plains and rugged hills, always encouraged by new vistas of cliffs, valleys, and the sea. A stream flows down from the heights and into the bay. Rio de Janeiro was derived from it. It is reported that this stream, the fastest on Elba, does not start on the island, but rather comes from Corsica, where it would then proceed through underground systems beneath the sea until it returned to the Rio. The leaves and branches of the chestnut trees carried by the stream would clearly reveal its Corsican provenance. Regardless, this new Arethusa appears to be poetically tied to Napoleon's fate.

Another factor ties Rio's mines with Corsica. Pietro Cireneo, a well-known Côrsian writer whose eventful existence as a fugitive is analogous to a novel, fled from his stepfather here in the 15th century.

The red ground we walked on told us that we were on iron-rich soil; everywhere there was nothing but this iron dust; the surrounding hills, dark and reddish, covered with uncountable aloè bushes, whose stiff, steel-blue leaves, ending in thorny points, looked like a swarm of daggers and swords. Everything we encountered had this iron colour, including the workers in Rio who were dyed red in their clothes, faces, and hands, as well as the canines who approached us. The port to which we descended was red with iron powder; mountains of ore sat on the sand, ready to be loaded aboard ships.

We went in search of the construction manager. He was German, which I discovered with delight. Only the German is a true miner; he alone is capable of delving into the well of life and seeing into nature's dark recesses for its innermost character. Here, he digs incessantly until he finds pure ore, and he has forgotten about the spring outside. He sometimes sleeps in the depths, like Epimenides, or Emperor Barbarossa in the Kyfthäuser, that old German miner with the golden crown and the long beard grown across the table, or Tannhäuser in the Venusberg (Mount of Venus).

Mr Ulrich, a martial man and a good German, came to greet us; his handshake was solid as well, his speech was brief and firm, and his voice was exceptionally powerful. He welcomed us as his countrymen, escorted us to the works, and explained their layout. The Elbe iron mines, which are run independently by a Tuscan firm, had recently fallen under his control. He received them in deplorable condition, but within a few months he had improved them so much that yearly production can now be computed at 35,000 tonnes, whereas they previously produced just 22,000 tonnes. 120,000 pounds of iron are mined daily, although the activity slows in the summer since the fields require labourers, the majority of whom are Rio residents. Work moves considerably more quickly in the winter.

The Rio mine has been worked since ancient times, and it still produces a lot today; it is a 500-foot-high mountain made entirely of iron stuff. There are several other rich resources nearby, including Terra Nera, Rio Albano, and Calamita, a real magnetic mountain. Already, the Etruscans utilised these quarries, transporting the material to Populonium, the island's ruler, and extracting the iron there. The lack of wood prohibited Elba from smelting, and iron is still smelted in factories near ancient Populonium, or it is exported to Naples, Genoa, Marseilles, and Bastia.

Mr Ulrich demonstrated how much money the ancients and their descendants had squandered on these deposits. The ore deposits were covered by entire hills of unusable ferruginous earth. This waste earth, on the other hand, is so rich in substance that it still produces wonderful stuff. Mr Ulrich took a handful of soil from where we were standing, showed it to us, and remarked, "Observe, the earth that I take here at the surface still yields better iron than that acquired by the French in the Auvergne, where digging is much more difficult." The ore is really above ground here, and you can stand and walk on it for kilometres. Rio's mines are wealthier than those owned by the Demidoff in Siberia, and no other mines can possibly compare.

The activities are still limited to the surface, and the subterranean works consist of only two tunnels; despite this, the most spectacular ore resources have been discovered. Anyone who expected to discover shafts of galleries and quarries with all the romantic accessories of miners in Rio, as I did before witnessing this magnificent mountain of iron, would be severely mistaken.

I looked about; there was melancholy everywhere, and the works themselves, these red and black hills, the iron-colored ground, and the sparkling iron powder, created the effect of a desert, similar to the lava and ash fields of a volcano. A crenellated tower loomed over the pits, looking down cruelly. It was Jupiter's tower. A monument to Napoleon was to be erected in front of these sinister mines, from which the fury of war has continuously brought swords, spears, and balls into the world, and from which the Iron Age appears to have emerged directly, as the poet has sung, placing on its pedestal that order of the King of the Etruscans, Porsenna, that iron should only be used to make implements for agriculture and the peaceful arts in the future.

The lovely narrative reminds me of another requirement of peace, a true fact from Greek antiquity. When Gelon imposed peace on the Carthaginians in Syracuse following the battle of Himera, one of his requirements was that they stop making sacrifices to Moloc. This edict should have also been posted on the pedestal of the iron colossus to be raised on Elba: no more sacrifices to the god Moloc!

But I'm not sure if such an icharic age will ever occur, or if Elihu Buritt's olives ever take root. The peoples appear to be morally no better than they were under the reigns of Porsenna and Gelon of Syracuse.- In honour of both the political and religious Moloc, nations fight one other today as they did then, while the blossom of their youth is permitted to ripen calmly, as if human life could reproduce itself a hundredfold like the hydra.

That is why we break away from the Iron Island with the scream of Porsenna: "No more swords or spears, but industry and agriculture, and no more human sacrifices to any idol."

SAN MARCO OF FLORENCE.

* * *

A side from its historical significance, the Dominican convent in San Marco in Florence has enormous artistic significance. One is due to Savonarola, and the other to two great painters, Angelico da Fiesole and Fra' Bartolomeo. The plaza on which the monastery stands is still one of the haunts of Florentine artistic life today, as it was during the reign of Lorenzo de' Medici, ranking third after the Uffizi and the Pitti Palace; in fact, the gallery of fine arts and the famous school of copper engravers are located there.

The Medici garden flourished in the contrada of San Marco during Lorenzo's time, and it housed the first collection of ancient statues, overseen by the old sculptor Bertoldo. There collected Florence's sharpest minds, as well as everything new in science and the arts, as well as everything that had previously achieved notoriety and enjoyed Lorenzo's favour. Sculptors came to this de' Medici garden to study the ancient school and entertain themselves with Angelo Poliziano, Pico della Mirandola, and Marsilio Ficino, just as painters went to the Brancaccio Chapel to learn to sketch from Masaccio's murals. Lorenzo, Florence's Pericles, was frequently seen walking from this garden to the convent of San Marco, where he would shut himself away in a cell and be free of sweet paganism. Elevated debates on Plato's worldly soul were held here, along with a disingenuous contemplation of Christ's succession. Savonarola, on the other hand, remained silent, mumbling, and did not respond to Lorenzo's calls.

The convent was worthy of the Medici; in fact, they had built it. In 1220, the founder of the Dominican order sent twelve disciples to Tuscany; from these, a number of convents were created, the most notable of which was that of Fiesole. The

Dominicans of St. Mark convent arose from the latter. The Silvestrians founded it in 1299, but by the time of the great plague in Florence, it had fallen into disrepair. The Dominicans of Fiesole were summoned to St Mark's by Cosimo dei Medici, who had recently returned from exile in Venice. Cosimo summoned the famed prior Antonino of Fiesole, the greatest saint of his time. He was born in the year 1389, the son of Florentine lawyer Nicol Pierozzi. In his sixteenth year, he entered the Dominican order in Fiesole, where he later became prior. Cosimo persuaded him to go to San Marco in 1436, after Michelozzo Michelozzi was commissioned to rebuild the old Silvestrian convent. He almost totally dismantled the ancient convent and built a new, majestic structure in its place. Two cells were also prepared here for Cosimo, as if he were a monk, cells that, like Savonarola's, can still be seen today as a historical curiosity. According to Father Marchese, Prior Antonino made the ambitious old man hear, with the candour of a friend and the authority that comes from the sanctity of his life, that truth that flattery always conceals from the powerful, and it is certainly due to the saint that Cosimo did not become a common despot.

The edifice was completed in 1443, and Cosimo established the famed San Marco library. Antonino was appointed Archbishop of Florence three years later. He died in 1459, after being respected by the entire world for his virtues and taking a strong interest in the reform of the clergy.

St. Mark's has two huge courtyards; the lunettes of these courtyards are frescoed and represent facts from Antonino's life painted by Gherardini, Dantini, Poccetti, and other painters. The convent's greatest asset, however, are the wall paintings by Fiesole, the eldest master of Giotto's school. His paintings may be found in almost all of the cells, the chapter house, the passageways, and several of the courtyard lunettes.

With Fra' Angelico began the unusual reactions that the reform-minded nuns launched against the new spirit of ancient Italian painting. Vasari recounted the biography of the legendary painter. However, Vincenzo Marchese, a Dominican from San Marco, described it in greater detail. Because of his book, "Unpublished Letters of Fra Girolamo Savonarola and Documents relating thereto," this scholar was accused of liberalism by some of his order's confreres, zealous inquisitors; and since it was threatened to send him to Rome, he went to Genoa in the year 1851 and headed the Society that now edits the new edition of Vasari's works in the "Raccolta artistica." He authored 'Ricordi degli esimi pittori, scultori, e architetti dei domenicani, with alcuni scritti sulle fine arti' in 1845. In the 16th century, Razzi wrote a history of the great Dominicans, which included biographies of some of the order's painters, sculptors, and architects.

The Marquis appears to have taken this concept and put it into action. The biographies he provides us with via his work begin with Fra' Ristoro and Fra' Sisto, prominent 13th century architects who erected the splendid Dominican cathedral of S. In Florence, Maria Novella. However, he recounted the lives of the painters Fra' Angelico and Fra' Bartolomeo in greater depth; his work concludes with a chapter on Savonarola's effort for the reform of the arts.

Closely related to this work is the most important copper engraving in Florence, which was started under Perfetti's supervision: 'S. Father Vincenzo Marchese wrote 'Marco, il convento dell'ordine dei predicatori di Firenze, illustrato ed inciso principalmente secondo le pitture del beato Giovanni Angelico, colla life del stesso maestro et un compendio storico di detto convento' (Florence, published at the expense of the Artistic Association, 1850).

In this work, the Marquis exaggerates Fra Angelico's importance, equating him to a prophet entrusted with the job of reviving dying religious painting. He hoped to achieve the same moral reform of people through his paintings as Antoninus and

Savonarola had accomplished through their writings and public activities.

It is unknown where Fra Angelico was born. The Marquis believes he came from Castel di Vicchio in Mugello, a few kilometres from Giotto's birthplace, Colle di Vespignano. Guido was born in 1387, and his name was Guido. In Florence, he first began to paint in miniature, like his brother Benedetto, who was adept in this craft. In contrast to the decidedly realistic inclinations of Florentine art, he soon developed an outspoken religious leaning. The Marquis boldly compares this outstanding artist to Thales, who, via the inspiration of his rhymes and rhythms, paved the way for Lycurgus' legislation, just as Fiesole's paintings paved the way for his buddy Antoninus' reform.

The two brothers entered the Dominican order in Fiesole in 1407 and stayed there for a while until the papal quarrel reached here as well. Guido, or Fra' Giovanni, as he was now known, next went from Foligno to Cortona, where he painted in the style of Giotto, Spinello, and Simone da Siena, before returning to Fiesole after a four-year hiatus. In 1436, he was summoned to the newly constructed convent of San Marco to decorate it with paintings. At the same time, Masaccio was painting the chapels of the Carmine church, Brunelleschi was constructing the Duomo dome, Ghiberti was preparing the Baptistery doors, and Donatello and Luca della Robbia were competing in sculpture.

Because Fra' Giovanni lacked sketching, perspective, and refining chiaroscuro, he first examined Masaccio's paintings and gained a lot from this outstanding artist who was much younger than him.

The famous painting of the Chapter House, which he finished in St. Mark's and is one of the most beautiful to have been done in the 15th century, belongs to this era; it is his masterpiece, the last flower of Giotto's school; its theme is the passion, with saints in devotion on both sides. The two thieves' personalities are perfectly portrayed there. Christ's head has suffered; his features are no longer distinct. At the foot of the cross, on the left, sits a group of astonishing eloquence: the mother, about to swoon and lose her head and arms; Mary Magdalene, kneeling before her, clasps her to her breast with both arms, her loose blond hair flowing over her shoulders. Mary is supported by John and one of the women. It is difficult to express the tragic effect in a more straightforward manner; sublimity occurs here immediately through the grandeur of the inner essence. Neither Perugino nor Francia, who were masters of movement, display such height.

In this regard, the ancients were far from flawless. Their indestructible glory is their great and secure notion of spiritual existence; they are epic and popular, later ones musical and dramatic. Later, the image of suffering gets more and more rich, but also more violent and one-sided. The other figures are likewise significant; they are placed rather naturally and unattached on both sides and act only through their singular expression. Dominic, Bernard, Francis, Ambrose, Thomas Aquinas, and Augustine are examples of saints, clerics, bishops, or order founders. The colouring is really mystical, reminiscent of Fra Angelico.

Despite the fact that he has painted many other superb works, none of them have achieved such magnitude and strength, which is occasionally lacking in his impressions, which become weak owing to their excessive delicacy. The Deposition from the Cross and the Last Judgement are regarded the best by the Academy of Fine Arts, which has a considerable number of Fiesole's works. This one, on the other hand, is not a composition of significant importance due to the depth of feeling and the suavity of the colours.

Fra Angelico's depiction of hell is the worst of all; his disposition is too infantile to be able to construct diabolic beings. His devils only cause laughter, not dread; he showed hell in seven compartments, according to Dante, and at the bottom he also painted Lucifer, who with his three teeth tears apart Judas, Brutus, and Cassius. Angelico was also influenced by Dante, who was Giotto's buddy and the Giotto of poetry. Furthermore, the 'Divine Comedy' has inspired all painters, beginning with Giotto. It sparked the artists' imaginations and filled them with sublime visions and poetic thoughts; their pictures had already been drawn in Dante's verse compositions, and countless scenes from Hell, Purgatory, and Paradise were just waiting to be translated into colours, to become living pictures. In general, I feel that religious painting in Italy could not have developed and achieved such heights without Dante.

His poetry dominated the art of painting throughout the 14th and 15th centuries, until religious painting thrived. Even Dante's fervent admirer, Michelangelo, adhered to him, much as Luca Signorelli had done before him in his Extreme Judgement in Orvieto Cathedral, which Fra Angelico had begun to paint. Dante subjects are also painted by many masters in several cathedrals, such as Orcagna's Inferno and Paradiso in Santa Maria Novella's Strozzi Chapel.

Together with the 'Divine Comedy,' Petrarch's 'Triumphs' had a significant impact on art, as evidenced by Orcagna's 'Triumph of Death' in the Camposanto in Pisa, among many other paintings.

Fiesole also painted the Descent of Christ into Limbo at St. Mark's, from which he drew the patriarchs: a work of extraordinary colour finesse. His 'Adoration of the Magi,' one of his rare works in which he shows a certain gaiety and worldly diversity, is no less interesting. This issue was discussed frequently and with great affection. There are few textiles more appealing to religious school painters, and it surpasses them all in terms of the depth of poetic life. The contrasts are dramatic, plain, and natural: a craftsman's infant in a stable, cow and donkey in the cradle; this child comes to revere the earth's mighty ones, leading such long procession of finely clothed halberdiers and pages, bearing wealth and diamonds. One of these monarchs is invariably an elderly man, and when he kneels before the kid, the poetry of the scene is heightened by the contrast of ages. The second king has a Moorish face, the third is of excellent complexion, young and noble, and the old painters appear to have wanted to symbolise the three continents. Add to that the mystery distance from which the fabled monarchs have come, the darkness of the night, and the star, which frequently provides an opportunity to add a few of astronomers to the procession, and you have a fascinating oriental narrative in which the impact of the Crusades is obvious.

This type of image is abundant in Tuscan painting. Two excellent paintings of this type can be found in the Uffizi, by Domenico Ghirlandaio and Filippino Lippi; two others, masterpieces of the highest beauty, are owed to Fra Angelico's pupils, Gentile da Fabriano and Benozzo Gozzoli. Gentile's artwork is in the Accademia delle Belle Arti, while Benozzo's is in the Riccardi Palace's Medici Chapel. He produced frescoes here that, together with his works in Pisa's Camposanto, rank among the best of his time. His unusual universality can already be seen here; he embraced all kinds of painting, from landscape to architecture, figures to animals, and all with exquisite harmony. He painted the opulent voyages of monarchs in the aforementioned Riccardi Chapel; on horseback, on foot, or on camel, they cross the lovely plains, mountains, and valleys in unending columns.

Fiesole, who taught Gentile and Benozzo, remains with his painting beneath them; he lacks the solemn magnificence and joyous richness that his disciples were able to convey.

Many more paintings in St. Mark's need to be mentioned, including the Oration in the Garden, the Baptism, the Coronation of the Virgin, which has Dante's Ascent, and his

Christ on a Pilgrimage; but enough of them. They all have the same means of expression, the same childish conception, and the deepest religiosity. Even his colours, which are predominantly white, light blue, and a delicate red, must be described as infantile. His most appealing figures are sometimes those painted in small, almost miniature form; they are quite graceful and of exquisite refinement, such as the little angels of an altar piece in the Uffizi and the figures on the Santa Maria Novella reliquary.

Fra Angelico died on March 18, 1455, in Rome; Nicholas V, who had summoned him to the Vatican to paint, had a sepulchral monument made for him in the Church of the Minerva.

The epigraph compares him to Apelles, to whom many painters have been compared. He was the last great master of Giotto's school, which was ended by the naturalists Maselino and Masaccio, who established the modern trend of painting. Titian, Giulio Romano, Correggio, and Michelangelo were the culmination of the old school that led to the representation of the naked with admiration for the forms of human nature.

Then, from St. Mark's cloister, which had found in Fiesole such a zealous advocate of holy painting, a backlash against the modern school arose, and its champion was Savonarola.

He used his own weapons to fight the Medici, who had fostered the ancient school. They formed the Platonic Academy and admired paganism; yet, Savonarola, Lorenzo, Pico, Poliziano, Marsilio Ficino, and many others were Platonic mystics.

From the pulpit in front of which stood the tombs of his companions Pico della Mirandola and Angelo Poliziano, the prior of St. Mark's conducted Platonic sermons on the essence of beauty and thundered against the nakedness of art. The Marchese quotes Savonarola in a lecture in which he considers the beautiful platonically as the soul and idea of the good. On the basis of this thesis, he waged a frenzied fight against the ancient school and the arts, which, he claimed, led the human race astray by focusing on worldly matters. Many artists who had before painted or sculpted happily were shaken by his words, and one witnessed the outstanding Sandro Botticelli, Cronaca, Robbia, Bartolomeo, Lorenzo di Eredi, and many others repentantly abandon their paganism at the feet of the prior. Only Mariotto Albertinelli and the weird Piero di Cosimo were unaffected, remaining pagans and ardent opponents of Savonarola and his moral religion.

To the tune of trumpets and drums, all the symbols of worldliness were paraded into the city square on February 21, 1497. A tree with many branches was erected there, to which were attached portraits of the most beautiful Florentines, masterpieces of painting, beautiful nudes, god sculptures, music books, harps and lutes, cymbals and violins, papers, silk and velvet dresses, the most expensive objects of gold and ivory, and even Petrarch and Boccaccio's poems were seen hanging. The enforcers of this fanatical tribunal, which was to evaluate human vanity, had examined the residences and were also scared turned over to them, and were freely given art and precious artefacts of all types as penance. A Venetian shopkeeper in Florence, who had no qualms about the moral essence of beauty, reasoned that it would be preferable to sell these valuable trade products rather than burn them. He thus offered the small sum of 20,000 scudi for all those materialistic vanities. Following this, the Lordship had him seized, placed on a chair, and painted by a Platonic painter, with his portrait set atop the stake. So, amid the celebration of the gathering, this tree was burned with all its jewels. This occurred on the same square where the great fanatic was burned a year later.

Savonarola's death broke the hearts of his contemporaries. Many artists ceased painting, notably Baccio della Porta, who left the world in 1500 as a sign of sadness and donned the Dominican cassock. Baccio, or Fra' Bartolomeo as he was known from then on, was immersed in grief for six years and did not touch his brushes. Following that, he felt revitalised and resumed his religious paintings at the prompting of his order brothers. Raphael was returning to Florence for the second time at the time. He befriended Brother Bartholomew and studied drawing and colour from him; under his influence, his Madonna del Baldacchino was begun, but never completed, and bears a strong resemblance to Bartholomew's technique. He was trained in the style of Michelangelo and Leonardo da Vinci, and instead of painting in the mild and delicate style of Fiesole, he became the polar opposite of his predecessor in S. Marco. Giotto's school was defeated. Bartolomeo demonstrated how much the knowledge of plasticity had influenced painting; his figures, especially his evangelist Marco in the Pitti Gallery, are often as grandiose as Michelangelo's and almost statuesque.

He died in 1517, and he left us a painting of Savonarola, which captures the fiery figure of this Renaissance prophet. Whatever the heights of this amazing man's ideas, he remained a monk, and more specifically a Dominican.

Fra' Bartolomeo was painting in St. Mark's while another ardent fan of Savonarola, the miniature painter Fra' Benedetto, was imprisoned there in a cell. Nothing is known about this unique man's paintings; nonetheless, he has left us with an original poem that he wrote in the solitary of his jail. This is the oldest epic poem about Savonarola, recounting his life and death. It's called "The Cedar of Lebanon." 'The Cedar of Lebanon, or the life of Girolamo Savonarola, described by Fra' Benedetto in Florence in the year 1510,' the Marquis just republished. According to the Marquis, several contemporaries, such as Burlamacchi and Count Francesco di Mirandola, have documented Savonarola's life, but they could not have experienced his intimacy and friendship, as was allowed to Fra' Benedetto for three years, during which he resided with the master in S. Marco. Savonarola had clothed him in the Dominican habit, and this disciple of his suffered and worked much for him, and defended him after his end with a love and constancy that earned him first exile and after many years of imprisonment in his cloister; a singular man, the type of which can only be found in those paladins of the Middle Ages, without stain and without fear, who were immortally sung in verse by Ariosto and Tasso.

The Marquis correctly assigns historical significance to this poem because it faithfully reports events, the majority of which the author witnessed with his own eyes; I therefore believe it is worthwhile to translate some passages from it, but not before providing some information about the simple poet's life.

Fra' Benedetto was born in Florence in 1470. His father, Paolo, was a jeweller, and his mother, as he describes her, was a lady of spirit and boldness. He led a dissolute life at first, but was converted by Savonarola's preaching and joined the Order of St Mark. He had been in the monastery for three years when, on April 8, 1498, the populace rose up in revolt against the reformer. Fra' Benedetto battled bravely alongside other monks and Savonarola partisans. Baccio della Porta happened to be in the monastery that evening, and he hid, terrified by the cries of the people and the violence of the battle. Benedetto, on the other hand, climbed onto the roof of the burning church and shattered as many opponents as he could with stones. Savonarola saw him and summoned him, pleading with him to put down his arms; similarly, when the prophet readily surrendered to his adversaries, Benedict desired to share his destiny, but Jerome forbade him.

He then describes how, among the master's followers, Malatesta Sacromoro da Rimini acted as a traitor by advising Savonarola to surrender to the people, while the latter (Fra' Benedetto) implored him in vain to imitate Paul by lowering himself with a rope and sought his own freedom in flight. Savonarola and Domenico were transported to the Palazzo della Signoria, while

Silvestro hid in the monastery. Malatesta, however, betrayed him the next day. On May 23, all three were set ablaze.

Benedetto initially escaped to Viterbo, but soon felt guilt for having rejected Savonarola's memory even for a short time; he subsequently returned to Florence and continued to valiantly defend his unhappy master's ideas, despite the anger of the opposing party. He spared no one and even launched an attack on Pope Alexander VI. As a result of this, he was expelled from the monastery and later imprisoned there. It is unknown if he endured here until the end of his life. In prison, he wrote in defence of Savonarola, on religion, and lastly "The Cedar of Lebanon."

This simple poem is composed in tercets and divided into eleven chapters. It does not have any poetic beauty; yet, it is notable for the consistency with which it identifies events and gives us an insight into life at the time. The disaster is recounted graphically and unquestionably factually.

Following an oration-like preface, the author describes his own life events:

Born of poor origins in the city of roses in the year 1470 in the area of S. Cross, etc.

Benedict then describes the corruption of his time: peace reigned across the world, but the devil planted wickedness, the people were full of vile deeds, and lust and violence were common. Alexander VI reigned, a man of greed and passion, and every priest looked up to him.

At this time, the Lord had dispatched a loyal servant named Jerome, etc., to my city.

The poet recalls how his mother, captivated by Savonarola's remarks, pushed him to attend one of his sermons. Regardless of how difficult this invitation seemed to him, he eventually succumbed and went to the church of San Marco. Here he sat, embarrassed and silent among the listeners, astonishing the audience, who had not expected to see the bird of delight there. And here he inserts Savonarola into the scene, preaching, as Lenau does in his work on Savonarola.

When my prophet, Savonarola, arrived, he respectfully ascended the pulpit, and I listened intently to his words, etc.

He then maintains this tone. It's the Noah's Ark sermon: Benedict's conscience was so deeply affected that he immediately retreated to an isolated location, where he initiated a discourse with himself, in which clear allegations are contained.

And I went away, weeping, tossing my light and dissolute self, as well as my instrument, away from me.

His former buddies insult him and label him a hypochondriac, invite him to social gatherings, and show him how he is liked by all and has many friends, and how nothing is missing from his life. Not only do his comrades taunt him, but his senses are eventually drawn into temptation, and he displays them as people:

I don't know what you think; you've conditioned me to run free, and freedom is what I want since it suits me. The ear told me, etc..

But Savonarola consoled him in his conversion, and he began his holy life by working as a nurse and undertaker in a hospital for a few months. Despite the devil's constant torment, he fought hard and eventually joined the order in his twenty-fifth year.

In the same way that Bartholomew represented Savonarola in colour, Benedict described him in verse:

Petite in stature, but in perfect health; with small limbs, etc.

This is followed with judgements on his soul, which one might easily understand, and a brief mention of his tenacity; then a lengthy sequence reminiscent of Klopstock, in which the poet has the devils collaborate against Savonarola:

When the haughty Lucifer, the prince of Hell, saw what fruits the priest was reaping, he roared loudly like a tearing beast, etc.

Later, Lucifer recounts what he has done wrong since his fall from heaven, including how he drove Adam out of paradise, bending all creatures under his dominion, how the people of Moses fell prey to idolatry as a result of his preparation, and how he sent out all the devils to exterminate the faith after Christ's birth:

And you lies, disgusting beasts, you haven't destroyed my faith. The first says, "Today I still do," while the second says, "Tomorrow," etc.

The demons flee with terrible howls on Lucifer's orders. Their activity is soon visible in the holy man's persecution, particularly on the side of the Minors of the Holy Cross, who interrupt his lectures in every way, inciting the people against him. The storming of St Mark's on April 8, 1498 is then described by Benedict.

It was on a Sunday, Palm Sunday, that Florence erupted with wild demands to take the monk alive or dead.

He subsequently relates how twenty of Savonarola's friends repulsed the attackers on their own, killing their commander and driving out the entire mob three times. The enraged mob returned to the assault three times.

The adversaries then set fire to the church and convent doors. The prophet was encircled by his brethren who were holding the

Sacrament, etc.

This is followed by the prophet's comforting and warning sermon, in which he informs the brethren that he has resolved to voluntarily submit himself into the hands of his foes, heeding Malatesta's perfidious advice.

I watched with my own eyes how he offered himself to the enemies with comrade Dominic, and how he stayed cool and tranquil in the midst of the enraged individuals who threatened him, etc.

Benedict then describes how, after Savonarola's death, his followers shamelessly abandoned his banner and repudiated his memory.

No one remained devoted to him, and I, too, began to waver. However, my cooling was brief, and my passion quickly returned, etc.

The final chapter is a lamentation over the prophet's death and how he died. The poem then concludes with an admonition to Savonarola to remember his pledge and protect the unfortunate author, which was undoubtedly to be followed by another part.

The Marquis, to whom we owe the publication of this old poem, did not create a special history of Savonarola, but simply added a description of his life to the wonderful work already stated on St. Mark's frescoes. It's intriguing to hear how a Dominican living today speaks of his convent's past prior. He begins by saying, "The reader will discover how a man, arguably the greatest of his time, met a horrific end." He will discover that neither his noble soul, nor the holiness of his life, nor the loftiness of his mission could save him. He will know what hopes died with him and what were the bitter fruits of his death, and how gallows and pyres were insufficient to quench his opponents' thirst for vengeance, a hunger that still blazed over his corpse and his memory. Nonetheless, his name is honoured now, after the wrath has been buried forever, and is treasured by everyone who are fearless friends of the truth. Fra Girolamo Savonarola is this magnificent and unhappy man.

The letters and records describing this sad reformer, provided by the Marquis himself, are significant additions to a history of Savonarola. Among these are letters to his mother, Elena Buonaccorsi, his friend Domenico, his sister Beatrice, Pico della Mirandola, and a letter from Louis XII to the Government of Florence, in which the monarch pleads for a stay of execution for Savonarola's sentence. 'Here we end our patient research into the life and death of Savonarola, in the hope that a purely Catholic, diligent and just writer may soon arise, free from all the prejudices of political and religious sects, who will finally present us with the true type of this great man, who in a difficult and corrupt time achieved such a high reputation that not even the calumnies of four centuries could diminise,' the Marquis says at the end of his introduction to the collections.

The Marchese's demand was answered when Pasquale Villari, a history professor at Pisa, wrote a valuable work titled "La storia di Girolamo Savonarola ed I suoi tempi.".

THE VOLUNTEER CAMPAIGN AROUND ROME.

* * *

I n the autumn of 1866, Italy was gripped by a frenzy comparable to that of 1859. Austria, the last surviving embodiment of German imperial power, had likewise been forced to hand over the final vestiges of its Italian territories to the Italian country. The day the Austrians set sail for Trieste and the Italians invaded Venice on October 19, was one of the greatest and most euphoric days in Italian history; it symbolised the return of the Italian country to its independence after more than three centuries of servitude.

The Italians attributed this lofty triumph to Prussian military prowess. The powerful connection of alliance, to which they had remained committed even when persuaded to quit it, had triumphed over the defeats of their army and fleet.

Following Venice's cession, Italy reformed as a single nation, its unity unbroken by the cession of Rome. Only foreign troops remained, Napoleon's occupying army. However, the Papacy's reliance on the French Emperor was about to shift.

Austria had previously surrounded the Vatican from the Po; the imposing quadrilateral was the Vatican's most prized trench. It had now fallen, and the connection of common interests that had held the Papacy and the Habsburg dynasty together had been severed. Austria discontinued its Italian policy and, as a result, its commitments to Rome. Italy therefore deepened its alliance with Prussia, which had become the continent's major power after weakening France and was now following the same objectives in Germany as Savoy had followed in Italy.

In the autumn of 1866, it was foretold that the result of these events would be the overthrow of the Popes' temporal power.

According to the agreement of 15 September 1864, the French occupation of Rome was coming to an end.

The question arose as to whether Napoleon would rigorously follow this agreement, i.e. remove his forces, and if so, what would happen to the Papacy. Would papal troops, a few Roman regiments, and a few foreign regiments be enough to maintain order in the state's provinces? These provinces were claimed to have taken secret pledges to respond to the first appeal of the Mazzinian Central Committee in Florence. Napoleon had organised the Legion of Antibo to defend the Pope personally. Colonel d'Argy's corps of 1,200 troops, largely French, had already landed at Civitavecchia in September 1866 and was garrisoned at Viterbo.

The fall of Palermo (16 September) into the hands of Bentivegna's gangs, with control remaining for six days, left a deep impression in Rome: could nothing comparable happen here after the withdrawal of the French troops? In October, the fervour reached a fever pitch. Several desertions were reported in Antibo's legion. The Pope got word of a communication from Napoleon in which, referring to the excesses of Palermo, he urged that an Italian garrison be welcomed in Rome following the withdrawal of his forces. There was talk of direct negotiations for reconciliation between Pius IX and Victor Emmanuel.

On October 29, the Pope delivered a speech to the cardinals that abruptly shattered all hopes in this regard. Pius IX protested against all of the Italian government's actions; additionally, after the peace of Prague, he did not want to know anything about the rights of the Italian nation; he considered the Italians to be heretical rebels, and finally expressed his intention to leave Rome if circumstances demanded it.

There was a fanatical group that sought to exile the Pope. The Jesuits, like the democratic party, wanted him to flee.

The latter wanted to position Rome at the forefront of the Revolution and to establish the Republic on the Capitol. They wanted nothing more than to plunge Italy into anarchy with the Pope's exile, to stir the protests and aid of Catholics all over the globe, and, finally, for the Powers to intervene and re-establish - potentially - the Church State, as in the year of grace 1815. Only the moderates, who made up the majority, agreed that the Pope should stay in Rome. Despite everything, they hoped for the possibility of reaching an agreement with the Pope, overcoming all the obstacles strictly inherent in the ecclesiastical system—an agreement with a Pontiff from whom they had taken a large part of his states, and whose seat, Rome, was claimed as the capital of the Italian nation. An act of sacrifice and self-denial was asked of this sovereign, an act for which no state or king in history could have supplied an example! Temporal authority is an anti-evangelical premise, but it is also a state of affairs that has persisted for over a thousand years and is so important to the Papacy's position that it can only be destroyed through a reform of European state relations. True, this has already begun, but no Pope will resign his temporal power until it is completed.

The Italian government appeared willing to engage in negotiations; it stated that, in accordance with the terms of the September Convention, it would not attack the papal dominion when the French withdrew, nor would it tolerate others attacking it. It dispatched troops to the borders to guard them, preventing volunteer bands from infiltrating the Papal States. Meanwhile, the French government considered reconciling the discrepancy in the Papal State's public debt, calculating the arrears for the Church regions ceded to Italy to be paid to the Pope at 12 million. He informed the Italian government that it was appropriate to bring the action party, whose signature on the September Convention was known to be deeply resolved to crush it underfoot at the first opportunity. The goal of the democrats was clearly not hidden;

would the Italian government have enough authority to limit their zeal? Following the French withdrawal, they intended to provoke the fall of the Papacy and the annexation of Rome to Italy as its capital, igniting revolution in the Papal States and forcing the Italian government to break the Convention and march on Rome, either with Napoleon's consent, if he wished to recognise a fait accompli for the second time, or without, if he intended to intervene and oppose the Italian army.

While the Curia worried about the French retreat and debated whether it was better for the Pope, who was defenceless against the revolution, to abandon or remain in the city, nationalists debated what the Roman people should do in this situation. The Senate of Rome and the Pope, a pamphlet produced in November, was discreetly distributed to Rome's ambassadors, cardinals, and notables. It reawakened ancient conceptions of municipal independence; the ghosts of Cola di Rienzo, Lorenzo Valla, and Stefano Porcari were once again calling to the Romans. However, it is unclear whether these shadows arose in Rome on their own or were conjured up in a Florentine cabinet and then sent to Rome. That writing attempted to demonstrate, through the study of Middle Ages history, that Rome had never been in a state of direct and proper subjection to the Pope, that it still retained its right to autonomy, and that, once the French had withdrawn, the Senate and the municipal authority of the people should be re-established on the Capitol, and Vittorio Emanuele should be crowned King of Italy by plebiscite.

The time for violence has passed; the French troops who have occupied Rome for sixteen years are on the verge of abandoning it; the Pope's Roman militia is faltering: weak in discipline and number, they feel the shame of serving under a banner that is not that of the fatherland; and the mercenary troops are few and treacherous, fearing the wrath of the people who will not tolerate being limited and prevented from exercising a sacred right by a group of adventurers. The Roman people desire to be a part of Italy's existence; the youth have already stated their intentions, and some patricians have enlisted under the King's flag. Finally, all residents want peace, order, and freedom, and they have no intention of relying on the whims of greedy condottieri or ultramontane madmen. The clergy, that simple, intelligent, and moral Roman priesthood that despises the Curia and outsiders, wishes to combine with the voices of Milan and Venice. In a nutshell, the moral revolution has been completed. If souls remain calm, if nothing has transpired thus far, it is because they do not want to disrupt the long-awaited evacuation of the French from Rome in any way through an inappropriate movement.

"However, once that is accomplished, the entire citizenry must, with the calm and dignity befitting the exercise of an inalienable right, re-establish its own municipality and administrative system, for the purpose of defending itself, maintaining order through the citizen militia, and declaring to the world its will." The Roman people, now masters of their own fate, must provide for their own and their country's, and exercise the right that was the highest policy of their conduct and the system of their Senate; a right that every civilised European people has now obtained, and the name of which the Romans themselves took: the Plebiscite! The Roman people will then turn to the King of Italy and say to him, "Sire, come to us to fulfil our fathers' vows; come and crown yourself with the laurel that Dante, Machiavelli, and Gioberti promised you, and that you have well deserved for the valour of your army, your valour, and the blood of so many martyrs." You have come to crown the efforts of many centuries, to realise the dream of countless generations, and to crown yourself on the Capitol with the iron crown that you won on the Po. We Romans will rejoice if, from today, we are called upon to protect this crown, symbol of civic liberty in national independence, alongside all the other peoples of Italy.

"However, the Roman people must turn to the Vatican and so speak to the Pontiff: Holy Father, the Italian revolution has fulfilled its course and achieved its aim." Now it stands in front of the venerable Basilica of the Apostles, and it wants you to know that it does not intend to plunder it, nor to shake the foundations of the Religion of Christ, which is the religion of all Italy, and of which you are the Primate, but rather that it intends to grant you the freedom you sought in vain from monarchs who based their power solely on the sword. You will be able to freely exercise your holy office under the aegis of the laws, in the shadow of a flag that reads: Freedom of the Church and of the State, no longer surrounded by foreign weapons, but defended and sustained by the reverence and homage of us who, if no longer your subjects, will remain your faithful children."

This paper was dated Rome, Day of the Dead; it was signed Stefano Porcari; and it was printed in Romae, ex aedibus Maximis 1866. It made a big impression; all the media talked about it, and it got as far as Paris.

Shortly afterwards, Ricasoli's circular letter of 15 November was distributed to all Prefects of Italy; in it, the Cabinet of Florence declared that it would strictly adhere to the September Convention; that the Pontiff's temporal power had become a strange anomaly in the midst of modern civilisation, and that it should be treated like any other secular power: the Pope alone, that is, in Rome; and that he would then regulate his relations with the Roman Catholic Church. In essence, the circular echoed Porcari's writing.

Ricasoli's statements appeared to the papalists to be a provocation. They were progressively advising the Pope to flee to exile. According to them, he had to leave Rome and go to Civitavecchia, surrounded by his troops, and wait there, following in the footsteps of the pontiffs of the Middle Ages who had long taken refuge in Viterbo or other towns in the province, for a change of direction or a political revolution to call him back to Rome. The fleets of the Powers would meet to defend him in the port of Civitavecchia, according to the Jesuit counsellors. In fact, a number of French, Spanish, and Austrian warships anchored in that harbour in November. Civitavecchia appeared to be the final Ptolemaid of the Papacy. But Pius IX shuddered at the prospect of leaving Rome again. Should this old man, who was nearing the end of his life, face the anguish of exile and escape once more? It was up to Emperor Napoleon, who had sent General Fleury to Florence, to confirm the Pope's conviction that he must remain in the Vatican; there he was weak; in exile he could have been strong, but he was exposing himself to a grave danger: Catholic France, and with it the entire Episcopate, would undoubtedly have been moved, forming a compact phalanx to defend the threatened Papacy. The news also spread that Empress Eugenie would be visiting Rome. But, because she, like Matilda of Canossa, could not stand in the breach that the French general Montebello was ready to abandon, she would only come as an ambassador of her husband to encourage the Pope to accept the article of agreement that had been formulated in Florence and to remain in Rome.

II.

The French troops had progressively retreated from their garrisons in the Province; they were on their way to Rome, where they would leave for Civitavecchia. There was also speculation that the Pope would travel to that city on December 4th to inspect the new port works and make a decision on his probable house there, which would be defended by his army. Many speculated that he was about to set sail.

Fra Giusto to the Romans was delivered as a flying leaflet. It claimed that Providence had chosen Rome to fuse and integrate the new civilisation with the ancient, freedom with faith, and to emancipate people via a work of social and religious renewal with the same eternal character as Roman Law and the Gospel. Roman liberty, cleansed of pagan materialism and purified by Christian emancipation, would serve as the foundation for ecclesiastical power, allowing it to blossom in all the purity of its new spiritual essence, free of the material forms of the principality. The Romans would meet Victor Emmanuel with dignity and serenity, knowing that only within the walls of Rome could he complete his job of rescuing Italy. This Roman optimist advised his fellow citizens to avoid any radical political parties. So he concluded:

"The threat of flight, which the wicked have sought to instil in the Pope, does not correspond to the goodness of his heart or the sacred responsibility of his apostolic office. Flight belongs to the leader of mercenary warriors, not the shepherd who must care for his flock, as Christ has clearly stated. Pius IX is far too aware of his responsibilities to leave in fear, or to allow the streets of this holy city to be defiled with the blood of his children in the presence of the vicar of a God of peace and love. But if his advisors' malice drove him from Rome, if the savagery of his generals and mercenaries poured Roman blood, God, the world, the judges of this cowardice and madness, would only expedite the final triumph of the Italian cause, validating every rightful and necessary defence.

The French were beginning to depart from Rome. General Montebello and his officers arrived in the Vatican on December 6 to take leave. The atmosphere was solemn. The Pope appeared solemn and mild on the outside. The General's speech, or rather his Emperor's speech, and the Pope's response are historically significant since they accurately portray the situation[1].

The general said:

"Holy Father, I am overcome with emotion as I return for

the final time to pay our profound devotion to Your Holiness and to seek Your Holy Blessing. There are times when the melancholy that comes with leaving transforms into actual and vivid sorrow. But one idea consoles me: if the Emperor withdraws his forces from Rome in accordance with his commitments, he does not withdraw his protection from the Holy See. Our 17-year occupation is being followed by a moral protection that will be no less impressive and effective, a brake for some and an encouragement for others.

"May the time, which in the hands of the most powerful God calms the passions and gives respite to sorrows, and builds more than it destroys, inspire in everyone that spirit of conciliation which alone can lead to the solution of the present difficulties and assure the supreme Head of religion the independence and security it requires to carry out its spiritual activity freely until the end of the worlds.

"I timidly prostrate myself at Your Holiness' feet with my wish, my reverence, and the expression of my heartfelt appreciation."

The Pope responded in French as follows:

"I've come to bid you farewell at the hour of your departure, my dear children.

"When our flag flew out of France to defend the rights of the Holy See, it was accompanied by the prayers and blessings of all Catholic hearts. It is now returning to France, and I hope it is received in the same manner. But I'm not sure if it will happen. They write to me that Catholics' hearts are affected by the terrible situation in which the Vicar of Christ, the Head of the Catholic Religion, finds himself.

"I've already told your comrades: we're not fooling ourselves; the revolution is coming.

"They've said it, assured it, declared it, and you've heard and read it. Italy is done, but not finished, according to a high-ranking member of the Italian administration. Perhaps he could have argued that it has not yet been entirely eradicated because there is still a territory where law, order, and religion reign.

"They may plant their flag on the Capitol, but keep in mind that the Tarpeian Rock is right next to it.

"They may be masters for a time and spread disaster everywhere. For what purpose?

"I was speaking with a French representative maybe five or six years ago. He asked me what I should say to the Emperor before leaving. I don't recall exactly what I said to him, but it went something like this: "I'll tell you a storey from the Church's history." St Augustine was bishop of Hippo, a city you may be familiar with because it is one of our African colonies, when it was besieged by a barbarian army. He knew that if the city fell, the population would be subjected to a slew of atrocities, so he pleaded with God, "I want to die before I witness such a dreadful thing." Please convey this to the Emperor on my behalf. The ambassador told me, "Your Holiness, these barbarians will not enter here."

"He was a worthy gentleman, not a prophet.
Another, who now has a high position, informed me that Rome cannot be the capital of a kingdom because it lacks everything needed to be so, but it does have everything needed to be the capital of the Catholic world. These are, without a doubt, good and confident statements, but I repeat: the Revolution may come, and I have no help on earth.

"However, I remain calm and resigned, relying in God to provide me with the necessary strength.

"Go, my children; I love and bless you, as well as your families and friends. Tell your Emperor, the Emperor of France, that I pray for him every day. They say his health is bad; I pray for his health; they say his soul is agitated; I pray for his peace.

"The Emperor is the ruler of a huge nation that carries the title Most Christian; it is a good title, but it must be earned; it cannot be the result of a simple and spontaneous expression of the heart.

"One must pray, and pray with humility, trust, and perseverance; even a nation's leader requires this trust in God if he is to be strong and obtain what he seeks.

"I'm not angry; in fact, I'm quite calm. But I notice that the globe is not at peace. I believe in God's assistance and wish you well. May my blessing be with you throughout your life!"
The former Pontiff's remarks left a lasting impression. Many French officials held firmly papal views, and many despised Italy; others despised the bond that had now united it to Germany, which had robbed Napoleon of the honour of carrying out the work of liberation of Italy, and now had succeeded France in the intimacy with this nation, and now perhaps joined it in arms against France. Many saw the withdrawal from Rome as a moral setback, a sudden abandoning of France's really imperial and hegemonic position. French troops flocked to the Vatican to receive blessed rosaries from Pope Francis.

The regimental departures began calmly and orderly on December 7. At daybreak, they could be heard crossing the city to the warlike sound of their march Partant pour Syrie. This was their farewell message. They had taken Rome with pomp and grit, and now they were abandoning it with timid serenity!

The Roman militia occupied all of the gates, the Capitol, and the guardhouse at Piazza Colonna. The city's physiognomy appeared to have transformed. After 17 years of seeing those magnificent French troops, the Romans were taken aback by the inept papal soldiers who had taken their place. The city of Rome fell silent. Everyone believed that a historical era had ended and that the Vatican was returning to its solitary. The French also cleared the last site, Castel Sant'Angelo, on December 11 at eight o'clock in the morning. A Zouaves lieutenant led half a company to the fortress gates, which were guarded by French sentries. They conversed. The appearance of a papal general. The French flag was hoisted, while the papal flag was lowered. The weapons were displayed; the French exited, and the Zouaves entered.

The bronze archangel, Michael, waved the Church's banner over Hadrian's mausoleum once more. This archangel, flying towards the city with his wings outstretched and a big sword in his sheath, is the Church's most beautiful image of the peace it must bring to the world, one of those ideals that sorrowful humanity generally communicates in myths. Is there anything in the history of symbols as profound as this angel, sheathing the sword in its scabbard, indicating Redemption and Peace, hovering over the sad burial of a Roman emperor, indeed over the entire everlasting city? On December 11, 1866, it appeared to take on a new symbolic meaning. Wasn't it the non-evangelical sword of the Popes' temporal power, whose dominion must not be of this world, that the Archangel hid forever? The sword fought by Arnaldo da Brescia, Dante, our Enrichi, and the Hohenstaufen? Was it merely the dagger France wielded in forsaking the Pope?

The withdrawal of the French left a significant hole. Seventeen years in Rome had rendered them, if not Roman citizens, at least city dwellers, and their warlike aspect had become a familiar element of the city. With tradition and their excellent behaviour, the Roman people's initial hostility toward them had progressively faded. This was undoubtedly the most bearable occupation of a country by foreign forces, all the more so because it did not represent a conquest, but rather the defence of the Papacy. It cost the country nothing; on the contrary, it profited it: the French circulated 12 million lire in Rome each year. Under normal circumstances, the Papacy would have delighted with the retreat of foreign troops, but instead had to lament its loss. The papal government, which had been allied with the French military command for 17 years, establishing another government with whom it frequently clashed, had finally regained its independence.

The last French forces embarked at Civitavecchia on 14 December 1866, and no foreign flags flew over Italy from the Alps to the sea on that day. This was a fresh new condition in the Peninsula's history, one that had not existed since 1494. While France was being compelled to submit and vacate Rome by the right of the Italian nation and popular opinion throughout Europe, after forcing Austria to evacuate Italy, a great new civil principle was clearly expressing itself.

On the same day, the National Secret Committee in Rome issued the following crucial proclamation in the form of a flying leaflet:

"Finally, the last French soldier, the last foreigner, has departed Italy, Romans. From the Alps to the sea, no foreign flag flies over Italy, offering undeserved protection or lordship. This spectacle, while unpleasant for our oppressors, brings comfort to those of us who, after 18 years, raise our brow and behold Rome as the arbiter of her fate. This glorious day will live on in the mind and heart of every Roman who feels honour for his formerly wretched motherland. This day, 14 December 1866, ushers in a new age, one that will see, alongside the purification and liberation of religion from authoritarianism, the liberation and development of Rome itself.

"This is our task, O Romans. A late justice has now placed the fate of this region in our hands! The occasion is sombre and decisive. The entire world is watching Rome, moved and disposed in numerous ways. We, firm in the strength of an unchangeable right, vowed to exercise it without infringing on the rights of spiritual power, keeping our minds, hearts, and, if necessary, our arms ready for the great event. There will be no vain talk, misguided movements, or distinct and unsuitable activities! Those who do not know how to contribute to our cause should remain outside our ranks. Our fatherland is full of bravery and civilised morality; the pivotal moment will demonstrate this. As a result, there will be no vain and chaotic demonstrations. For this is what our adversaries want, those who bank on our mistakes to return Italy to ancient slavery; they are numerous and twisted, and they surround us, spy on us, and undermine us. But don't worry; the eyes of those who are waiting for our deliverance are on them. However, against them, we must utilise union and order, as well as a firm, decisive, and tranquil demeanour during the time that separates us from the fulfilment of our aspirations.

"Let us join hands and make a sturdy chain in the honour and glory of Rome. Let not one particle of our power be lost in the name of the fatherland at this grave moment.

"So, huddled together, we wait for the proper moment. Victory is assured. The days of priestly dictatorship are quickly coming to an end. Your committee will be prepared to offer advice and take action as needed.

The Roman National Committee.

Rome, December'.

III.

Fears that the French withdrawal might spark an uprising, if not in Rome, then in the nearby towns, particularly Viterbo, were unfounded; peace reigned supreme. This was owed in part to the superb behaviour of the newly organised papal forces, as well as the command that came from Florence to the Roman National Committee. To demonstrate its good intentions, the Italian government had made preparations for all bishops who had been pushed out or arrested to return to their positions. It had also dispatched Tonello to Rome, not only to reach an agreement on the issue of the bishops' oath and the royal exequatur, but also to bring the proposal of that grand financial project, which consisted in converting Italy's ecclesiastical property, valued at two billion lire, into a movable annuity, granting the Church true independence from the State. These conversations, albeit not followed by results, drew widespread attention and enhanced the belief of those who remained hopeful for conciliation. After the French withdrew, the Roman dilemma shifted from a European to a domestic Italian one. The Papacy was now surrounded and crushed all around by Italy, alone in the face of its claims: this situation appeared so intolerable that many believed an accord between Rome and Italy had to be established somehow.

The city's Italian party had formed the Roman National Committee, which received its address from the government in Florence and served as its organ. Its goals were as follows: accord with the Papacy, deprived of temporal power; plebiscite annexation of Rome to Italy; and designation of Rome as capital with the Savoy dynasty. As a result, he campaigned for the importance of peace and order, as well as passive resistance.

The Mazzinian faction, which intended to remove the Papacy and establish the Republic in Rome, had been opposing this since the end of 1866, believing that it would spark a social revolution in all of Europe, if not all of humanity. These parties began to fight bitterly against each other, and this schism in the revolutionaries' camp was a cause of more than just the preservation of Rome's tranquillity and order.

Because of the National Committee's peaceful aims, the Mazzinians dubbed it the Mallow. Both of these parties published fliers and secret periodicals, the Nationals under the name Roma dei Romani and the Mazzinians under the name Sveglia. The lives and covert workings of these underground administrations, of revolutionary subterranean Rome, escaped the authorities, who were unable to find the leaders, premises, or printers. Those newspapers were possibly never printed in Rome, but rather in other cities.

Mazzinians and Italian emigrants, some of whom belonged to their sect, held lively meetings throughout Umbria and the Neapolitan area. They established these associations throughout Italy and used the cities to propagate propaganda for the armed invasion of the Church States. Since January, an arms depot had been established in Terni, and Roman emigrants from Lombardy had been summoned there. The weapons were to be introduced secretly into the Roman, i.e. Viterbo. The French Foreign Minister, Moustier, alerted the Emperor's embassy in Florence about what was planned, so that he may draw the attention of the Italian authorities.

The Mazzinians gave the city its first glimmer of life on the night of February 10, 1867, with the explosion of many firecrackers. It was the anniversary of the Roman Republic's proclamation in 1849. Furthermore, there were no excesses; only the National Committee prohibited theatrical visits and Carnival celebrations, resulting in the most melancholy Carnival ever seen. Outside, and even at Rome's gates, brigandage was on the rise. All roads were dangerous; finally, the Papal Government stepped in with a zealous statute and efficient military actions.

Throughout Italy, agitation was on the rise. Following the rejection of Scialoia's financial initiative by the democrats and radicals, the adversaries of all Church freedom, the Italian Chamber was dissolved; new elections inflamed the entire country and threatened to push it to revolution. The Italian administration appeared to be shaken to its foundations since the transfer of the capital; the Monarchy, notwithstanding the gain of Venice, was tottering; and the sad war of 1866 had increased the disaffection into which it had fallen. Dishonesty throughout the administration, quick ministry changes, financial difficulties, and internal dissolution all contributed to a scenario verging on anarchy, and the government lost all moral prestige as a result. The Action Party was always calling for the violation of the September Convention; it not only formed secret committees, but also open associations in the Church States for an invasion. Committees of this type sprang up in Florence, Genoa, Bologna, and elsewhere, with no action taken by the government. Garibaldi had grown close to the Mazzinians and had been following their plans. On the 23rd of February, during the election for the new Chamber, he rushed from Caprera to Florence to assist the democratic party in its win. He then travelled to the Italian cities as an agitator, inciting the populace to a murderous battle against the priest, from whose grasp Rome now had to be freed.

On March 22, the King convened the new parliament, which was mostly constituted of the same members as the previous one; there was no mention of the Roman question. At the beginning of April, Urbano Rattazzi assumed the Presidency of the Council, and the revolutionary party hoped that under him, they would be able to accomplish what Ricasoli had failed to accomplish, despite the fact that it was Rattazzi who had organised the tragedy of Aspromonte at Napoleon's command.

As a result, another democratic organisation, Garibaldi's action party, was forming, with the stated goal of invading Rome. Garibaldi was elected as its head, and specifically by a Mazzinian Committee, with a letter dated from Rome (Centre for the Insurrection of Rome), despite the fact that the existence of that Committee, in this particular city, was somewhat dubious. This Committee invited the Romans to rise up and overthrow the priests' government on April 1st; it assured that other cities in the Church States would rise up at the same time, because everything was ready; and it proclaimed Garibaldi as the leader of the uprising, Garibaldi who, after his nomination by the people of Rome in 1849, had rightly remained a Roman general. In response, Garibaldi issued a letter dated S. to the Centre of the Insurrection. Fiorano 22 March, in which he declared his pride in the title of Roman general and announced that he had already chosen the top of the Roman diaspora to Florence.

In response to the radicals' appeal, the National Committee issued a protest on April 9, advising Romans not to be led to act with guilty and dangerous levity, and to wait for the appropriate time to act. In fact, the peace was not disturbed; and even the 12th of April, the anniversary of the Pontiff's return from exile as well as his miraculous escape from the collapse of the hall at St Agnes, was celebrated with illuminations and passed off peacefully, as is customary.

However, the foreshadowing symptoms of an invasion by volunteer troops, as clearly shown in Garibaldi's letter, gave the Roman government cause for concern; Cardinal Antonelli sent a note to the French envoy in Rome, Count Sartiges, on 26 April, expressing his concerns. According to the September treaty agreements, the French Cabinet advised the Florentine Cabinet to keep watch over the revolutionary meetings, and received assurances from Rattazzi that they were keeping watch and that there was nothing to fear because the revolutionary committees were weak and lacking in means. Rattazzi stated at an interpellation in Parliament that he would pursue the course of action outlined in the Treaty of September in the Roman dispute.

Meanwhile, the French authorities was alerted of the radical party's continuous spread. He had heard of a convoy of arms to Viterbo, as well as Garibaldi's plan to arm ships in Genoa and disembark them on the Roman coast, while droves of immigrants were to pass the Neapolitan border, and revolutionaries' emissaries were to stir up the insurrection in Rome. In fact, Garibaldi openly led the invasion; at the end of April, he sent a circular to the ministers of England, Prussia, and Russia in Florence, protesting against the Pontiff's sovereignty and recalling that the Constituent Assembly of 1849 had appointed him as governor of Rome, and affirmed that this power entrusted to him was still legitimate, and could only be taken away by an assembly of representatives of the Roman people.

The movement on the borders and the work of the committees increased in May. Following the notes from France, Rattazzi responded that Garibaldi was unwell at Signa and had no intention of embarking on any risky ventures, and that the government was keeping an eye on him. One can trust that this was his genuine opinion, even if he secretly considered leveraging the revolutionary movement to change the September Convention. Rattazzi, in fact, arranged for the Roman emigrants to be removed from Bologna, the epicentre of the insurgency. Meanwhile, Cardinal Antonelli permitted papal troops to join forces with Italian troops for border patrol. An initial group of 200 volunteers were detained by the Italian government in June after attempting to cross the borders at Terni. Sixty volunteers were imprisoned, while the rest were dispersed. This made a favourable impression and reassured many people. The Roman invasion was postponed not just due to a lack of soldiers and weaponry, but also because the peace between France and Russia changed the political environment. The Italian democracy had banked on a war of those powers following the Luxembourg dispute, but this threat had passed with the Treaty of London of 11 May.

Keeping the peace preserved the Pope's temporal power from destruction, which would have occurred if France had gone to war with Germany. The huge Centenarium Petri feasts may now be staged without risk. In the midst of Italian instability at the danger of an invasion of the Papal States, this jubilee of the prince of the Apostles, whose successors the popes claim to be, was to assert that Rome was the metropolis of the Church and the capital of the Catholic world. From the beginning of June, hordes of priests made their way to Rome via all of Italy's trains. Four hundred and ninety bishops and prelates, as well as over ten thousand priests, assembled in Rome, where nothing like this had ever happened before the railways. The clergy were swarming the hotels, houses, and streets. After the feared invasion of Garibaldi's red shirts, Rome now appeared to be undergoing another invasion of black shirts; a whole people rushed to defend their city.

Several nationalities could be identified in this crowd, although French, Italians, and Spaniards predominated, as if confirming the Roman-ness of the Catholic Church once more. In the midst of this throng, the Germans were lost. The archbishops of Mainz, Cologne, Posen, Salzburg, Prague, and Olmütz were present; the archbishop of Vienna was not. On that occasion, all of Christendom's customs were visible. The pompous and grand patriarchs of the East were appreciated, as their presence emphasised the Christian cult's ties with Asia and the Old Testament. There were also Chinese and Moors.

Never before, not even during Leo X's Papacy, had there been processions in Rome comparable to those held for Corpus Christi and St. Peter's Day in the year 1867. These feasts marked the Pope's most magnificent and spectacular appraisal of his clergy.

On St. Peter's Day, the grand procession out of the cathedral into the square and back into the church lasted two hours. Banners 20 feet high were carried, representing the new saints, either dying or performing a miracle, and none piqued the interest of the Japanese missionaries more than Pedro Arbues, the terrible inquisitor of Spain, whose assumption into the heaven of the blessed was judged abroad as an open and clear declaration of war on the laws of humanity and civilisation. Throughout the day, a silent flood of individuals entered through one door of the shrine and exited through the other.

Five hundred hymns were sung from the inner circle of Michelangelo's dome. On June 29, the illumination of this golden glittering vault was enchanting and magical, just as the effect of the temple sparkling with fire and light was magical: it resembled, in fact, a celestial sphere in which innumerable stars sprouted fire amidst a golden mist.

According to mythology, the Apostle sat on the Petri Chair, which was moved from the bishop's throne in the Tribuna, which Alexander VII had enclosed, to a dedicated chapel and exposed to public worship. It was rediscovered after two centuries. Ivory plaques portraying Hercules' labours adorn the front of this old wooden chair. The throng went to great lengths to rub fabric or rings against it, hoping that it would take on the properties of amulets.

Rome honoured the occasion for eight days with processions, illuminations, scholarly and musical performances. The cult's grandest manifestations were collected in Rome in the same year that the World's Fair in Paris displayed the fruits of our century's labour and ingenuity.

The apostolic feast of the Church's unity, consecrated by history at its centre in Rome, was to demonstrate, with massive clergy manifestation, that in the cog of the hierarchical machine, not a single wheel was missing, that between the head and the members all reigned a perfect and unalterable harmony, maintained without effort or constraint. On this occasion, Emperors, Kings, and Princes were not to be found in Rome, as they were in Paris; however, pilgrims from all over the world flocked here. Representatives of Europe's oldest genuine aristocracy had arrived, not without gifts, to pay tribute to the Pontiff.

On that occasion, millions of dollars were donated to the Vatican, both through individual collections from various dioceses and private contributions. In Rome, there were counted from 50,000 to 70,000 foreigners from all areas of the Kingdom of Italy attended. This demonstrated that the schism between the Italian people and the Church was not as serious as it was made out to be.

The chains of St. Peter still bind a portion of humanity, and it has never worn other chains longer!

The Papacy's paladins were filled with joy and pride. Wasn't it supposed to be demonstrated that Rome could not be the capital of a kingdom? Were not those celebrations the clearest evidence of this? The thousands of priests who crowded around the Pope and fraternised among their Church's extravagant festivities were all filled with the same exuberant feeling. Wouldn't they have taken that enthusiasm and disseminated it throughout their countries and communities? The tremendous reaction and triumph of the Church over all the antagonistic powers of the universe was to begin with this centennial feast. So said Louis Veuillot in the Universe. No one could have predicted that such fervour in the Church would be followed by such blatant disillusionment!
Pius IX announced the Council in his addresses to the gathering bishops on June 26 and July 1.

In the war against what he termed the Century and what we call the spirit of civilisation, it was inevitable for the Pope to draw the entire hierarchy closer around him and strive to magnify his authority in the organism of the Church. The old dogma of the Pope's infallibility has now returned more forcefully to the organs of the Jesuits. The Gregorian Papacy's crowning glory is infallibility. And didn't this dogma also signify the end of the Church's great ideal force in history? If it was to be the Papacy's apotheosis, it is well known that apotheosis is expensive.

Civiltà Cattolica had solemnly urged that all priests and believers who came to Rome for the centenary make a promise at the tomb of the Apostle to maintain the pontiff's infallibility in life and death. Catholics had previously only sent St. Peter material sacrifices and offerings, both their wealth and their blood, it claimed cynically; now it was a matter of sacrificing reason itself to the prince of the Apostles! It was believed that by doing so, the entire clergy would be solidly bound in the bonds of this promise, forming nearly a holy league of Knights of St. Peter in Christendom; but, the Jesuits' plan was not accepted.

There were no new declarations made by the gathering bishops respecting the temporal Dominion. They simply stated in their address to the Pope, dictated by Heinald, that they wanted to reaffirm what they had already stated in 1862, namely that they wanted to believe what the Pope believes and reject what the Pope rejects. Wasn't this a proclamation of his infallibility?

During these festivities, word of Archduke Maximilian's execution in Mexico reached Rome. It left a lasting effect. Many clerics voiced their joy that the death of this unfortunate prince was a kind of Medusa's head for Emperor Napoleon; as he had betrayed Maximilian, he was ready to betray the papacy! He recalled with awe the Roman satire that had welcomed the archduke in 1864, when he had visited Rome before embarking on his perilous expedition to Mexico, and his prophetic verses:

Maximilian, do not trust; return to Miramare as soon as possible. Montezuma's contentious throne is Gallic nappa full with froth. Danaos timeo, who has forgotten, discovers the rope beneath the chlamys.

IV.

These magnificent celebrations were followed by completely different events. There are few examples in history of such a sudden and stark contrast as Rome provided in just a few months. If we imagine that among the pilgrims who flocked to Rome was an Asian or African who was completely unaware of European politics, this foreigner could have said of Rome at the end of June: 'Rome, the very ancient capital of the Catholic world, is not only the richest and noblest city on earth, but also the happiest. All peoples go to her, bringing gifts and tribute, not in response to a stern and terrible rebuke from their sovereign, as in ancient Rome or the empires of Asia or Egypt, but voluntarily, to magnify their love for Him. Thousands of visitors travel there to prostrate themselves in prayer before the tomb of the Prince of the Apostles and witness unbelievable magnificence rites in his sublime shrine. It appears that the love of all men crowns Rome with festivities and honours, at the beckoning of which the bishops of the earth and seventy thousand priests have flocked to tell him that they believe what he believes, that they reprove what he reproves, as have thousands of other men who are not priests and who have also come to pay him divine honours.

If the same stranger returned to the same city three months later, he would not have believed his senses and would have assumed he was the victim of a spell. For he would have discovered that city, which had been full of festive tumult and garlanded with flowers and covered with carpets and paintings not long before, almost contaminated by the plague, immersed in astonishment, anxiety, and terror, at night from the bursting of bombs and mines, during the day from patrols of frightened soldiers, gathering hordes of arrested men. They would have told him that the old man, whom he had just seen exalted to heaven, was now full of panic praying in the lonely and wretched Vatican, asking God to save him from imminent peril, and already splitting himself into Castel Sant'Angelo and confining himself there. He would have seen the gates of Rome locked and reinforced on the inside with ramparts, the battlements of the fortresses defended by sacks of earth; and he would have heard that innumerable battered, starving, ill-armed bands, dressed in red shirts, were marching towards Rome, shouting: Rome or death! ... seize Christendom's capital and jail the Holy Father, or to force him into exile around the world.

Meanwhile, the colèra had already showed itself in June, and it became more violent in July. It erupted with unusual force on August 6 in Albano, where many Roman families had gone to spend the summer. The queen-widow of Naples, Maria Theresa, daughter of Archduke Charles, died there on August 8. Panic gripped Albano, and both locals and visitors fled in terror. Cardinal Altieri, who had gone there as the local bishop to calm the populace, was victimised by his self-denial. The Zouaves stationed there kept discipline on their own, and they should be applauded for their efforts.

Even in the rest of Italy, the colèra raged, but it did not derail the revolutionary movement of the party of action, which had been energised by the festivities in Rome and was eager to put its plans into action as soon as possible. Meanwhile, the French government's behaviour bolstered the Italians' concordant aspirations; that administration appeared to begin with the assumption that the occupation of Rome would continue through Antibo's legion. Not only had General Dumond arrived in Rome to examine this legion, which had been partially disbanded due to frequent desertions, but the publishing of a letter from Marshal Wiel to Colonel d'Argy demonstrated that these troops in the service of the Pontiff were still considered a French corps. This prompted Rattazzi to write to the Paris Cabinet at the end of August, vowing that the French government would not add to Italy's difficulties by bringing up the Roman question and jeopardising the

September Convention.

The democratic press declared angrily that France had violated the Convention and that, as a result, Italy was also entitled to disregard it. The government, which by this time was considering renouncing Rome and recognising the sovereignty of the Pope in support of the September Convention, and was also constantly threatening Italy with a new French intervention, found itself in contradiction with itself, while feeling too weak to withstand the pressure of the party of action at a time when, after the disgraceful financial project, it saw its own embarrassments grow out of all proportion.

Garibaldi returned to Italy, openly discussing a campaign against Rome, where the National Committee and the Insurrection Centre had already joined and united in the Roman National Council on 13 July. Arms and money were amassed all the way to England, where one of Garibaldi's sons had fled. Umbria's boundaries began to fill with strange people. The Agitator arrived in Orvieto on August 26. Here he assembled the people to hear him, assailed the government of Florence as vehemently as the government of Paris in his address, surrounded by cries of Rome or death, and eventually announced that, despite the September Convention, Rome had to be conquered by the people rising in armies. He then travelled to Rapallo, and on September 8, he found himself in Geneva, at the Peace Congress, where the leaders of European democracy had convened to lay the groundwork for a future European community. Garibaldi was hailed with universal honours and named honorary president of this Parliament.

His speeches from the balcony of the Fazy house, as well as those for the inauguration of the Congress, were so powerful that they shocked many of his supporters. He intended to forget that the city of Calvin and Rousseau had many Catholics among its residents, as well as aristocratic and traditional attitudes. His angry outbursts against the Papacy and the Church elicited loud protests from the Catholic citizens; among the Reformed, the moderates were no less fearful; a split arose in the Congress, and Garibaldi left Geneva on September 11, nearly clandestinely and thoroughly disillusioned.

He then went to Genestrelle, intent on carrying out the Roman invasion. Since his stay in Orvieto, he had been secretly working on the preparations and strategic plans for this audacious venture. Ancona, Foligno, Bologna, Florence, the Abruzzi, and Naples all had volunteer troops. Weapons deposits were secretly transported to the borders and into the Church States. According to the September Convention, volunteers came from all over to patrol the borders, which were guarded by Italian troops on the front lines.

The obvious nature of these armaments in front of the government's eyes, the invective of Mazzini's press, the proclamations of the national committees, Garibaldi's letters, and the messages of the legates of Rome and Florence urged the French government to excite the Italian ministry to prompt and effective action, making it aware of the serious difficulties that could arise if this state of affairs continued, difficulties that the Emperor wished to spare himself and the King. And Napoleon's difficulties were numerous. In light of the ever-increasing threat of war with Prussia, he did not want to alienate Italy from himself; by distancing himself from France, Italy would have drawn closer to its ally of Padua; if he had allowed the September Convention to be violated, he would have suffered a new setback, making himself the figure of an accomplice or a scoundrel. If he decided to intervene in accordance with the Pope's wishes, he would seriously harm France's liberal party, possibly provoking a desperate defence war in Italy or throwing it back into anarchy, destroying his own work of 1859.

Following urgent dispatches from Paris, action was taken against the revolutionary party. Victor Emmanuel dispatched envoys to encourage Garibaldi, in the name of the monarch, to abandon his hasty preparations and retire to Caprera. However, he left Florence to travel to Arezzo through Sinalunga and then to the States of the Church.

However, on the orders of the administration, the general was captured in Sinalunga on September 23 and transported by rail to the Alexandria stronghold. This unexpected information abruptly altered the situation, and it appears that the invasion project with it.

Garibaldi's aim had been to use his agents to incite a revolt in Viterbo, but following his arrest, the papal authorities seized them and the correspondence they had with them. Garibaldi's operatives were also active in Rome, but after much futile effort, they had to convince themselves that there was nothing to be done in this city. There were also mass arrests conducted here. Flyers were distributed throughout the city announcing that the National Council had dissolved on September 22nd and that on September 27th, the so-called section chiefs had formed another in its place,'so that the city would not be left without a government in such difficult times'. The capture of Garibaldi was welcomed abroad; the Italian government was congratulated on regaining control of an unfortunate state of affairs in which a leader of the people was allowed to place himself above the laws of the State, to form his own government within the State itself, to carry out his own plans, to spill the blood of the people, to ruin the money entrusted to him, and to lead them to revolution, thus determining the outcome. Indeed, it was rumoured that a French fleet was waiting to sail in the port of Toulon. Garibaldi's esteem and consideration had long since dwindled. His numerous proclamations, his eccentricities (he had even gone so far as to baptise children himself as a future priest), the ceaseless raging of his thunder without the flash of action, and the fact that he had become closer to Mazzini's movement had made the halo of the great agitator, who had played such a heroic role in the Italian redemption, pale. At the time, it was regretted that he had not perished at Capua or Aspromonte, thereby finishing his life as a popular hero rather than surviving. The liberals in Rome welcomed his detention as a prelude to diplomatic negotiations by the Italian government aimed at definite liberation from interference, even moral involvement, by France, and a change of the September Convention. And it was only Italy that could defend the Church States by keeping the ranks of volunteers from infiltrating them.

But the action party erupted, demanding the release of its leader, an inviolable member of parliament. Under the threat of riots in Florence and other cities, Garibaldi was taken from Alessandria to Genoa and almost certainly set free, as he himself declared, -that is, embarked on a war-boat on September 27 for Caprera. Was his incarceration truly serious? Had it not been a ruse to silence, shall we say, the French government while concealing the actual violation of the September Convention? Hadn't the invasion's leader been made to vanish, so that the invasion could follow its path more freely and less openly, and so that, instead of an officially disowned and sometimes covertly supported general, as at Marsala, Capua, and the Marche, other generals could lead it in the name of Italy? Was the Italian government truly incapable of dispersing the ranks of volunteers gathered on the borders? Although there were numerous troops of all ranks clutching the line of the Roman borders, this chain of militia frequently thinned out its links for various reasons, allowing armed bands to easily break into the Papal States. As soon as it became known outside Italy that the Italian government had prevented the execution of Garibaldi's plans and imprisoned him, they were informed that the daring enterprise of the invasion had begun and was openly continuing with the

Italian government's support.

V.

The invasion of the Church State by volunteer ranks, which lasted more than five weeks, will go down in history as a remarkable and highly dramatic episode in the history of Rome and the Papacy. In the history of Italy it will be a painful page, which will certainly not do credit to the government of that time, whose Macchiavellianism and profound weakness it showed. If, in the future, the difficult questions of our time find a solution in a regime of liberty, people will look back with the same astonishment that we now have for mediaeval and feudal forms of anarchy.

And indeed, in the year 1867, the mediaeval companies of fortune and those condottieri of the past, who, independently of the state, led their armies through the countryside, suddenly seemed to be resurrected with all their characters. Whoever was then in Rome and witnessed this state of affairs, believed he had suddenly returned to live in the Middle Ages, and in a country where the power of laws was now null and void; he saw things and figures that he had already encountered in the chronicles of that time, to which this extraordinary epoch could exactly resemble. Garibaldi, the most modern man of his time, according to his ideal, is also among the Italians of our time the one whose psychic figure is most deeply linked to mediaeval forms and sentiments, which partly explains his great popularity. He stands outside the state; like a condottiere; he lives, a hermit agitator, on a lonely island, far from the continent. He only appears in his homeland to carry out his designs, in defiance of the state, by means of popular agitation and ranks of volunteers. Monreale, Sforza Attendolo, Piccinino and Fortebraccio would certainly have recognised in him a colleague, a valiant captain of bands; in their time, he would have formed a military republic, or won a ducal crown. Today, however, he is distinguished from those leaders by the fact that he has put his sword at the service of his country and his people. He fights with republican disinterest for the ideas of the present, indeed perhaps for the ideas of the future. He wants to overthrow the idol of absolutism and tyranny, both spiritual and temporal, but he wants to put in its place another idol, whose despotism could not possibly be less. He, too, with the carelessness of a tyrant of ancient times, has sacrificed the bold youth of his homeland, exploiting them as a tool for his own aims.

The Roman question, so deeply connected to the whole complicated machinery of the European world, seemed, to this man of war, a Gordian knot that the sword alone could solve. Simply he did not have Alexander's sword, and even if this were but a symbol of contemporary reality, like Columbus' egg, European opinion would never have accepted Garibaldi or Mazzini and his party as its spokesmen and sponsors.

And indeed, it appears to us a fantastic dream that ranks of troops, jumbled together, poorly armed and without discipline, and such that the ancient leaders of Italy would have despised taking them into their service, should pretend to conquer Rome, like a Constable of Bourbon! But such a design was possible in our time, and it wasn't long before this dream became a reality. One day this will be a myth in the history of Rome.

And the ardent and noble patriotism of a Garibaldi-type warrior, as well as the sublime audacity that drove his ranks to their deaths, will be recognised and admired even by those who condemned his enterprise as detrimental to the homeland, and trembled at the thought that the principle of brigand-like freedom of the Americans of the Plata or Chili could also find expression in a civilised Europe. But that's all there is to say about it. Instead, the dispassionate judgement of the warmest friend of the Italian nation and of the freedom of peoples will always regard, with contempt and disdain, those who followed, in this false game, the rules of the "Machiavelli's 'Prince', for one must proclaim to the ends of the earth the justness of Washington's maxim, and prove that the best policy is the truth. In 1867, the history of politics was enriched with such a comedy that mankind will have to search its annals for a similar one for a long time to come; and if crimes have often been committed in the name of freedom, such fundamental trifles have rarely been committed in its name.

The Italian Cabinet, due to its weakness and a kind of strange illusion, was led to tolerate the dangerous design of the invasion, then even to accept and accelerate it, which threw Italy into the most terrible crisis, jeopardised the monarchy and the unity of the country, and produced a frightening demoralisation throughout the nation. Thus, amidst a diplomacy without power and a heroic rage of leaders, tremendous errors evolved. A Roman uprising was hoped for, but it did not happen. There was none in the Church's states, and even less so in Rome and Viterbo, where agents of the revolutionary party tried in vain to incite it. Only a genuine revolution in the Church's states might, if the people's desire had been clearly expressed, transform the situation, justify an intervention by Italy, and completely rule out French participation. But since this did not happen, and the populace of the Roman empire remained quiet, it would have been in vain to pass off an invasion by voluntary troops from other provinces as a popular rebellion. It was counted on the inability and weak character of the papal troops, as well as on the desertion of the Italian element; but these soldiers, foreigners and peasants, fought with unexpected valour, remaining faithful to the flag on which they had sworn. They also counted on the mistakes of the Papal Government, but it rarely showed such reasonableness and strength as it did then, and was able to maintain, under such difficult conditions, such a legitimate and expedient demeanour, which made an excellent impression on European public opinion, especially as it contrasted with that of the Italian Government.

One hoped, in particular, for the protector of France's tacit approval and his consent to the modification of the September treaty. Rumours were flying around England that this change was on the way for the coming summer, and that Napoleon would reconsider and decide to intervene once he learned of Rattazzi's specific offers to Prussia. However, Napoleon could not allow the revolutionary side, against which he had risen, to tamper with a treaty that he had confirmed and acknowledged; he intervened - because the Roman State had not risen - in favour of the Pope and the spiritual power, with which he wished to maintain good friendship, at first hesitating and stalling, then with inconsiderate gravity.

According to Garibaldi's plan, the invasion was to proceed from three sides; from Sabina and Umbria, from Tuscia and Lazio, the armies were to head for their destination: Rome. The first route was the shortest and led directly to Rome, as the borders here, at Corese and Scandriglia, were only two hours away by train from the city. Garibaldi's son, Menotti, took command of the armies arriving from Umbria. The second road passes through Viterbo, the first destination of the troops that followed, today the second city of the state, situated in a rich countryside and inhabited by a population that was always considered bold, proud and fond of novelty. Here Acerbi was to take command. On the third road, Nicotera was to direct the invasion against Rome through the Monti Latini. The latter two leaders were to be Italian Parliament deputies. In addition, minor maniples were to lead these roads from various points to assault the papal garrisons here and there, to keep the entire papal army occupied and scattered with the system of guerrilla warfare.

The bulk of these ranks were made up of people jumbled together, a large proportion of whom could barely handle a rifle. Their condition, which would have made a novelist or a

Salvator Rosa go into raptures, made every man of war doubt and bewildered; they were footmen, coachmen, servants, student scribes, peasants, tailors, shoemakers, factory workers of all kinds, all sorts of hungry people. In their ranks were also men and young men of extensive cultivation, nobility and wealth, and even emancipated ladies, who followed the small army on horseback. Such feats are only performed in Italy, because here the unique character of the population responds to them. Certainly, the leverage that moved all these people was, for the most part, need and the spirit of adventure, but it would be unfair to consider these ranks merely as a gathering of rogues and scoundrels. Patriotism had spread from democratic circles to the lowest classes of the population, and the poor workers fought valiantly at Mentana. Finally, there were among them well-known patriots and noble spirits, who, full of patriotic sentiment, had resolved to sacrifice everything, even their lives, for their country. And these grew in number from hand to hand; all the states and provinces of Italy had their representatives there; finally real Italian soldiers, secretly discharged, came to strengthen these bands of volunteers.

They were divided into battalions. Their uniform was supposed to be the red shirt, but not all of them had one; many wore a piece of red cloth on their clothing. All had a rooster or falcon feather on their hats. Weapons were lacking and in poor condition. Many were armed only with spears, daggers, and sabres. Some battalions had used weapons that had come out of the National Guards' stores. The method of supply and provisioning of this army was as primitive as that of its armament. They relied on the contributions of the places they occupied, but everyone knows that the castles of the Sabine and Latium districts are mostly inhabited by very poor farmers, who live off the grain of their fields, the income from their vineyards, olive groves and chestnut groves. And one could indeed well have prophesied that Garibaldi's patriotic fanaticism would have thrown so many thousands of people into misery, as it did at the time of Aspromonte, if he had not succeeded, as he did then, in dragging all the Italian people behind him and getting the people of the Papal States to take up arms.

The army that the Pope could confront these lines of volunteers then comprised 12,981 soldiers and 929 horses, of which 8000 were actually fit and ready to battle. The corps, arranged according to the number of men, were in this order: regiment of zouaves, 2237; legion of indigenous gendarmes, 2082; regiment of line, also indigenous, 1595; battalion of foreign carabineers, 1233; French legion of Antibes, 1096; battalion of hunters, 956 infantrymen and 442 horses; finally 5 batteries of artillery.

This army was composed of Italians from the Papal States as well as immigrants of various nationalities. Since the Papacy had found itself in significant difficulties after the French army retreated, all regions of the world had committed themselves, with great Catholic zeal, to the restoration of the papal army.
Numerous Belgian, French, and even American associations sent boxes full of money and weapons to Rome as tribute. The Catholic press gave the new recruits the dramatic title of St Peter's Crusaders, jubilating over the revival of the crusade. In fact, the small papal army represented the effort of the whole of Christendom; many faces and many nationalities were represented: Scots, Irish, Poles, Germans, French, Dutch, Belgians, Canadians, Moors from Africa, Italians, Spaniards mingled under the banner of the archangel Michael; and even in this cosmopolitan army it was not only religious zeal that drove so many people; in some it was rather the spirit of adventure, need, or a past to be redeemed.

The Zouaves were the chosen corps of St Peter's militia, the actual guard of the Knights of the Cross. When the Pontiff summoned Lamoricière to Rome as the Temporal Power's rescuer in 1866, he established this corps in remembrance of his African battles. Many sons of ancient legitimist families from France and Belgium served in this army as officers or as ordinary foot soldiers. Their colonel was De Charette, a descendent of the famed captain of the Royalist Vendée. The corps was largely French and Belgian, and spoke French. Their half-Turkish outfit, somewhat theatrical and colourful, was enthusiastically donned by many gentlemen. Most of these officers of the Zouaves, and also of the simple soldiers, were full of Catholic sentiments and mediaeval ideals; they were burning with the desire to come to blows with the Italian rebels, the red-shirted democrats, the heretics, and to avenge all the insults suffered by the Pontiff in recent years.

General Kanzler, a former officer in the Baden army and long in the service of the Pope, led the papal army. A skilful retreat of his battalion after the battle of Castelfidardo had drawn attention to him, so that he was promoted in rank and appointed deputy minister of war. The Papal War Ministry had hitherto been entrusted to prelates; most recently to Merode, Montalembert's brother-in-law, and this custom could not have been very beneficial to the organisation of the army. The visible difference was immediately noticeable when it was finally entrusted to a man of arms. The general's seriousness and activity quickly reorganised the troops, and the Papal States owed it to the Kanzler if they could withstand the invaders' forces for so long.

The Church State was divided into military zones, which included Viterbo, Civitavecchia, Tivoli, Sabina, Campagna, and Marittima. These formed together a half division under the command of General De Courten; the other half division, a two thousand men, resided in Rome, under General Zappi. Companies were located in larger cities, but gendarmerie postings were frequently found in smaller towns. The

Campagna garrison was reinforced by volunteers from the Campagnola population, known as auxiliaries or squadriglieri, who formed militarily organised corps while wearing their picturesque Ciociaria costume and distinctive sandals. They had previously been militarily constituted during the fight against brigandage in 1866-67, when they provided valuable services to the Latium region. A battalion of them, totaling 638 men, was stationed in Frosinone and the borders of Naples. Others had, elsewhere, incorporated themselves into the gendarmerie. In total, their strength amounted to 1,200 men.

At the end of September, Latium offered a strange and comical appearance. While the Papal State was preparing to oppose the occupation of Rome and the entire territory with all its forces, 10,000 to 20,000 Italian soldiers were making their rounds on the borders, in an equivocal and mysterious attitude, who were supposed to keep the volunteer ranks away from the borders, but on the contrary, they were blatantly letting them in and out, while they themselves sang patriotic hymns with the refrain: "We will go to Holy Rome". They stood, arms at their feet, quietly watching hundreds of red shirts, divided into small bands, roaming around the borders, burning with the desire to break into the papal region, while their duce, the leader of the movement, whose name alone was a war cry, was still relegated to the rock of Caprera. Seven Italian warships were circumnavigating this island in the same way that English warships had circumnavigated Elba, envious of a bigger man who was preparing daring exploits against the continent.

On 29 September, the announcement came to Rome that the invasion had begun. During the night, 40 Garibaldians had crossed the border at Grotte S. Stefano in the province of Viterbo, disarmed that gendarmerie post, ripped off the papal coats of arms, and planted the Italian flag. Then they had headed for Bomarzo, where the same scene had repeated itself. From then on, they frequently carried out little incursions of this type in various locations. On the 29th, others occupied Bagnorea and Torre Alfina, and on the following day the most important place, Acquapendente. The gendarme barracks defended themselves in this town for a good three hours, then surrendered. The Garibaldini seized the public coffers, arrested the Magistrate and levied taxes. They declared themselves General Acerbi's vanguard, led by Count Pagliacci, who had emigrated from Viterbo.

When the occupation of Acquapendente was announced, Colonel Azzanesi moved from Viterbo with troops; he swooped down on the Garibaldini on 2 October at S. Lorenzo, put them to flight, took many prisoners and reoccupied Acquapendente. The fugitives gathered and Bagnorea, the ancient Balneum Regis. A corps of 95 Zouaves attacked them by surprise, but was repulsed with losses until papal reinforcements arrived. Bagnorea was attacked on 5 October; the Garibaldians, 500 in number, retreated, leaving 100 dead and wounded and 178 prisoners. This was the first notable fact about the guerrilla war. It demonstrated, against all odds, that the papal soldiers knew how to fight with gallantry and seriousness, and that they were as good and fit for battle as their opponents.

Every day, troops left Rome; the city appeared to be devoid of militia, and reports of new attacks in the Latium region arrived on a daily basis. The city began to experience unusual excitement, not least because news of defeats, victories, and hypothetical uprisings were artfully spread from time to time.

The volunteer armies, driven out of Bagnorea, had thrown themselves on Torre Alfina, a small village on the Tuscan border, very strong due to the nature of the place. General Acerbi gathered his forces here, as if in a command post, to swoop down on Viterbo as soon as possible. At the same time, other bands fortified themselves in Nerola, Moricone,

Montemaggiore, Montelibretti; small and deserted places in Sabina. They are true clusters of houses atop rugged cliffs, from which emerge the church, and a few crumbling mediaeval towers, and the grand baronial castle, from the time when the Orsini dominated so much of Sabina.

The young Menotti led 600 men there, with whom he hoped to break into the campaign towards Tivoli, if supported by other troops, and favoured by the concerted conquest of Subiaco that was to join him with the Abruzzi. Garibaldi had appointed his son as his lieutenant, with a decree from Caprera; there was also a kind of Garibaldian dynasty, and, while the old lion roared closed in Caprera, at least his sons, Ricciotti and Menotti, were to fight for the national cause. But, when Colonel Carette marched on Menotti's troops on 7 October, they fell back in Fara. They were pursued, driven out, and dispersed after a short fight; they then retreated to the borders, where they were graciously received by the Italian troops. They returned, reinforced, renewing guerrilla warfare here and there. The papal troops sent prisoners to Castel Sant'Angelo every day, but the continuous marches and countermarches, and the losses they suffered, were beginning to tyre them out. The war of invasion had begun in the Papal States like an intermittent fever in a sick body: could it not have soon spread to the head, the already murky Rome?

From the beginning of September, Garibaldi's agents were actively working in Rome to prepare and provoke an uprising. To achieve the goal, no means were spared. Weapons, bombs, powder were ready in concealed places. The Roman National Committee, which had already been dissolved, reconstituted itself and issued a proclamation on 8 October, which said: 'Romans, the provinces have already risen; soon the uprising will be general. We must join this movement and support it with all our strength, because the victory of the provinces will prepare and facilitate the victory of Rome. We are therefore all ready. Let the blood of our brothers that the papal zouaves still shed in the provinces be the spark that will set our spirits on fire. Romans, the decisive hour is approaching. In the name of the Fatherland let us unite, and let each one obey only the command that will come to us from the Central Committee. Unity and discipline, that is what forms strength. Every inconsiderate, irregular and isolated movement can be of great harm. Trust that Committee, which has already proven its strength, acuity and firm will. Now that the great moment has come, it will know how to fulfil its duty. Let us unite confidently and boldly; let us work disciplined, and the cause of civilisation will be won.

Meanwhile, the facts showed that all the exaggerated reports in Garibaldi's papers were shameless inventions. Not in one place was there an uprising in the provinces. After all, did undisciplined bands that attacked and ruined communities, only to run as soon as the papal troops approached, have sufficient moral force to bring the people into common cause with them and go down with them? Was Italy behind those bands? Was there no fear of French intervention with its unavoidable consequences in this case? Neither citizen nor countryman desired to know about the uprising. The invasion resembled a fatuous fire that flickered at the borders, and was lit briefly, here and there, without result. It would have been dubbed a major war against brigandage.

On 11 October, Subiaco was taken; the bishop and the supreme magistrate were put under surveillance; in vain the fortress was commanded to surrender. Some Zouaves emerged, and the Garibaldini retreated, swiftly abandoning the city.

On 13 October, Menotti was snatched from the strong position of Montelibretti, where he had returned. The volunteer ranks made no progress anywhere. Nicotera, who had to penetrate the Liri valley through the Neapolitan borders, could only move on 13th October and occupied Falvaterra. However, on the 15th, he was beaten and driven out of the province of Frosinone. The prisoner population at Castel Sant'Angelo was high. The Pope commanded that they be lavishly fed. To those men, prostrated by hunger and fatigue, he sent cloaks to shelter them from the night frost. He also visited them one day and said to them: "Here I am: I am he whom you consider your enemy and whose death you have sworn. And who are you up against? An old and weak man. They knelt before him, and many kissed the hem of his garment. "He is good," the Romans observed of Pius IX at the time, "but he has two souls: one obeys Italy and one obeys the Jesuits.

The Mazzinian press gave atrocious reports on the treatment of these prisoners; but they were false. In the hospitals and prisons they treated them humanely and benignly. The only thing the prisoners could complain about were the visits and sermons of confessors and priests sent to them to reconcile them with God.

VI.

Meanwhile, the threat to Rome grew stronger by the day. The invasion was the hydra with a hundred heads. Always new bands appeared, and they were more and more openly sponsored by the Italian army. Enlistments were being made in the cities of the Kingdom; weapons were coming to them from the warehouses of the National Guard. The railways were at their service, and hundreds of red shirts were transported by trains to the borders every day. Even in Rome, an increasing number of mystery foreigners were detected; big preventive arrests were made, but they were unable to reach the epicentre of the commotion. Every day, the city's appearance deteriorated; commerce ceased; and monetary money vanished. There was talk of impending violent riots, and the Roman garrison, tired and diminished by sickness and desertions, had to undergo a strenuous patrol duty.

On October 17, the Pope issued an encyclical to the Catholic clergy in which he described Rome's dire situation. In the usual declamatory pomposity of these acts, one noticed, strange to say, that the very first sentence of the encyclical coincided with that: Levate in circuitu oculos vestros ,[3] with which the great enemy of the papacy, Frederick II of Hohenstaufen, had once begun his encyclical to Christendom against Gregory IX: "Raise, O venerable brethren, your eyes around and you will see, and you will grieve with Us, the horrible abominations that presently bedevil wretched Italy. But We humbly defer to the inscrutable Divine wills, who wished to make us live in such sad times, in which, by the work of some men, and precisely those who govern public affairs in Italy, the precepts of God and the laws of the Church are trampled underfoot, and unbelief triumphs with impunity. From this state of affairs derive all the injustices and all the evils to which we are sorrowful witnesses; in this state of affairs those numerous bands of atheists who unfurl the banners of Satan, and who bear written on their foreheads, find nourishment and spur: Lies; who blaspheme against Heaven in the name of rebellion, who defile all that is holy, who trample underfoot every divine and human right, who, like wolves in search of prey, shed blood, corrupt souls in their delirium, demand the reward of their wickedness, they rob their brethren, they make the poor and the weak more miserable, they increase the number of widows and orphans, for money they exalt injustice, and, seeking in every way to satisfy their perverse lusts, they spread desolation and death in the nation.

"O Venerable Brethren, today we find ourselves encircled by this diabolical genius. Yes, these men want, moved by a diabolical spirit, to raise the flag of lies in this enlightened city of ours, in the chair of Peter, in the centre of Catholic faith and unity. And the representatives of the Subalpine government, who should be working to curb these people, do not hesitate to help them, to provide weapons and everything necessary to facilitate their coming to Rome. But these people-they even occupy a high rank in the civil hierarchy-are afraid that they will soon be punished for their behaviour. If, on the one hand, we beseech God in our humility to turn his benign gaze upon all these unfortunates, to lead them back to the path of Justice and Goodness, we cannot remain silent about the grave dangers that loom over us in this hour of darkness. We await events with a calm spirit, despite being moved by so much deception, slander, and lies, trusting in God, in God who is our salvation and our strength, and who will not allow those who trust in him to fall victim to so many unworthy unbelievers, whom he will crush and destroy. However, O venerable brothers, and all of you, O faithful ones, who have entrusted yourselves to us in the meantime, we do not wish to conceal from you the sad situation and danger in which we find ourselves at the hands of the Subalpine Government. And although we have been defended so far by the valour of our faithful army, a valour that has already shown itself in a thousand deeds of arms, we also think that, in the face of the ever-increasing number of invaders, it will not be able to resist for long. Our subjects' piety and fidelity also entrusts us not insignificantly in these sad and impious times, but we suffer deeply to see them exposed to dangers of all kinds by those wicked men who threaten, plunder, and torment them with every means..."

The Pope did not mention France, but his deliberate quiet was possibly more effective than a clear call to the forces that be for assistance.

All eyes were on Napoleon, who was also silent and appeared to have reverted to the mysterious Sphinx. Everyone wondered what he would do in the face of such a blatant breach of the Treaty of September. The liberals in Rome murmured that everything had to be settled at Biarritz; that the September

Convention had to be changed, that the Emperor, on the verge of entering the next inevitable war with Germany, couldn't afford to lose the Italian alliance, and that the price of this alliance had to be the Church's state, which would be all conquered in a few weeks.

But on 17 October, the very day the Pope published this encyclical, a telegram was sent from the Foreign Ministry in Paris to the French plenipotentiary in Rome, Armand: 'The Papal Government will continue to defend itself energetically; it will not lack the help of France'. This dispatch astounded the Roman National Committee and made the conservatives ecstatic. Napoleon dispatched General Prudon to Rome to inform the Pope that intervention had been determined, and Cardinal Antonelli directed the nuncio to thank the Emperor on the Pope's behalf.

The French government had previously kept the events in Italy under wraps, only advising the Italian government. The latter had repeatedly stated that border surveillance was impossible due to their length and natural configuration; as there was no other option to resolve the situation, it proposed that part of the Papal States be invaded by the Italian army. Nigra,[4] the King's plenipotentiary at the French Court, was tasked with carrying out this mission while also pointing out that a second French expedition into the Papal States not only violated the September Convention, but was also the most risky for resolving the Roman situation. By occupying a portion of the Papal States, Italy did not intend to interfere with the rights of papal sovereignty in any way; it only desired to restore the disturbed order and reach an agreement with France regarding the independence of the Pope, with the Italian government prepared to convene a Congress for this purpose.

The French Cabinet replied: 'that it was pleased that Italy recognised the sovereignty of the Pope; that it had nothing against a Congress of Powers being held; but could this

Congress be held if Italian troops occupied the Papal States, undoubtedly forcing the Pope into exile? The withdrawal of French troops from Rome had been a consequence of the September Convention and the Emperor's confidence that the Italian government would protect the Papal domain from invasion. The same treaty gave the Emperor the right to take measures to defend the Papal State, demonstrating the Italian government's inability to do so."

France's unequivocal rejection of Rattazzi's offer compelled the Italian government to proclaim its desire to keep the agreement. On October 19, the Emperor issued an ultimatum to Florence; his representative told Rattazzi that Napoleon demanded proof of the government's sincerity, namely the suppression of conscription, the dissolution of committees supporting the revolutionary work, and a royal proclamation declaring that Garibaldi's volunteers should be disarmed and interned.

On the same day, General De Failly left Paris for Toulon to take command of the expedition; the army was prepared to leave on the squad awaiting orders in Toulon if the Italian government did not accept the ultimatum.

The Rattazzi Ministry found itself in a difficult situation; not only did France oppose it, but all the powers were determined not to obstruct French action. Prussia itself, which he could relied on, would only be sympathetic to him when Napoleon became engaged in the Italian situation again and therefore lost Italy's final affections. Rattazzi couldn't possibly occupy the Papal States' territory. There was no movement in Rome that could provide him with an occasion or a pretext. On that day of October 19, I found only an anonymous writing in the Roman Senate's correspondence boxes, which stated that the situation in Rome was so dangerous that it required the intervention of Italian troops in the capital; the senator had to present the proposal to the Pope; and thousands of citizens who had left their names at a notary public were ready to declare that this was the will of the city of Rome. In the absence of Senator Marquis Cavalletti, the four conservatives sent this letter to the Pope, declaring, however, that they believed it would be a good idea to give it to His Holiness, not dividing in any way the ideas expressed in the letter, ideas that they believed were not in keeping with the dignity of the government.

And could an anonymous letter of dubious Roman origin, too closely related to the draught sent to Paris by Rattazzi, really be considered a genuine expression of the people and Senate of Rome?

Rattazzi was fired on the evening of October 19, the day of the crisis, and the King commissioned General Cialdini to form a new Cabinet. Cialdini was the man of Castelfidardo, but also of Aspromonte, a principled opponent of the volunteer ranks, and thus liked by France. In Florence the excitement was growing; and in the dilemma: to return to the convention and obey France; or to side with the revolution and break with Napoleon; it was not known which way was less dangerous. In the meantime, while Cialdini was unsuccessfully working on the composition of the Ministry, Rattazzi was still carrying out the business of ordinary administration; during this pause, forces could be set in motion that led to catastrophe.

The French Emperor, always hesitant, always doubly so, wished not to be forced into intervention. He was delighted when his plenipotentiary telegraphed from Rome on the 20th that no more volunteer troops were to be found in the Papal States that day.

In fact, it had succeeded, with great effort, in driving them back across the borders. The so-called Roman legion, with which an émigré, the former major Ghirelli of the royal army, had taken Orte on 17th October, had been driven out;

Menotti's volunteer troops, after the violent clash of arms on 18th October, had had to evacuate Nerola with great losses; Nicotera's bands, on the 19th, were driven out of Vallecorsa in Lazio. Following that telegram announcing all these facts, Napoleon, on the 21st, gave the order to suspend embarkation in Toulon. On the 22nd, the Moniteur gave news of this in an article that also expressed the conviction that the invasion of the Papal State had reached its end, and that the Italian government was resolved to the safe fulfilment of the September Convention.

So the surgery was cancelled, much to the grief of those who had so eagerly hoped for it.

VII.

Meanwhile, Garibaldi had remained at Caprera, in painful anxiety. Letters from his sons and revolutionary agents had informed him of the failure of the Roman expedition; he had also been warned of Napoleon's preparations for the intervention that the Italian government was about to undergo. He had already once attempted to escape to Livorno, and the cruising warships had prevented him from doing so. He immediately devised a strategy to place himself at the head of the volunteer ranks, march on Rome, enlist the Papacy at the base, and, if unsuccessful, leave his body between it and Italy.

As Napoleon had already escaped from Elba, he happily left Caprera on his boat on October 16th. With or without the complicity of the Italian warships, he reached the island of La Maddalena, where an English lady gave him hospitality; he then passed on to Sardinia, from where, disguised, he left and on 19 October, the decisive day, he landed on the Maremma of Livorno, near the tower of Vada. He arrived in Florence on the 20th. Nobody dared to obstruct his path. Rattazzi was no longer in power; the new Ministry had not yet been formed; the government was in complete anarchy.

He gave public speeches in the square of Santa Maria Novella; he aroused the people to fight against the Papacy and against all those who through error or weakness stood in the way of the holy patriotic cause. He was enthusiastically acclaimed.

The French chargé d'affaires immediately demanded his arrest in order to prevent him from crossing the border and leading the ranks of the volunteers, thereby destroying the diplomatic agreements that had been painstakingly negotiated between the two governments. This was obviously anticipated. However, Garibaldi quickly left Florence on October 22, despite the fact that arrest warrants were issued for him. The royal gendarmerie was pursuing him and was about to apprehend him in Rieti when he fled.

On the 23rd of October, he travelled to Passo Corese and, via Scandriglia, entered the Papal States, where his two sons and other leaders, such as Solomon and Frigesy, had assembled thousands of troops. Garibaldi was then informed about the events that had occurred in Rome the previous day, which he was familiar with, but which fell far short of his expectations.

It was now up to Rome to stage a coup before the French landed and covered it up; if feasible, it would have to rise up. A revolution in Rome would have been decisive. It had been predicted a hundred times but never happened. Mazzinian agents had been active in the city for some weeks. Francesco Cucchi, a Bergamo native, was assigned to carry out this task. Arms caches had been discreetly created, one near San Giovanni de' Fiorentini and another under San Paolo, in the Matteini vineyard. Romans had also lent themselves and favoured the movement. Even at Castel S. Angelo they had managed to bribe two artillerymen, who, at a given signal, were to blow up the powder magazine. Then, in many places where the papal troops had their barracks, in the Serristori palace, in the Borgo, in the Cimarra palace, in the Monti, and also in the barracks of the Svizzeri, in the Vatican, mines were to be placed. 21 October was set for the rebellion. On that day, the Giunta Insurrezionale Romana (Roman Insurrectional Council), which had taken over from the National Committee, published the following energetic call to revolt:

"Romans, to arms! to arms! for our freedom, for our right, for the unity of the Italian fatherland and for the honour of the Roman name. Let our war cry be: Death to the Temporal Power of the Popes! Long live Rome, long live Italy's capital! We want to respect all religious beliefs, but we also want to be free of a tyranny that forcibly separates us from the Italian family and wants to perpetuate the notion that Rome is foreign to the right to nationality and belongs to the entire world, but not to Italy! Our brothers have already raised the flag of holy rebellion and stained the Via Sacra, which leads to Rome, with their blood for several days. Let us not leave them alone any longer. Let us answer their call of heroes with the bell of the Capitol. The commonality of the cause for which we fight, as well as the tradition of Rome, demand it. Call to arms! Run to the fight anyone who can carry a rifle! Every home will be a fortress, and every iron will be a weapon! The elderly, women, and children can construct barricades; the young will defend them. "Long live Italy and Rome!""

The propagation of this proclamation was answered by a stony stillness. Those who wrote it were unaware of the state of the public mood in Rome. They could only rely on the few hundred men who had been covertly introduced into the city, as well as the few Romans who had been persuaded by word of mouth to support and back the attempted insurgency. Rome was no longer a Middle Ages city. Back then, Rome had a citizenry strongly enclosed in the trade guilds, who defended the ideal of an autonomous political republic; a militia divided into the numerous militias of the districts, at the service of the Capitoline magistrate, and an aristocracy partially Ghibelline, always ready to fight. At the time, the city frequently rose up against the despised popes, driving them out or forcing them to recognise its political rights. Conditions had completely changed in today's Rome of 220,000 people. Citizenship no longer had any political meaning; the nobility lived a life of meaningless leisure (exceptions were rare), which is disgraceful but historically explicable. For the most part, they belonged to families that were benefited and illustrated by the popes who came out of them. But part of the Roman populace was devoted to the papal government, in whose service it was, which nourished it, keeping it necessarily subject, through the clergy. Did they really believe, then, the Mazzinians, that a compact mass of Italian sentiment would be found in Rome, who would rise to their call to build barricades, to be shot by the Zouaves, or in any case, after a bloody repression by the French army, to end their lives in exile or in prison?

There were about 3,000 men garrisoned in the city, under the command of Marquis Zappi, and distributed in such a way as to be able to put down the riot in a short time, if it broke out. There were orders for five cannon blasts to raise the alarm from Castel Sant'Angelo. Many defensive measures were implemented, primarily on the advice of General Prudon, who had arrived in Rome on October 20 to assure the Pope of France's unwavering protection and to persuade him to remain in Rome until the French fleet from Toulon arrived in Civitavecchia. He also suggested forsaking the provinces and concentrating the forces distributed there in Rome to protect this city, the primary purpose of the movement. They began barricading the gates on the night of October 21-22, placing trenches in front of those that remained open and tamping down those that could be closed from the inside with embankments. In the Middle Ages, this was known as gate-making. Maggiore, Salara, S. Lorenzo, S. Paolo, S. Pancrazio, and S. Sebastiano gates were all closed. The Ponte Rotto and the new Lungara bridge were made impassable by removing the boards that covered them. On the road to Tivoli, three bridges were destroyed: the Aniene, Salaro, Nomentano, and

Mammolo. Loopholes were made in the walls, and also at the Pincio, and cannon batteries were established. One was placed at the point when the railway entered the city. The pits of Castel Sant'Angelo were filled with water.

The night of October 22nd passed quietly, with only the bursting of firecrackers and the alarm of sentries and the firing of their weapons heard in many streets.

There was a feverish tension in everyone's minds. Rome felt separated from the world: the telegraphs were down, the mail was irregular; the railways were partly interrupted at the borders by the papal army itself. There were dark rumours circulating. What a difference between the glorious Rome of June and the squalid Rome of now!

On the evening of October 22, there was open talk in the hotels and cafés that a revolt would break out in the city. It was known that Garibaldi had gone to Florence; it was said that he would place himself at the head of the volunteer ranks, that Rome would rise up, and that he would make his triumphal entry. All the horrors of a civil war in the streets, all the excesses that take place in a revolution, possibly even a potential plunder, filled many with anxiety and pain. Fear reigned supreme in many homes where retaliation from the action party was to be dreaded. The city still remembered the famous sack of Rome by the Bourbon gangs.

Towards evening the appearance of Rome became frightening. Shops and doors were closed; here and there arrests were made; the entrances to the deserted avenue were barred by sentries; patrols on foot and on horseback roamed the streets.

A man hurriedly threw a bomb at the guardhouse at Piazza Colonna, signalling the start of the insurrection. Then there were frequent bursts of firecrackers, a clatter of musketry, and a dull rumble. The mine at Palazzo Serristori exploded in Borgo; part of the large building, where the Zouaves had their main quarters, blew up, burying more than twenty people, mostly young musicians from the corps and orphans from the city. Fortunately, the mines placed under the other barracks could not be set on fire. The artillerymen who had been won to the revolutionary cause, in Castel Sant'Angelo, had already been detected and imprisoned. According to their plan, the revolutionaries, numbering no more than 500 men, would form small bands and take over various military posts. The guardhouse of the Capitol was to be forced, and the bell of the tower was to be rung to call the Romans to arms. The 50 Garibaldians who moved against the Capitol were dispersed by a couple of shots. Every other attempt had the same result. Only at St. Paul's Gate did the Garibaldians, 400 in number, under the command, it is said, of an Italian deputy, succeed in seizing the guardhouse. Some of them occupied the fortified, rock-shaped gate, while others marched towards S. Paolo in order to seize the arms depot in the Matteini vineyard. But the cops had already found it and taken it away. Another cache, hidden in a pozzolan quarry near the basilica, could not be traced by those who had established it there. The ranks, returning towards the gate, battled with the papists and dispersed after a short fight. The papal forces also reclaimed the gate. The assault on the gasometer near the Circus Maximus, attempted in order to plunge Rome into darkness, also failed.

The small band of volunteers led by the Cairoli brothers along the Tiber towards the city, intending to land at Ripetta, did not arrive, but instead occupied, outside the walls, a villa on the Acqua Acetosa heights.

Without the weapons scattered here and there, the tattered clothes thrown on the street, the traces of blood, and especially without the ruin of the Serristori palace, the vast majority of Roman citizens would not have known, on the morning of 23 October, that there had been fighting during the night. That very morning troops moved from the Porta del Popolo towards the Acqua Acetosa to rout Cairoli's ranks. There, near the confluence of the Tiber and the Aniene, rise verdant hills that slope down in quiet meadows to the Tiber, which flows majestically between two low banks, in view of the distant and picturesque Sabina mountains. A few country houses stand in those hills known as Parioli. On these, in Villa Glori, the 70 volunteers had stopped, among whom were patriots, men of culture and daring, principally rural landowners and engineers, students, warriors. The two Cairoli brothers led them, Enrico, a Member of Parliament, and Benedetto, an artillery captain in the Italian army. Among them was also a Count Colloredo, a Neapolitan from the House of Acton. When the papal carabinieri attacked them unexpectedly, the Garibaldini defended themselves like heroes in a hand-to-hand fight. After Enrico and many others were killed or put out of action, the rest dispersed or were taken prisoner.

VIII.

Garibaldi had just reached Scandriglia, when he gave orders to Acerbi to march on Viterbo, and to Nicotera to raid the Roman Campagna. He was to lead 4,000 men to Rome and seize Monte Rotondo.

On October 23, Acerbi entered Viterbo through Torre Alfina with barely 800 men. There were about 200 pontificii under Azzanesi's command in that city. When Viterbo was besieged at its six gates on the night of the 24th, one of which, Porta della Verità, was set on fire, the latter successfully repelled the attackers. The Garibaldini suffered heavy losses in their retreat.

Garibaldi took over Monte Maggiore and Passo Corese, from which he threatened Monte Rotondo. The volunteers were moving throughout the entire line, according to telegraphs from the frontiers of Lazio.

The situation in Rome was deteriorating. The 3,000 men

that were there, exhausted as they were, could not have defended it if Garibaldi's army had assembled on all sides under its walls. Furthermore, it was not certain that a second, more successful revolt could not occur. Hundreds of suspects had been apprehended, but every night since October 22nd demonstrated that the city was still teeming with revolutionaries. The firecracker game did indeed begin with the darkness. At the most sacred hour in Italy, when the bells rang out the Ave Maria chimes, it seemed that Rome was filled with devils from wherever, heralded by the vivid and dense crackling of the firecrackers, which joined the solemn sound of the bells. What could be more strange and evocative than this sinister harmony of bombs and bells, expressing better than words the irreconcilable conflict of those forces of the time, fighting today for possession of Rome, and having fought for so many centuries?

To relieve the fatigue of patrol troops, clerical citizens formed a national militia, which included princely house sons. Following the tracks of an insurgent hearth in Trastevere, a weapons depot was discovered in the house of cloth-maker Aiani on October 25. The Zouaves stormed the house, slaughtering almost all of the Garibaldians and the owner. A few were taken prisoner. On the same day, Rome's military governor declared the city to be under siege and ordered the surrender of all privately owned weapons.

Meanwhile, on the night of the 24th, Garibaldi appeared above Monte Rotondo, a charming village on a charming hill overlooking the Tiber valley as far as Corese and the countryside as far as the city, which was only three German miles away. He had cut the telegraph lines that connected the village to Rome in order to isolate the 370 Italians stationed there under Captain Cortes' command. The location was fortified and surrounded by mediaeval walls, and the baronial castle of the Orsini, now of the Ludovisi, could function as a fortress. Garibaldi launched an attack on Monte Rotondo with 400 men but no artillery. The Pontiffs used two cannons to successfully repel the attackers. Garibaldi led his force back to the assault after being repulsed several times; a gate was set on fire, and the Garibaldini ultimately entered the town, while the defenders escaped inside the castle. After being mined, the small garrison surrendered on the morning of October 26th, after a valiant twenty-seven-hour defence.

Garibaldi rode into Monte Rotondo Cathedral on horseback, expecting to lay his head there, and in this, too, he presented himself as a fully mediaeval figure. So did Francesco Sforza ride into the cathedral of conquered Milan, as did King Ladislaus of Naples ride into the church of St. John Lateran after conquering Rome. The prisoners were also led into the cathedral in Garibaldi's presence, and as they uncovered their heads, he made them sign to cover them, believing they did so out of respect for him i[5]. He then complimented the prisoners' bravery, saying it was worthy of a greater cause; he also shielded them from the wrath of the Garibaldians, who had already killed some of them, and had them brought to the borders, from which the king's troops transported them to Spezia, to Fort Varignano. Garibaldi spent the night in a confessional while the red shirts destroyed the cathedral in the same way that the savage ranks of the Bourbon constable had destroyed St. Peter's.

Garibaldi held the strongest position in the province; now Hannibal was at the gates. But he had achieved this, the only notable result of the entire campaign, despite having 400 dead and wounded and having lost valuable time. The small garrison at Monte Rotondo had done Rome the greatest service; if it hadn't held Garibaldi back by resisting him vehemently, he would have accelerated his march on Rome. Taking Monte Rotondo, on the other hand, was vital since it connected the Roman Campagna roads with the road to

Umbria. An army that had captured it possessed control of the road to Rome and the Passo Corese, as well as an easy escape to the Tivoli and Abbruzzo mountains.

Garibaldi may have had the city in his hands if he had a few thousand well-armed men to throw against the walls of Rome before the pontificii, recalled, returned from various areas in the province. In the Middle Ages, how many times had its frail Aurelian walls been breached by a swarm of invaders in some less guarded location at night? The same thing could happen now. The papal forces would not have been able to protect Rome's massive walls. Those who had seen the pale and tired Belgians and Dutchmen dragging themselves armed through the city might have concluded that they would be incapable of repelling a volunteer attack on the walls or effectively opposing them when they entered. They could only have barricaded themselves in the Lion City to protect the Pope in Castel Sant'Angelo until help arrived from France. Pius IX would have withdrawn from Castel Sant'Angelo, like Clement VII, through the underground corridor that connects with the Vatican, and might have witnessed a second sack of Rome from its battlements.

This city, which found itself, after three centuries, in a similar condition to that of 1527, threatened as it was then by volunteer armies, offered the viewer, in 1867, a picture of indescribable strangeness, similar to what it must have offered in 1527. One would have said that only names and customs had changed. Instead of the Constable of Bourbon, Garibaldi was under the walls of Rome, and perhaps would have fallen in the assault on the city, and, by an irony of fate, could, dying, have repeated the very words of the Bourbon: à Rome! à Rome! Instead of Pope Clement VII, Pius IX was absorbed in prayer in the halls of the Vatican. The same war cry that had guided the ranks of Bourbon and Frundsberg, a cry of hatred and desperation, was now the cry of Garibaldi's army: Rome or death! Just as men of all nations were mixed in the ranks of the Bourbon, so here democrats from all parts of Europe had entered. An equal contempt for the Church and its sacred functions, an equal cry of fury against the Pope and the clergy, resounded then as now. However, the Lutherans of 1527 and the Spaniards and Italians who mingled with them were less radical in their destruction mania than the Garibaldians of today. The same magical effect, which the name and figure of the Bourbon had produced on its ranks, was now produced by the figure and name of Garibaldi. They enthusiastically sang the verse as they marched singing songs glorifying the constable:

Garibaldi said it, And this is truth,
He who dies for his country
To heaven he goes.

When the Garibaldi ranks were in Monterotondo's cathedral, one of them climbed up to the pulpit, grabbed the crucifix, and began a burlesque sermon peppered with countless filthy blasphemies, eventually inviting the audience to invoke the God Garibaldi. The preacher then exclaimed, "And in the name of Garibaldi, I give you a blessing." The audience was not shy in making obscene gestures and mocking the sacred relics; the one who climbed onto the pulpit made the sign of the cross with the crucifix, then threw it to the ground, smashing it to pieces.

This is told by the Dominican prisoner, chaplain of the Zuav I[6], who says: "The Garibaldini belong to all social classes; there are nobles, plebeians, educated, uneducated and all kinds of brigands. They belong to every nation and have all come together with the aim of waging a campaign of destruction against the Church and Christian society; in short, they are the cosmopolitan army of the Devil, the terrifying caricature of the Catholic army. Many of them have a good Christian upbringing and excellent parents. Many are also witty and cultured, with refined and gentlemanly manners. But the mass is made up of men who lead unworthy and misguided lives, leftovers from prisons, or young men who have slipped into secret sects, or vagabonds from the big cities, with no fixed employment, who earn their bread by chance, serving as coachmen, errand boys, porters, clerks and so on. Others are labourers and workers. All of them sign up to try their luck, to kill or be killed, without knowing why. A fever, a vain delirium, draws them to the fight, and they are not aware of it. It would be in vain to look for any cohesion or unity of thought among them. Some want to destroy the Papacy, as they told me; others want to unite Italy; others want to deprive the Pope of his temporal power, which they consider to be contrary to the Gospel; others want to overthrow all thrones and all kings; and many, finally, want to steal. From this variety of intentions arises an indescribable confusion, so that it is no wonder that they sometimes mistreat and harm each other."

If among their commanders one orders one thing, another orders another, hence the habit of disregarding and transgressing commands. Each one thinks himself an authority, and they all want to rule. Many of them would not be bad, but, in those moments of fever, they are capable of excesses; I unfortunately witnessed this in Monterotondo, and its churches bear the deplorable traces. Their clothes are in tune with their ideas and opinions. It would be difficult to find two men among them dressed in the same way. Many wear a red shirt or a red cap; some are dressed in red from head to toe, but all have a red rag somewhere. Of religiosity they show no traces; many flaunt hatred of all religious forms; in several one could easily find an exact image of the devils, so sinister does their flaming robe appear, especially when combined with a wild and daring look.

There is only one name that electrifies them: Garibaldi. It has such a fascinating authority over all of them, that, since it is not possible to discern any real causes, one can truly suppose a diabolical power at the service of the secret sect ."[7]

The same monk describes his conversations with Pantaleone, a frank, good-humoured, and extremely lively Sicilian who was formerly a Franciscan and, after Marsala, Garibaldi's chaplain, to whom he served as secretary and wrote proclamations. It was he who found, for the first, the battle cry: Rome or death! Of which he himself boasted to our monk, who owed his salvation to him. Pantaleone was strong and well-built; he wore a bearskin cap, called the Orsini cap, without a brim, in the Armenian manner; over his red shirt he wore, especially in battle, a black buttoned jacket, so as not to offer a target to the enemy. He then had dark boots and trousers, at his hip a large sabre and around his neck, attached to a chain, a whistle for signalling. He spoke with surprising ease, in a figurative and elegant style, on an infinite number of subjects. He used to say, quite often, that the Catholic religion is against nature, that the papacy is a lie, a fraud that has had its day and should be taken away. He added that priests do not love their families, that they renounce conjugal love, that they depress and keep people down by means of a thousand lies, and so on. Asked by the naive monk if he had already contracted marriage, he replied: "I have found no woman so far who has won my heart, and I do not know when this will happen... but it cannot be long before it happens, if I do not die first. Take away this cowl,' he then said to the monk-symbol of ignominy and lies, and follow us who are the men of truth. We are the first men of the revolution; it is our task to destroy the papacy and to teach the simple doctrines of the true Christ, without miracles and without humiliation "[8].

IX.

The seizure of Monterotondo caused fear in Rome, where more than one thought to secure their valuables.

The Roman Insurrectional Council published this proclamation (27 October):

"Romans! For three days you have been spreading-without weapons, without ammunition, animated only by the sentiment of duty, strong in your right-you have been spreading fear and harm in the ranks of a fierce soldiery, which stands ready to fight in its quarters, and thus you show Italy and the world that Rome, though defenceless, cannot attack an open battle, knows how to write in its own blood the protest against its martyrdom. On the first night of the 22nd, you uncovered and took away the few weapons that were needed for your defence; you forced the enemy to open the St Paul's Gate, you resolutely assaulted the guard of the Capitol and thus avenged your dead, knocking down all those adversaries who were able to reach your weapons. Part of the barracks, Serristori blew up, undermined by your hand, and buried not a few enemies under the ruins.

"In all hand-to-hand combat, the enemy bowed under your blows. Above all, your Orsini bombs struck terror into the enemy ranks. On the night of the 23rd, when the enemy had already set up their defences, you dared to assault the patrols accompanying the prisoners at S. Pietro and Tommaso, and succeeded in freeing them. At the Monti, the blood of the zouaves reddened the streets; at Ripetta, near the Clementine, on the Sforza Cesarini square and in other places, officers and soldiers fell by your hand. The papal government, in the vain hope of making deceived Europe believe that Rome is at peace, has, for a week now, kept you in an effective state of siege, without daring to proclaim it; but this game could not last long, in the face of your animated demeanour, and your oppressors were forced to recognise and declare your rebellion and their fear.

"Yesterday a state of siege was declared and the order for general disarmament given, but with that hypocrisy which is

the main characteristic of the Pretender government. Rome is placed in a state of siege and disarmed, not because the Romans fight and die, but because a band of men, secretly introduced into the city, disturbs public order and spreads terror among a garrison of thousands of soldiers. O lie! Romans were killed at the Capitol, Romans the 200 prisoners at the gate
S. Paolo, Romani the old woman and child killed in the Sora barracks.

"While that lie was becoming more and more evident every day, the people of Trastevere, mindful of their past, took the field, and grasping with a feverish hand the few remaining weapons in their power, locked themselves in one of their houses like a fortress, and challenged the whole papal army to a fair and bloody fight. They were fifty against a thousand; every tool, every contraption was a weapon, and for four hours they resisted. The defenceless people tried to bring them aid, but all access was closed; it was impossible to approach the combatants. Numbers finally outweighed valour; the Zouaves succeeded, while they had already seen the road sown with the corpses of their comrades, in penetrating into the interior of the house, and then they gave no quarter. No ferocity could compare with that of these crusaders of the vicar of Christ. Everything was slaughtered: the Aiani family, women and children, mercilessly slaughtered; the wounded with a few blows finished off. The Pope King can bless this bloody bath and thank the Lord.

"Romans! It was necessary to give a bloody answer to the proclamation of the state of siege, and you have given it; it was necessary to place between you and the Pope a barrier of corpses, and just one of the massacred of Trastevere would be enough to prove to the world that conciliation between Rome and its tyrants is no longer possible. If this is not enough, if Italy does not hurry and hesitate, if victory should not yet come to us, it will not be our fault; we will have fulfilled our duty in full, and this page will remain in our history. But have faith: Garibaldi is at the gates; French intervention seems to have been averted; the whole of Italy, Government and People, is about to unite its forces for a single purpose: Rome. We will not be abandoned. It is impossible for this hesitation to be prolonged; it is impossible for this conflict not to end with the proclamation of Rome as capital of Italy'.

Rome, 27 October 1867.

But the hope of having averted French intervention soon had to be abandoned. Public opinion in France seemed to be in favour of this; only ministers Duruy and La Valette were against it, and spoke in favour of the Italian cause.

On 24 October, the Pope received, through his nuncio in Paris, a clear declaration from the Emperor, to whom he had made known the desperate conditions in Rome, and Monstier, on the 25th, told the powers that be that France was intervening because an infringement of the September treaty had been committed. In vain Victor Emmanuel had tried to provoke a mixed intervention, obtaining only to delay the departure of the fleet from Toulon; but on 26 October the command was given, and the French battleships sailed towards Civitavecchia.

In this crisis, on the outcome of which the fate of his monarchy seemed to depend, the king finally resolved to take the step that he should have taken a long time ago, namely to deliberately place himself on the side of legality, and to put a stop, by means of violence, to Garibaldi's revolutionary movement.

Calling Menabrea to the new ministry on 27 October, he put an end to ministerial anarchy and issued the following proclamation: 'Italians! Troops of volunteers, exalted and dragged by a party, have, without my and my government's authorisation, crossed the borders of the state. The respect that all citizens owe to international laws and treaties, approved by me and my Parliament, demands of us, on this occasion, the fulfilment of an indeclinable duty.

"Europe knows that the flag unfurled in the country neighbouring ours, and on which is written destruction of the highest spiritual authority, that of the Head of the Catholic Religion, is not mine. This attack placed the motherland in grave risk and obliges me at the same time to safeguard the honour of the country and to prevent the confusion of two different purposes and directions.

"Italy must be made safe from the dangers that threaten it; Europe must see that Italy, true to its commitments, cannot and will not be the disturber of public order.

"A fight with our allies would be a fraternal struggle between two armies that have fought for the same cause side by side."

"I, who am the arbiter of peace and war, could not tolerate this. I therefore trust that the voice of reason will be heard, and that those citizens of Italy, who forgot their duties, will soon return to the ranks of our army.

"The dangers, to which the disturbance of order and inappropriate resolutions could expose us, must be averted, and the prestige of the government and the inviolability of the laws strictly maintained.

"The honour of the country rests in my hands, and I cannot, now, lack that trust that the nation placed in me in the days of its deepest mourning.

"As soon as peace has returned to the souls and public order is fully restored, my government will work with sincere vigour, in collaboration with the French government, to reach a practical agreement to put an end to the grave Roman question.

"Italians! I do not doubt your prudence, that prudence that you always showed for the love of your King, and for this Great Country, which we, thanks to our common sacrifices, have seen once again become one of the nations, and which we want to hand down unharmed and honoured to future generations.

Feverish was the agitation in Florence. People were rioting in the streets. People shouted: "Down with the Menabrea Ministry! We want Crispi, and we want to move on! " People wanted war with France: "We want Rome, capital of Italy! Long live Garibaldi! Long live the Italian army on the Capitol! " The troops maintained order. Strict commands were sent to the borders to disarm the bands and drive them into the interior. Now only the enlistment offices were closed and the Revolutionary Committee dissolved.

Nothing could stop Garibaldi's ranks from advancing where they retreated; on the 28th, Nicotera occupied Frosinone and, the next day, Velletri; Acerbi re-entered Viterbo; Antinori, Pianciani, and Orsini entered Palestrina, Subiaco, and Tivoli, where provisional governments were being formed; Antinori, Pianciani, and Orsini entered Palestrin

Only the Aniene now separated Garibaldi from Rome. The Salaro bridge had been blown up. The Goths had once destroyed this bridge and Narses had rebuilt it; many times over the centuries it had been cut and restored; the last time it had been blown up was by the Neapolitans retreating from Rome in 1798; even Narses' inscription was lost. Now its arches are again ruined in the current, offering a picturesque spectacle to the traveller.

Garibaldi entrenched Monte Rotondo and Mentana, undecided of what to do. He immediately went to Marciano and Casino Santa Colomba, on the railway road, seven miles from Rome.

His bersaglieri outposts were on the other bank of the Aniene, across the bridge, near the beautiful Pazzi tower, and they ventured cautiously up to the river banks, to exchange a few shots with the papal troops.

The old folk hero wandered around the walls of Rome, while memories of 1848 were still alive. It was said in Rome that he had entered the city in disguise and spent two nights in the Palazzo Piombino. It was said that he had sworn to enter Rome through that same Porta San Giovanni through which he had withdrawn in 1849. It was then that his escape to San Marino and the pine forest of Ravenna laid the foundations of the fame of this national duce, who so wonderfully renewed in our time the exploits of the ancient condottieri. Eighteen years had passed since that time. How many upheavals had taken place in Italy in this space of time, how many strange events in its existence! First, unhappy years of reaction and despair, but also of incessant conspiracies, of covert efforts to achieve the national ideal. Then, after the fall of Venice destroyed even the last dream of Italian liberation, Garibaldi's exile in America, where with honourable work he had to earn his bread; then, seven years later, the first ray of hope with Piedmont's participation in the Crimean War; Garibaldi's return; France's alliance in the unexpected war of independence; the precipitous collapse of the Italian thrones; his expedition to Sicily with the Thousand; his entry into Naples, which was the most brilliant moment of his entire life, facts that resembled a Norman romance more than historical truth; the violent annexation of Marche, Romagna, Umbria; Italian Unity; the September convention; Florence as capital; Garibaldi in new conflict with the government, in the solitude of Caprera; the desperate catastrophe of Aspromonte; imprisonment and anguish at Varignano; Caprera again; the second unhoped-for war of Independence, with the help of Prussia! Free Venice, free Italy, all the way to the Adriatic; all that remained was Rome, to fulfil the 19th century dream of unity.

Garibaldi was now, after 18 years, seeing this Rome again; he stood before it, at the head of new ranks of volunteers, having again conceived the audacious design to conquer it. He justified his unlawful present enterprise with that very date: 1849, and called himself General of the Romans, as others had once called themselves King of the Romans. But the circumstances had completely changed; he had defended Rome eighteen years before; now he was besieged and had to fight with those Frenchmen who, eighteen years before, had fought under the walls of Rome; and this time, too, they had landed at Civitavecchia in order to penetrate into Rome. Napoleon himself sent them to defend Pius IX, and under his protection lived that Francis II, whom he had driven out of Naples. Of the men of '48 there still remained Pius IX, Napoleon, Garibaldi, Mazzini, all still at the head of the various tendencies and currents of the time. Others had died, including Manin, Balbo, Gioberti, and Cavour.

The French fleet arrived in Civitavecchia on October 28; the rough sea delayed the landing by a few hours on the 29th, which greatly impressed the clerical party.

A proclamation by Commander General De Failly, who had been preceded in Rome by Generals Polhès and Dumont, was posted on the 30th in the streets of Rome; it read as follows: 'Romans! The Emperor Napoleon is sending an expeditionary force to Rome for the second time to defend the Holy Father and the papal throne from attacks by revolutionary bands. You have known us for a long time; we only fulfil a moral and disinterested mission. We will help to re-establish tranquillity and confidence in the citizenry. Our soldiers will respect, as before, your people, your customs, your laws.

"Civitavecchia, 29 October.

"The General Commander

121

of the French Expeditionary Corps DE FAILLY'.

The proclamation was read by some with satisfaction, by others with mute disdain.

Here is the order of the day issued by Garibaldi in Santa Colomba on October 29, before he learned that the French had already arrived in Civitavecchia.

"ITALIAN VOLUNTEER CORPS."

"HQ St. Columba, 29 October. "

The Americans struggled for 14 years to conquer independence, and to make themselves the freest and most powerful people on earth; the Greeks struggled 11 years and more, and so do all nations, who wish to redeem themselves to independence and unity, and not to bend and fall into that prostration, to which our fatherland was condemned by foreign preponderance. The Italian people, after the sublime impetus of '48, was exhausted in a few months, and the small failure of Custoza set it back a long way on the glorious road.

'The battle of Novara ended the disgrace of Italy, and without the famous defences of Venice and Rome, the history of that war would have been more than sad for us.

"We are fighting the most intolerable of all governments, while another, similar to it, stands behind us." Corruption, dishonesty, and cowardice surround us. While one government spreads lies about the other, one and the other seek an excuse to crush this handful of volunteers, who are the magnanimous heralds of the national conscience.

"From the disorder of our organisation first came conflicts, the repetition of which would be shameful, and even in this I recognise the hand of treachery, which wants to destroy us.

"An attitude worthy of their lofty mission is required of

these ranks of volunteers, who offer the world such a noble spectacle and who have already forced mercenary armies to come from abroad to Rome and blow up the bridges leading there." Sorrows, privations, dangers will be a welcome theme of your speeches, when you return to your families; and to your women, O young men, you will recount with a prouder brow the heroic deeds you have accomplished. And now let us hasten to the enterprise we hope propitious!"

The liberals had hoped that the French occupation would be limited to Civitavecchia; but they were deceived. Napoleon had now found the courage to declare himself an ally of the Jesuits and saviour of the Papacy. On 30 October in the afternoon, the first French battalions entered Rome to the sound of fanfares. They descended from the Quirinal, surrounded by the legitimists and the papalists, who had gone to meet them as far as the railway station, to celebrate a long-awaited triumph. The appearance of these troops was gloomy and pointingly familiar, like that of people entering enemy territory and feeling their hatred upon themselves. Many people were in the streets, but silent. Not a voice was raised.

30 October 1867 was a sad day in the history of Italy; it marked a deep moral breakdown and a great regression. A year had not yet passed since the French were forced to abandon Rome due to political circumstances and the logic of opinion and facts. The entire world rejoiced with Italy because, after centuries of aspiration and effort, this day of independence from foreign dominance had finally arrived. This too had been illusion. The French had once again landed in the country, and their new occupation seemed to tell the world that Italy, unable to maintain its freedom, had fallen again through its own weakness into the vassalage of a foreign lord.

The bitterness, shame and despair of the patriots had no limits. He waited for the news of the outbreak of revolution in Florence and the fall of Victor Emmanuel. Perhaps he was saved in this crisis by the government's resolution to allow the Italian army to cross the borders of the Papal States. The Italians reached there 30 Acquapendente, then Civita Castellana, Ceprano and Frosinone, where they re-established the papal coats of arms and nearby raised the tricolour flag. This was the only protest against the French invasion that the Italian government could muster; however, a categorical order from Paris arrived shortly afterwards, ordering the Italians to recross the borders.

X.

Following the return of the French, the Papal government dispatched troops to occupy the various locations throughout the province from which they had been summoned to defend the capital, and on 30 October General de Courten himself moved on Albano and Velletri, where Nicotera's bands had established a provisional government.

They then wanted to assault Garibaldi himself with all their forces, dislodge him from his strong position and drive him back across the borders. He had gathered around Monte Rotondo and Mentana about 8,000 men. There he witnessed events that disheartened his homeland and forced him to retreat back to the Italian troops and lay down his arms or boldly attack the French and the Papists and succumb.

His situation was desperate and untenable. He had to aggravate the Sabina villages, which were very poor and opposed to the invasion, which offered them no benefit but only the saddest consequences of the revolution; while he had not even succeeded in lessening the harshness of the conditions and the deplorable misery of his starving cohorts. Excesses were also committed in Monte Rotondo itself. To give an example, Garibaldi had two volunteers shot. The people of the countryside had little sympathy for him, and it was difficult to get news and information. His troops were therefore not in a position to sustain a serious clash with the disciplined and well-armed Papal army, backed by French troops. They had then had time to recover from the exertions of the guard in Rome, and were fresh and rested.

Garibaldi's hopes and plans vanished. A man of such violent passions that he could admit of no separation between idea and deed, he had hoped to seize Rome as long as only the papal troops defended it, but after the coming of the French, the boldest fantasy had to come to a halt. The French intervention and the crossing of the borders by the Italian army now deprived him of any ground for further extra-legal action. He saw in these events a concerted plan of reaction, and judged himself a victim of it. First they had used him, now they wanted to crush him. The king's and Menabrea's proclamation showed him that he had to expect a second Aspromonte. They brought him the sharp intimation from Florence to lay down his arms and return to the state. He refused, and on 1 November published this order of the day:

"The government of Florence has left to occupy the Roman domain that we had at the price of precious blood conquered, taken from the enemies of Italy. We must welcome our brothers in the army with the usual cordiality, and help them drive out of Rome the foreign soldiers who support tyranny. If then shameful negotiations, a continuation of the vile convention of September, can so far empower Jesuitism and the filthy Consorteria, as to force us to lay down our arms in homage and obedience to 2 December, then I will be able to remind the world that I, a Roman general, created with full powers by the only legitimate government of the Roman Republic, by unanimous election, I alone have the right here to defend myself with arms on the ground of my jurisdiction; and that if these volunteers of mine, champions of liberty and of the unity of Italy, demand Rome as capital of Italy, faithful to the vote of Parliament and of the Nation, they will only lay down their arms when the homeland is accomplished, freedom of conscience and of worship raised on the ruins of Necromantism, and the mercenaries of tyrants outside the borders".

Garibaldi, finding himself between the two enemy armies, could have withdrawn, as was hoped, to Corese, to lay down his arms there before being attacked by the French and the Papists. It is said that, finally, at a certain moment, he really wanted to take this party. But why did he want to take his troops obligatorily towards the Apennines and not directly to Corese, where the road does not pass through Mentana? It must be believed that he wanted to go to any place in the kingdom to await events there, or perhaps even try to drag the nation along, although the memory of Aspromonte must have warned him of the improbability of a good success. Indeed, news from Italian sources explain that Garibaldi had conceived the plan to retreat with his 8,000 to Tivoli, to gather there with Nicotera and Orsini's bands, and to throw himself into the Abruzzi. They say that with this intention on the night of 2 November he gave the order to march on Tivoli by way of Mentana. It should be noted that some of the volunteers had already gone to Corese, most likely those who were no longer fit to fight, in order to return home from there. In opposition to this version, which is that of Garibaldi's officers Fabrizi, Mario, Missori, Menotti and others, we have that of the French party in Rome, which affirms that the strong positions, in which the Garibaldini were attacked on 3 November, Monte Rotondo and Mentana, prove that they were not surprised in their retreat, but that they were waiting there for the enemy.

The Italian version was also confirmed by reports from the Roman Ministry of War, which stated that while the Garibaldini wanted to operate at Tivoli their joint, they were attacked. Garibaldi later corroborated this version himself.
He therefore did not seek battle, but was forced into it; the

reproach that has been made against him for having wanted to use the blood of his soldiers for no purpose at Mentana is therefore unjust; and the same can be said of the accusation of having wanted to start a war between Italy and France with that battle; he evidently had no inkling on 3 November that the French would have to support the Papists in the imminent attack. It is also certain that, if he wished to assert himself as a separate and superior force to the nation, he had implicitly made the clash possible and did not wish to avoid it.

By the act of 3 November, 3,000 Papists led by General Kanzler had marched out of Rome, followed by the 2,000-strong French brigade Polhès, to seize Monterotondo and drive out the volunteer ranks. Garibaldi was to take this. Around noon the Pontifici attacked Garibaldi's outposts near Mentana (the French were in reserve). The surprise of the volunteers, to whom the news of the enemy's approach came very late, and who were on the march to Tivoli, was great. They did not even know of the existence of French troops in the surroundings. The combat was engaged with equal fury on both sides. Two great princes of the present world fought on that day, mortal enemies; on the one hand the leader of the national revolution and democracy, at the head of his volunteer ranks also composed of patriots of ancient stock; on the other hand the defender of the temporal power of the Popes, with volunteer soldiers from the most Catholic regions of Europe, many of them animated by the ardent zeal of crusaders, full of hatred against Italy and the revolution; these in large part children of the ancient legitimist houses of France, Belgium and Poland.

The proportions of the Mentana battle might in other times have earned it the name of battle; but now it seems to us of no great numerical magnitude, if we think of the colossal troop movements of other contemporary battles. Nevertheless, this battle will have important significance in history for two reasons. Firstly, because in it we faced two tendencies, two principles, two clearly opposing forces of our time; secondly, because it closed an entire period of the history of Italy and the temporal papacy.

The volunteers, poorly armed, weakened by hunger and cold - some were 15 or 17 year old boys - fought with heroic valour, with pike, sword and bayonet; but they were dislodged from their positions by the Zouaves regiment. They threw themselves under the fortifications of the Vigna Santucci in front of Mentana, and even from there they had to flee. The pontifical and French cannons brought up there then furiously battered the walls of the castle, while Garibaldi's two cannons, which had been fired at Monterotondo, ran out of ammunition after 50 or 60 shots. Under these conditions, the volunteers made a desperate effort to catch the enemy on the flanks with two strong columns, an attempt which succeeded, and at about half past two in the afternoon the papal troops were in a bad way, and the battle would clearly have changed their fortunes if the Roman general had not called the French brigade to the rescue. Even if their support had been useless, it would have shown that the French were there and were validly helping the papalini. They advanced, raining down bullets from their chassepots on the Garibaldini.

The French general himself, writing to the Ministry of War, wrote les chassepots ont fait merveille, a terribly unsuitable word, indeed indelicate and unpleasant, which Italy will never forget. The volunteers were overwhelmed; and at first they did not believe the new assailants to be French, but legionaries of Antibo; so far was it from them that Napoleon would allow his soldiers to shed Italian blood. But as word spread that the French themselves were attacking, the volunteers put down their arms and scattered in flight. Only one battalion stayed to protect the buildings, barricades and the baronial fortress of Mentana. Thus it protected the retreat that Garibaldi had started on Monterotondo. The Pontificii and the French were unable to break through the stronghold. They surrounded it at night, intending to re-attack the next morning, but at 5 o'clock the white flag was raised: a Garibaldian captain asked, speaking to the French colonel of the 59th line, for freedom of exit with arms and baggage; freedom of exit was granted, but without arms and baggage. A French company was to take the Mentana garrison, prisoners of war, to Corese and hand them over to the Italian troops. As a result, the fight was not dishonourable. The victors themselves had to recognise the valour shown by the vanquished.

Garibaldi himself, who had not been in the front ranks during the fight but had had to give the commands seated in a carriage, had already retreated with about two thousand soldiers when the assault on Mentana was made.

According to Crispi, an eye-witness, on the evening of 3 November Garibaldi arrived at the Corese bridge with 5000 nomini, if this figure is correct. He surrendered his arms there, and the next day he was imprisoned at Figline near Arezzo by superior order. When the papal and imperial troops moved towards Monterotondo on the morning of the 4th, they found the place had been cleared. Garibaldi's losses were great; 1000 men lay dead or wounded; about 1400 prisoners. French losses amounted, according to official reports, only to 2 dead and 36 wounded, those of the Pontiffs to 30 dead and 103 wounded.

The news of Garibaldi's defeat and retreat reached Rome on the evening of the 3rd and spread the following morning. It caused excitement of various kinds. The nationals trembled at the thought that the French, Italy's allies, had taken part in the fight as the Pope's gendarmes, had thrown themselves at the Italians like ferocious beasts, and had experienced the qualities of their chassepots on the almost defenceless volunteers. They were moved by the thought that the King's regular army, which was stationed a few miles away in Mentana, must have witnessed the battle, arms at their feet.

They did not know for which of the two nations this fact of arms should be considered more shameful, for Italy or for France. In the history of France, the marvel of Mentana would certainly remain, a tragic chapter in the Gesta clericorum for Francos.

The Via Nomentana had a peculiar appearance on 4 November. Hundreds of carriages had been brought in during the night to search for the wounded. These had already begun to gather in groups or at a standstill since the morning, a sorrowful sight, and amid them were also tiny lines of lighter injured, on foot or on horseback. Many and many Romans were moving towards them. I will never forget the appearance of two Garibaldians lying on a slowly proceeding cart, I don't know whether dying or already dead. Their faces, already blackened by death, still seemed to contract in the last spasm of grief and rage.

Around noon, the first group of prisoners, about 400 in number, arrived, escorted by papal and Frenchmen. They walked casually, with ostentatious tranquillity. One of their officers, a handsome young man in a red shirt, walked haughtily before them. The people pointed at him, saying he was Menotti Garibaldi; however it seems he was not. The men had finally reached the longed-for Rome, but in a different condition from the one they had dreamed of; they passed through the silent crowd to the prison on the Quirinal.

They were almost all ragged or poorly dressed; very few wore red shirts; among them were many extraordinarily young. Their appearance told of an odyssey of hardship and pain; on some pale faces one could still read: Rome or Death! They made an impression of deep emotion, which they would not have done had they been well armed and well dressed.

I observed the second batch of convicts, approximately 600 men, pass the Nomentano Bridge over the Aniene. They appeared to be in better shape than the first. Most of them wore red shirts and red caps; some had feathers on them; the whole street was lit up with these colours. There were also some mature, grey-haired men in the uniform of the Italian National Guard among them. The captains still carried swords, proof that they had surrendered honourably. They were all silent; many looked shyly at the crowd that had come to meet them from Rome. A signal from the horn signalled that it was time to rest; the escorting soldiers lay down in the ditches; of the prisoners, most of them stood on the road; some threw themselves on the bare ground of Rome; others took their places beside the papal men, who let them do so in silence; the whole scene was a singular historical picture on the picturesque landscape of the Aniene, near the ancient and turreted bridge in memory of Belisarius. On it are engraved the arms of that most notable pontiff who was Nicholas V, against whose government Stefano Porcari conspired, only to die in Castel S. Angelo, at the hands of the executioner. The sun's diffuse and luminous gold irradiated the solemn countryside, against which the majestic Abruzzo peaks were already white with snow.

The march to Rome of these sons of Italy destined for the prison of Castel S. Angelo brought back my thoughts to the memories of my early childhood, when I saw the defeated defenders of Poland, of Gielgrid's army, in their thousands, pass the border as prisoners, accompanied by Prussian troops.

Before my eyes again all the tragic struggles of the peoples fought on this great territory of Rome, the barbaric centuries of the Middle Ages passed over this city, whose history I had already been writing for years and still write; and an infinite sadness came over me when I looked again at all those prisoners of war on their way to Rome.

XI.

I went to Mentana to see some Roman friends five days after the battle. It was a beautiful walk through the peaceful countryside in the November sunshine. Only groups of soldiers kept the Via Nomentana alive. Lookouts in France were still waiting for the Aniene. Carriages transporting the injured were still passing by.

Ancient Roman tombs in ruins stand in the fields that one crosses, where, according to the remote custom of the forefathers, the Abruzzi shepherds led their flocks to graze. The bleating of the sheep and the soft notes of the shepherds' bagpipes fill the air with lament and the traveller's heart with mystery, a feeling that remains eternally in everyone who has passed through that sacred place.

Here and there stands a crumbling baronial tower, on top of a green hill, reminiscent of feudal times, when Rome was still a republic and the pope was not absolute ruler in it. Rarely does one come across a few isolated farmhouses, some of which are used as inns, with a mediaeval tower on the side and a rustic chapel. There is one eight miles from Rome, called Capo Bianco, which also serves as a tavern, and has a grove of green laurels at the door. Not a living creature was evident; everything surrounding seemed dead. Count L. had sent spare horses there, so that he could continue the journey quickly.

A strange and profound gravity invaded the whole group as we approached the bloody fields of Mentana. I remembered Petrarch's sublime ode:

Italia mia, benché il parlar è indarno... What do so many peregrine swords do here?

Donna E. said the verses of the noble Leopardi: Piangi, che ben n'hai d'onde, Italia mia...

And so the same complaint descends from Dante and Petrarch to Leopardi and the present day; when will it finally cease?

From Capo Bianco we advance on the gentle slopes of the hills. The Sabine landscape unfolds before our eyes as a grand panorama of high mountains, towards which rises a majestic expanse of fields, violet in colour in the distance, over which one can follow with one's gaze the flight of the eagles of Lazio. Nearby rises the mighty pyramid of Monte Gennaro above Tivoli; to the right the Prenestini Mountains, the Volsci Mountains, and the beautiful heights of Frascati, all suffused with a soft hyacinth colour and filled with a placid and classical majesty.

Here and there on the road are vestiges of the ancient paving of the Via Nomentana, in well-connected basalt polygons. Ten miles from Rome, on a hill to the left, is a solitary Guelph tower without adjacent buildings, built partly in black peperino, partly in red brick, which is a property of the region.

Monte Gentile, a lovely farmhouse with a tower, was once the castle of the Orsini family, as its name suggests; in the 15th century, Capocci and Stefaneschi destroyed and abandoned it. There is nothing more attractive than these turreted Roman farmhouses, lost in the melancholy of this deserted and grandiose countryside, so singular and so classical, which Walter Scott would certainly have fallen in love with.

Passing over a rise, we came to the Mentana forest, a wood of German oak trees, which have remained dwarfed here. Already in this location, and then all the way to the settlement, we noticed an unusually large number of cartridges in the ditches and bushes. Because the dead had already been buried and the wounded had been admitted to hospitals, these and the felled trees were the only traces of the fighting.

Mentana appears behind this thicket; first the Vigna Santucci with its white walls, where they fought so bitterly; then a chapel on the road, still full of straw, on which more than one wounded man found death. The baronial palace of the Orsini family stands in the distance, like a fortress, with turrets and battlements, on the green slope of a hill, lonely and haughty like a shelter for brigands; the settlement is still covered by little hills. Below, the valley is gloomy, encircled by hills dotted here and there with olive trees and vineyards; nevertheless everything has a wild, ominous but charming air.

A road leads up a protrusion of yellowish cliffs. Now one can see the village, a row of uninteresting houses, similar to the castles of the Sabine mountains, which exude so much misery and desolation; they are said to be dependencies of the feudal castle, which the lord once annexed for his own convenience, and gave to his vassals for habitation. In front of the palace stands the aristocratic church. It was open and already reconsecrated, and many injured had died there; among others, a Belgian who had arrived to Rome and joined the Zouaves a few days before the fight. A ball had cracked his skull; seventeen wounds had pierced his body. On a piece of paper, found near him, was written: le comte d'Erb, fils du du duque d'Erb.

The church door leads to the square in front of the castle, where one can see a column without a capital, around which lie some military bisques. Here and there, marble ruins of the ancient Nomentum. A mutilated statue known as St George can be found on the church's outside wall. The castle was full of French soldiers, who practised with their needle guns, which they boasted so much, claiming that without them the Pontificii would never have taken Mentana.

We entered the castle, which displays architecture from several eras. The oldest part, formed by round towers, demonstrates the 13th century style of construction known as Saracen in Rome; that is, these towers are made of fragments of peperino and various other filling materials, including pieces of marble. The front of the castle, on the other hand, is much newer and features Renaissance-style windows. The battlements are half destroyed, with parts broken by cannonballs. Overall, the structure appears to be a magnificent Middle Ages baronial castle. The arms of Sixtus V, or rather his nephew Michele Peretti, to whom the Orsini had sold Mentana, are displayed on the portal. The remains of Garibaldi's rifles remained on the door, which the besieged had broken before surrendering, as was customary in wartime.

Inside, there were ruined staircases and rooms with bomb-damaged walls. The French guards were preparing lunch in the castle courtyard, all bustling around a fire that they were stoking with the sticks of Garibaldi's rifles. Rifle balls were brought to us, which we could easily have picked up on the ground, cone-shaped, rifled or chassepot weapons; rarely were there any of the usual round ones from Garibaldi's rifles. We went to the isolated little settlement. Its residents had been hiding in their cellars for 15 hours, terrified, as the balls rained down like hail. There was one exception: a bomb had ripped through the wall of a room where women and children were found sitting quietly, as if nothing had happened. The Garibaldini were said to have occupied the village for eight days. One woman told us that among them were some lovely people who paid what they wanted, and she added that one captain had paid a chicken 25 soldi, which she was quite delighted with. Others had been unable to pay anything because they did not have a single penny in their pockets.

We reflected on the historical events of this small Sabine village, which had now returned to play a role in history that was not independent of the one it had previously played; we remembered that the Franks had once come here to save a threatened pope and his temporal power; and that this saviour had been Charlemagne. The location made it simple to reconstruct its history.

It was known as Nomentum in antiquity. This gave its name to the road, Nomentana, which did not belong to the main

Roman roads because it connected the Via Salara at present-day Monterotondo at Ereto, below Nomentum.

The Romans considered it to be one of the colonies of the Latin king Silvio of Albalonga, who certainly conquered that Sabine region. It was older than Rome itself and contemporaneous with Fidene and Crustumeria. He joined the Latins' alliance against Rome in support of the exiled Tarquinii. Nomentum became a Roman municipium following the battle of Lake Regillus, which established the Roman Republic's hegemony over Latium. However, this Sabine city was too small to play an important part in the history of Rome. Ovid, Seneca, and Martial are known to have had possessions in its territory. The air was clean, the wine was delicious, and there were thermal springs nearby.

In the Christian era of the Germanic Empire, Nomentum soon became a bishopric; close by were the other bishoprics of Fidene, today Castel Giubileo, Cures, and Forum Novum, which still remains. The series of Nomentum bishops runs from 415 to 964, in which year the appointment of bishops was suspended, which proves that the city had completely fallen into decay. It had, moreover, for unknown reasons, lasted longer than the other ancient cities in the immediate vicinity of Rome, which disappeared at the time of the barbarian invasions. Eretum Crostumeria, Fidene, Gabii, Ficulea, and Antemna all vanished. Even Numa's homeland, the ancient and famous Cures, fell victim to the Lombards and now exists only in the name of Correse.

Nomentana still existed in the year 800 with its ancient name, although it had already changed radically; on 23 November of that year Charlemagne, who was on his way to Rome to be crowned at St Peter's, stopped there. His staying there, in the same month of November, in which 1067 years later bands of Italian volunteers were attempting to overthrow the papal dominion, which Charlemagne had founded, seems to us a rather strange and remarkable fact.

The struggle of the Italians and the Romans against the temporal power of the popes already began at that time, as that temporal power had been established by the first intervention of Pepin in Italy in favour of the city of Rome, threatened by the Lombards. There has never been another long-lasting struggle in human history centred on a single, unchanging principle.

The reason for Charlemagne's trip to Rome was as follows. Pope Leo III, Hadrian's successor, had been, following a conspiracy of Roman nobles, among whom Hadrian's own nephews excelled, driven out of Rome after an attempt to kill him. He had fled first to Spoleto, and from there retired to Paderborn. The great monarch first sent the fugitive back with Frankish ambassadors to Rome, where the aristocrats, who had seized the government, put no obstacle in the way of his return: but, frightened by the imminent intervention, they submitted themselves to the trial and judgement of these plenipotentiaries. They decided in favour of the pope, but the condemned rebels appealed to Charles, and he came only a year later, as he had promised Leo, to hold his tribunal in Rome, which the pope, his subordinate in all temporal matters, equally recognised.

Charles descended with his army into Sabina, and stopped at Mentana to come to Rome, not by the Via Salara, but by the Nomentana.

This only goes to show how important the location was even back then, as it was the only episcopal see in the Sabine region. We can deduce from this that Monterotondo, which is only a half-hour drive from Mentana and is much larger and more habitable, did not exist in the nineteenth century. Actually, it was thought to recognise the ancient Eretum in Monterotondo; nevertheless, Nibby has spoken out, with serious strong arguments, against this opinion, and has proven that that area only existed in the later Middle Ages. Sabina originally formed a part of the Duchy of Spoleto; Charlemagne had given it to the Pope, and only much later did he take it into his power. But very relative was this power of his over the Sabine territory close to Rome. The whole region had been frightfully devastated in the 4th century by the invasion of the Lombards: its towns had already almost all decayed; in the 8th and 9th centuries, the documents of the dioceses show that they were no longer towns, but hamlets.

Leo III had solemnly gone to meet Charles at Nomentum with the major dignitaries of the church, a part of the nobility and the city militia, and many of the people. On November 23, 800, Charles arrived in Nomentum. He dined with the Pope, after which he returned to Rome to plan the monarch's ceremonial reception in St. Peter's for the following day, while Charles slept overnight in the village. In which palace did Charles have his lunch with the Pope, and where did he spend the night?

Nomentum was certainly more populated a thousand years ago than it is now, and if the ancient city stood in the same location, where the miserable row of houses near the Orsini castle stands today, it could offer, in a small way, the appearance of all other cities of that time: antiquity ruins, temples destroyed or converted to other worship, and palaces of ancient lordship, next to tugurines inhabited by a new generation.

A count did not reside in Nomentum; perhaps a tribune, by analogy with other cities, had jurisdiction there, if the country, however-which I doubt-was still large enough to be the seat of a tribune. There were no baronial lineages yet, in the sense of the Middle Ages closer to us. Only 150 years later is the Crescenzi lineage found in Nomentum, rich and therefore dominant. As a result, Charles undoubtedly resided in the bishop's curia, the bishop of Mentana's unquestionably patriarchal residence.

It was therefore from there that the greatest ruler of the West came down to Rome, on 24 November 800, and it was there that he stayed before going to his coronation. A month later Leo III anointed him King of the Romans.

The renewal of the Western Empire in the Frankish Dynasty, apart from other more general and elevated reasons, had also become necessary for the Popes for this reason, that it gave them a way to maintain their temporal dominion over Rome and the provinces. The popes would not have been able to assert their lordship over the Roman region without the protection of imperial authority, without the security of ever-ready Frankish intervention. This fact had already manifested itself manifestly then, but the later history of the Dominium temporale only offered further irrefragable proof.

In the tenth century, this dominion was threatened by a great danger: that of the noble house of the Crescenzi, which had great authority in Mentana. It appears for the first time in 901, and, from that year on, many Crescenzi are found among the most notable lords of the city. That this house already owned land in Sabina is shown by the fact that a Crescenzio, in 967, was count and rector of the Sabina province by order of the Pope.

Crescentius de Theodora seized power in Rome in 974, and his son John Crescentius later led the Roman national party. His storey is part of the well-known Crescenzio Nomentano episode during Otto III's reign. His family, which resided almost all in the Sabine region and near Farfa in particular, must therefore have been in possession of that place, and John Crescentius was either born in the possessions of his fathers, or Nomentum had particularly fallen to him by inheritance. Precisely at that time, it seems that this bishopric was suppressed; and since it is known that the last bishop was a certain John, it can be assumed that, as this name was usual in the Crescentian family, the last bishop of Nomentum was also a member of that family. At that time there were already hereditary counts in the papal territory. Therefore, already in 980 Giovanni Crescenzio could have been count of Nomentum and owned his fortress there, in the same place where the castle of the Orsini family, which still stands there, was built.

In 985, Crescentius took the title of Roman patrician and ruled Rome as its temporal ruler during Otto III's minority, but his power crumbled when Otto came to Rome in 996 to receive the imperial crown from Gregory V, the first German pope he had elevated to that position. Crescentius, condemned to death as a rebel, took an oath of allegiance to the young emperor, and was pardoned. But Otto had barely left, when the cunning Roman broke his oath, banished the German Pope and seized his imperial rights. In this usurpation he was supported by his relatives from Sabina, Count Benedict and his sons John and Crescentius. The usurper met a sad end after Otto III had brought the Pope back to Rome with a goodly number of soldiers. Crescentius defended himself heroically in Castel Sant'Angelo, until he had to surrender. He was beheaded, his body thrown from the battlements of Castel Sant'Angelo and then hung from a gallows on Monte Mario. For centuries, Castel Sant'Angelo was nicknamed the tower of Crescenzio.

After the death of Otto III, the Romans named his son John a Roman patrician, a power he retained until 1012, the year he died. The Crescenzi family remained in Sabina and Rome after then, but no longer rose to prominence. Patrician power passed instead, after 1012, to the Counts of Tusculum, who were able to arbitrate the temporal power of the Pope and the Holy See itself.

Thus in the history of the Papal State Nomentum is classic for having been the seat of a very ancient lineage rebelling against the power of the popes. Was this known to the last descendant of the Crescenzi family, who on 3 November 1867 fought with the popes and fell on the hill of Mentana in defence of the Holy See?

After the Crescenzi period, Nomentum is rarely mentioned in the documents of Rome's history; it is called Castrum Nomentane, hence the name Mentana or La Mentana. Already the change of civitas into castrum, to designate it, as we read in the papal bulls of the 13th century, says that the town had decayed so much that it was no more than a dismantled village. It belonged to the monks of San Paolo, who handed it over in the 12th century to the powerful Capocci family, until Nicolò III, of the Orsini family, gave Mentana to his nephew Orso. The Orsini seized control of many Sabine towns in the 13th century. They also owned nearby Monterotondo, Monte Gentile and Nerola. They built the castle in Nomentum, the present fortress, probably on the foundations of the ancient fortress, and remained there for more than three centuries; then, in 1595, they sold it to a nephew of Sixtus V, Michele Peretti, prince of Venafro. It was later acquired by the Borghese family, who still own it.

XII.

Monterotondo is less than a half-hour drive from Mentana along a very good road through bushes and vineyards. The great baronial castle, once owned by the Orsini family and now owned by the Prince of Piombino, is an imposing and beautiful edifice with a grandiose tower that rises almost to the top of the town. It was full of French soldiers. More than a thousand Garibaldian rifles lay in the courtyard, piled in disorder; bad percussion weapons, perhaps of the National Guard, piles of bayonets, sheaths of sabres, batons could be seen scattered on the ground. They had been collected in Monterotondo and on the nearby roads.

I was taken to the house where Garibaldi had lived; this was in the lower square, not far from the cathedral. Here he had two small rooms on the upper floor. On his bed, covered with a yellow blanket, hung a holy image and a crystal pitcher with holy water, which he used as much as the mirror in the canterano. Now this room is inhabited by a French captain.

We also saw the cathedral, St Magdalena, where the volunteers had quartered. On the altars we could still see shattered church ornaments, tattered church vestments, crucifixes and broken candles. Everything in the sacristy was in disarray: the cupboards were strained, the missals and registers were torn and scattered on the floor. A woman who led us in there pointed out, with signs of fright, the Tabernacle of the high altar, from which the chalice had disappeared. We were told of other desecrations, which we do not think it appropriate to report; something similar to the Sack of Rome by the Bourbon. Two volunteers were seen standing guard at the door, one with a mitre on his head, the other with a crosier in his hand. These volunteers buried their dead in bulk, in the churches themselves; the officials lowered them into the tombs, wrapped in brocade and gold vestments.

In Monte Rotondo, the fearful excitement of the war-torn towns was more visible than in Mentana; the latter only had just 500 inhabitants; the former 1300. The people were not in favour of Garibaldini: 'The invasion has ruined us,' an employee at the town hall assured us, making grand gestures and speaking forcefully of all the taxes in money, fodder, horses, exacted by Garibaldi, taxes that some of his unworthy subordinates sometimes took for themselves.

The small village is placed, high and strong, on the back of a hill, from which there is a great view of the Sabine highlands, as far as Monte Gennaro. Close by are Tivoli, Sant'Angelo, and Monticelli; further away are the white Palombara, Montelibretti, and even Nerola, and in the midst of the mountains is the Benedictine abbey of Farfa, which was destroyed by the Lombards of Spoleto in ancient times and then magnificently rebuilt. The toothed Soratte dominates the landscape to the north, beneath which the Tiber meanders, leaving Umbria to continue its winding path to Rome, accompanied on both banks by two Roman roads, the Flaminia and the Salara. Of Rome, at such a great distance, one can still see, as barely perceptible lines, the towers of St. Mary Major and the Lateran; but the dome of St. Peter's dominates whole and full, the solemn countryside, like a dark sphere. When the pilgrims who come from the East by this route, have come in sight of these grandiose landmarks of the Church, they can gladly kneel down and worship! There are several paintings showing such scenes. Today, a brilliant artist could use this dramatic contrast as his subject: Garibaldi's volunteers in red shirts, who see the dome of St. Peter's for the first time from the heights of Monte Rotondo.

It must have looked to them the emblem of the objective so fiercely pursued, as the city of Rome, seen in the distance, must have seemed to the Goths of Alaric or to the famished warriors of the Bourbon and Frundsberg. Their leader may have often pointed out that sublime dome to them; and he may have spoken to them of it in words blazing with patriotism - as he had spoken of it in Geneva, at the Peace Congress, from which Garibaldi - for an irony of history - almost immediately stepped onto the battlefield at Mentana!

It is full of interest to depict the thoughts that must have stirred the soul of this extraordinary man as he approached Rome, this man of such varied destiny and fortune, whose life was a struggle for freedom fought in two parts of the world! a man who would certainly have played a more remarkable part in history, if nature had coupled his disinterestedness as an ancient Roman, and his incomparable activity and vigour of character, with the genius of a statesman.

When Garibaldi saw Rome again, he would have remembered with amazement the time when he defended the world's metropolis against the French. Returning to the Tivoli campaign, he will recall himself retreating from Rome with other ranks of volunteers, slightly better armed and disciplined than the current ones, towards the Apennines. It was July 30, 1849.

He smiled at the thought of now entering the Rome he had already had to leave, and which formed the most ardent longing of his life. But he did not enter Rome; he did not plant the Republic's standard or the Italian tricolour on the Capitol. He was taken prisoner of state at Varignano after being beaten by the Pope's and Napoleon's troops at Mentana. They tried him, who couldn't be tried because he had too many accomplices, the series of which began at Palazzo Pitti.

The world that values patriotism and character had allowed Garibaldi, Italy's spoiled and terrible child, to engage in his campaigns in the name of the Ideal at his leisure, without their failure diminishing sympathy for him. But everything has a limit, like Machiavelli's maxim in The Prince: 'It is the end that must be considered, not the means'. Garibaldi's romantic audacity may certainly exalt the youth who have read Plutarch, but it tyres the mature judgement of the statesman and conscious citizen. That a national hero, so celebrated and cherished, should continually claim the privilege of being an exception, outside the framework and laws of the state, and of constituting a power unto himself, would be an absurdity and an impossibility in any well-ordered European state.

The Italian monarchy and the thought of unity overcame the terrible crisis (which Garibaldi's Demagogy had provoked) quickly and happily. If the Day of Mentana had the merit of liberating Italy from the anarchy of a revolutionary power opposed to the government, this should be regarded as a significant benefit. The invasion of the volunteers taught us other things as well: it revealed Italy's weakness and immorality, and diminished Europe's sympathies for it; it demonstrated that the Temporal Power could not last long in the form assigned to it by the September Convention; and it restored to Italy a principle that Europe had hoped to have permanently removed from her. I do not speak of the misery and ruin, into which the war of the volunteers threw thousands of people, on this side and on the other side of the Roman borders. If this war then, as Garibaldi believed, should be considered as a national war of Italy, against the Papacy for the possession of Rome, then we would say that its outcome showed that in 1867 the Papacy was still stronger than Italy, and that the Roman question could not be resolved by violence alone. Will this matter, which with the Treaty of September was, with regard to Italy, contained within the bounds of a question of geographical expediency, be raised again and brought back into the field of European diplomacy?

And what an intractable issue! Is there in human affairs anything impossible to solve? An astute mocker consoled a patriot by observing that Italians rise up as victors after the defeats that are supposed to weaken other peoples. Even if we cannot agree with this fine spirit, we see no reason to despair that one day a modus vivendi will be found that will be able to reconcile the spiritual independence of the Papacy with the needs of the nation. The day when this squaring of the circle will be found, mankind will be able to celebrate it solemnly, because it will mark the beginning of a new era of peace, an era to which all the peoples of Europe confidently aspire.

XIII.

The previous pages were written three years ago. The square of the Roman circle has not been discovered, but the sword has severed the Gordian knot. Therefore, the Volunteers' Campaign around Rome needs an appendix.

If it can be drawn from diplomatic material and enriched here and there with faithful portraits of the most eminent personages who played a part in this tragedy, the description of these last three years of Rome and the dying Papacy will one day constitute a remarkable page of our time's history. Its proper title should be "History of the Last Years and Days of Temporal Power."

To wrap things up, I'll mention a few dates.

At the end of 1867, the victory of Mentana completely reassured minds. Napoleon was drawn into reaction, into open conflict with democracy and demagoguery, with delight. It was consequently desired that he remain firmly in authority. The pope created Lucien Bonaparte cardinal on 13 March 1868, the first Bonaparte to attain the purple! All that was needed to consummate that family's incredible fortune was for him to visit the Holy See.

Rome was quiet. In the Patrimonium Petri were the French again: about 5000 men. Only papal troops garrisoned the city. The Roman Curia was now preoccupied with the concept of the Council, whose uninterrupted meeting was finally possible as a result of the French return and victory at Mentana. With this Council, which had already been prepared for many years, the Jesuits intended to crown their work by placing the fourth and supreme crown, that of infallibility, on the Pope's head. The bull summoning the Council to meet on December 8, 1869, was published on June 29, 1868.

As chance would have it, a solemn national holiday was celebrated in Germany on 8 June of that same year; the great Luther monument was unveiled in Worms in the presence of the King of Prussia, the shield of the Protestant church, the head of the German nation, and the now certain restorer of the Empire.

The fight against Protestant Germany, the Germany of intellect and science, had long been on the Jesuits' agenda; extraordinary plans were developed in this direction. They dreamt of a new epoch in history, an epoch of nationhood and crusade to Catholicise the world; the Papacy master of the earth, according to the statements of the Syllabus and the decrees of the forthcoming Council. And what better than a war of France against Germany could have opened the way for all this? This war to be waged by Napoleon's invincible legions, armed with the chassepots and machine-guns, so well experienced at Mentana, would certainly have annihilated the power of Protestantism in Europe, and made the unification of Germany under the Hohenzollern impossible. From the certain victory of France would follow the new division of Italy into its parts, and the re-establishment of the Church State, as in the time of Consalvi. Then Napoleon, the saviour and protector of the Church, would become a new Charlemagne, and pacified humanity would gather around the two great metropolises of the earth; Paris, the seat of Caesar's despotism, centralising human civilisation in itself; Rome, the infallible source of divine truth, manifested in Jesuitism.

The Spanish revolution and the violent fall of the bigoted Queen Isabella was the first blow against these designs. And who suspected that a bid for the Spanish throne would become a factor in world history?

The year of the Council arrived, 1869. Preparations were in full swing in Rome.

Nothing yet predicted coming storms, except perhaps in Germany, a lively opposition to the Council, whose necessity was denied and partisan spirit was condemned. The infallibilists and their opponents were forming camps.

The old pontiff celebrated his 50th jubilee since becoming a priest on April 11, and deputations, addresses, good wishes, and gifts poured in from all over Christendom. The rally was magnificent and serious, and Rome was transformed into a joyous theatre, as it had been in 1867. The pope, who was thus celebrated, believed himself honoured by the whole world as its spiritual leader. These festivities seemed to him to be a good omen for the upcoming Council.

On 8 December 1869, this solemn ecclesiastical gathering opened in St. Peter's. It was pouring down rain, but the temple barely contained the crowds that had flocked there. Rome, like all of Italy, was then quiet. Napoleon's troops were guarding the Council, which became the great event of the day, in which the world feared a crisis of awakening in the life of the assembled Church, while two hundred priests solemnly declared the attributes of divine power.

Everyone knows how this Council was constituted, the means by which the majority was obtained, how the minority was crushed, the struggles and debates of its parties. Its history was accompanied by a special literature such as had never been seen in previous synods. The Council was watched closely by public opinion; it met at this Roman parliament, whose most secret thoughts, plans, and manoeuvres it knew how to reveal and even direct.

Serious Catholic believers have been heard to cry scandal over this Council. They sadly acknowledge, and in spite of themselves, that its convocation was an incalculable error, its work a harmful challenge to schism. Its history will one day be a very instructive page in our history, showing future generations how great the blindness, how deep the spiritual poverty, and how exhausted the Roman element of the Church was at the time, as Catholics have already stated.

The summer of the great year 1870 arrived. Already the attention of the world had been diverted from the Council, where the strenuous opposition of the German minority and public opinion itself had been forced to give way. At the same time, while the Church had to gather all its energies in its Head, leaving its members useless and powerless forever,

France, with a new plebiscite, was centralising in the imperial power. Then the political horizon was suddenly troubled by the candidature for the Spanish throne.

The new dogma of papal infallibility was published on July 18, 1870. St. Peter's temple found itself empty and deserted on that occasion. A deluge of tropical violence was unleashed upon the city. Amid thunder and lightning it was announced to humanity that the Pope was infallible.

Only one day later, on 19 July, the storm was unleashed on France! Emperor Napoleon declared the craziest of wars on Prussia and the Northern Confederation.

Then came the great days of punishment for boasting and pride. History has recorded them, just and solemn. Germany erupted in an instant, compact, massive, and enraged. The strength of the German people defeated in battles that were slaughter, the French Empire. On 2 September, Napoleon surrendered to the magnanimity of the great German king, whom he had so cruelly offended. The whole of Europe trembled from the backlash of this unprecedented war; all that was fractious and deadly in it had to break away.

The Republic was proclaimed in Paris. The Italians insistently demanded Rome. But the old hero of the 1867 Volunteer Campaign had gone to France to fight alongside his enemies at Mentana, with Colonel Charette of the Zouaves, under the same flag:-for a shadow and a name. He, like Lucan, could exclaim: Tuumque nomen, libertas, et inanem prosequar umbram; a noble dreamer and a steadfast adherent to his principles.

The French troops had retreated from Rome to protect the motherland, leaving the Papal States vulnerable to invasion once more. The Italian government declared the Treaty of September null and void with the fall of Napoleon that had concluded it, and arranged for the occupation of Rome by the king's troops, justifying it as a necessity for the preservation of the state and as the will of the people of Italy.

Strange and admirable logical event concatenation!

On 19 September, the Germans tightened their iron ring around Paris, metropolis of the world; on the same day thirty thousand Italians were at the gates of Rome, metropolis of the world. The first shot was fired against the Porta Pia walls at five o'clock in the morning on September 20. The fight with the papal troops was short and simple. The Pope sat in the Vatican with cardinals and foreign diplomats he had summoned. The attack's cannon shots were heard. Cardinal Antonelli received and transmitted communications. The last one came, announcing that all was over.

The Italians entered Rome through the breach at Porta Pia on 20 September at 11 a.m., to the indescribable jubilation of the population, while, as if by magic, the whole city was covered in tricolours.

The Popes' thousand-year temporal rule ended barely unrecognised. What would have been a monumental world event in another era was achieved as an anecdote against the backdrop of the great Franco-German war. This unseen and stealthy death of Europe's oldest and most venerable authority is terribly terrible. Wasn't the world's silence a criticism of the Papal State? Many voices in Europe may still have been raised in its favour if the Council had not abruptly decreased regard for the Papacy to its lowest ebb. The demise of its temporal power was the legitimate outcome of the most horrific demand ever put on human reason.

On October 2, the Romans voted to annex Rome to Italy in a plebiscite. The King came to visit the city so cruelly damaged by the Tiber flooding for the first time at the end of the year, a welcome pretext for that painful visit. The Romans greeted him with joy. He stayed for a few hours and penned a letter to Pope Francis. In the Quirinal Palace-the papal palace from which Pius IX twenty-four years earlier had been acclaimed by the people as the Sun of the new Italy, rising to the throne-Victor Emmanuel signed his first decree in Rome, noting the plebiscite. The year 1870 had come to an end. With it, a significant epoch in the history of the city and the pope came to an end.

A tragic fate befell the weak Pope, who had experienced so many changes of fortune and so many vicissitudes as few pontiffs before him. A consenting prisoner, he laments in the dismal Vatican, neglected now in his Rome, of which he had been the idol. All human greatness is such a small thing!

Pius IX occupied his throne for a longer period of time than any of his predecessors, regardless of their importance in the globe! The last temporal sovereign Pope also ruled Rome for the longest period of time!

These are just facts. We are standing in front of the locked doors of an unknown future. The squaring of the Roman circle has not yet been found; the moral process is not yet resolved. Only this can be said with certainty, that mankind, in the memorable 1870s, has definitively freed itself from an ancient order of things.

CONTEMPORARY ROMAN POETS.(1858).

* * *

One may argue that the Muses, as shown by Raphael in one of the Vatican's apartments with the greatest poets, always selected Rome unwillingly and only in passing. After all, it is understandable that a city like ancient Rome could not be a very suitable hotel for poetry: poetic sentiment could not flourish in the hubbub of that world; but satire, because its element is the ugly and the ridiculous, could be highly regarded there.

Indeed, apart from the ancients, what notable poets has Christian Rome produced? This is what I asked a Roman poet, a friend of mine, one day, and after recalling Vittoria Colonna and Metastasio, he introduced me to other poetic productions of the city that I was completely unfamiliar with. Giusto de' Conti wrote a canzoniere, La Bella Mano, in the early 15th century; Meo Patacca, a popular epic, in the early 18th century; and, more recently, the improviser Gianni, who celebrated Napoleon's wars; Marsuzi, author of the tragedies Caracalla and Alfred the Great; and finally Luigi Bondi, translator of Virgil's Georgics.

Poetry adores the dynamic and passionate life, but Rome has not been a suitable setting for it for many years. The clamour of factions is more pleasing to the Muses than the solemn clangour of bells and the murmur of litanies in processions; the narcotic odour of incense, which pervades the entire city of Rome, is not an efficient inspirer of poetry. The profound severity of antiquity's ruins provides an object of thought for philosophers and historians, yet the blooms of poetry wither beneath the melancholy shadow of so many tombs. Stones are mightier than men in Rome; the past is massive; the present is small; and the future is shrouded in an impenetrable veil.

One evening, while wandering through the Trastevere, I heard a girl sitting alone on the steps of a deserted house, singing, serious and pensive:

"You are no longer, ancient Rome, illustrious Rome!"

These sorrowful words from the mouth of a young girl seemed to me full of meaning. Could not a lyrical, lively and naive genius have arisen in the ruins of Rome? Would he perhaps have been suffocated by the historical melancholy of the ruins? Perhaps; but even a Muse shrouded in sadness could have been beautiful and sublime, not like the swollen and rhetorical Muse of Verri's Roman nights, but like Lord Byron's in Childe Harold, in his apostrophes of a northern artist and a free man.

But let us be fair to the Romans; they could never sing and celebrate their ruins, because they were never allowed to regret them and judge the present by the leftovers of the past. They, in short, could not use their poetic dress.
Antiquity, like the Middle Ages, is full of heroic and tragic motifs in Rome, and a city poet would only use them skilfully to invariably arouse enthusiasm. Often, as I witnessed in the Mausoleum of Augustus (now the Corea Theatre) the jumps of the clowns in their curious pantomimes, or, with rare luck, saw Schiller's Maria Stuarda performed in Maffei's translation, I thought: what an impression a Roman tragedy about Brutus or Virginia would make in this place! How a tragedy concerning Cola di Rienzo might draw the Romans to enthusiasm, just here, in the Mausoleum of Augustus, where the body of that tribune was one day cremated!

The Romans left this matter of Roman theatre to Shakespeare, Corneille, Racine, Voltaire, then Alfieri; and on the Roman theatre those works are not even seen, and among the busts of illustrious men adorning the Pincio, that of Alfieri is missing! It was there, for a moment; then it was suddenly removed by the police - a fact I witnessed myself and report here, to spare myself a longer chat, tending to demonstrate the impossibility of a Roman national drama of the historical genre.

If, in addition to several other reasons of a political and physiological nature, which impede the development of poetic sentiment in Rome, one thinks of the stagnant literary culture, the lack of journalism and criticism, the decadence of the book market, -which is only slightly raised in the affairs of the antiquarian -if one thinks of all these factual conditions, any poetic activity of this people will seem all the more interesting and worthy of study.

The Romans, like all Italians, have never lost their love of poetry; people of all social classes pour out sonnets and songs whenever the opportunity arises. Is there a wedding? Sonnets. A child is born? Sonnets. A student graduates? Sonnets. What does a nun wear? Sonnets. Is a dead man buried? Sonnets. Is a saint commemorated? Sonnets pour down. A monsignor is made a bishop? He walks on a carpet of sonnets in his purple socks! These poetic parts of occasion used to gather in the Academies, in which wits were legalised and received the stamp of the traditional poetic school. The furor academicus, a real plague in the 17th century not only in Italy but also outside, has now completely subsided, and if there are still Arcadians, Quirites, Tiberini, and even academics of the Holy Conception in Rome, one should not look for literary intentions in them. The Arcadia was founded at the end of the 17th century by Crescimbeni and Gravina, Metastasio's master and protector. Its name and its symbol, a bagpipe, well delineate the harmless fields, in which the poetry of the Romans sought asylum, and it also fits well with the history of the city, whose Forum, the ancient ruler of the world, became a Campo Vaccino, whose countryside became covered with innumerable flocks, as in an immense idyll, and whose people, finally, changed from a host of rulers into a herd of pious sheep, which the Pope, a good shepherd, led to pasture among the ruins. In the days of Göethe, whom the shepherds welcomed into their choir with great festivities, Arcadia still enjoyed a certain fame; today, fortunately, it has passed into the background of curiosity, although from time to time its bagpipe returns to be heard. The amount of poetry that are created at those gatherings can only be equaled by their total insults: reading them, one suddenly seems to hear a multiform chorus of bleating and chirping.

Although there is no poetic genius in Rome who does not shut himself up in one of the Academies, where he is provided the opportunity to be heard reciting his verses in a vast hall, these Academies have drastically decreased and lost their influence. Even in Rome, a new generation is gravitating toward a more personal shape and meaning.

Grown amidst the upheavals of past decades, which shook the Romans out of their lethargic slumber, it embodies the hopes of today and attempts, even in Rome, under such unfavourable conditions, a renewal of poetry, a renewal that will only be possible when poetic genius, instead of wearing the old livery of the sonneteers, is clothed in a new form, devoid of artifice and throbbing with life.

The keynote of this young Roman school is above all the lyrical note of the poetry of feeling. The realistic and political Muse is mute in Rome, despite the fact that recent events have provided her with plenty fodder; this is not to be regretted, as it avoids immature judgments and boring and familiar phrases. It is impossible to find an original and powerful voice like that of the Florentine Giuseppe Giusti in Rome. Only philosophical lyricism prevails here, which is largely a reflection of Leopardi's poetry and an echo of England's and Germany's universal grief.

Leopardi's influence on today's young poets is enormous - they still adore him - but perhaps not entirely healthy. His classical and pure form, his beautiful language can be taken as a model of perfect style, but the imagination can draw little from a poet who composes lyrics without images or metaphors, but only with thoughts; the mind cannot too exalt itself to the desperate nihilism of a noble soul, corroded by doubt and despondency. The poetry of this elevated and solitary spirit is shaped by the heartrending cry not only of his homeland, but of humanity as a whole, which weeps over the unique and, dare we say, exceptional fate of one man: the poet. His way of considering existence is the worst school that can be offered to a being who has to struggle in existence.

The Italian poets trained in the school of Byron, Shelley and Lenau lack, due to the particular nature of the southern soul, a sentiment that balances and counterbalances the irony and humour that are particular to them, a sentiment that, in the final analysis, lifts the man from the North above his pain. The southern character has extraordinarily sharp contours, and does not know how to produce that agreement between extreme and opposite feelings and tendencies, which the northern soul perfectly achieves with its sentimentality, using this word in its best sense.

It is also a matter of wonder to see a German element introduced into modern-day Roman poetry.

While the Neapolitans devoted themselves with great devotion to the study of the German philosophy of Kant, Hegel, and Schelling, the study of German poetry extended rapidly in northern and central Italy, and took on a genuine drive. Maffei's magnificent translations introduced Schiller, not only to the stage, but to families, and the best current lyricists, Heine, Lenau, Uhland, are not unknown in Rome. Many contemporary Roman poets speak or understand German and read our authors in their original language. What especially attracts them to our poets is their serious character, so different from the poetry of bargain sonnets and pithy little poems; it is the musical vivacity of the sentiment, the warm lyrical throb, the happy painting of the various moments, the richness of the psychological states described in their most intimate nuances, and, finally, the pantheistic worship of nature. The latter holds a specific interest for Italians, who experience it in a unique and distinct manner. The beautiful, clear, sharp, and plastic form of Italian poetry, like the language itself, subordinates the content to itself, whereas with us, the sentiment overflows beyond the lines of form. The essence of that is harmony; the melody of our poetry, which is the richest in songs in the world. 'Desire,' a Roman poet told me, "is what characterises German poetry; this feeling would renew our poetry if it could be transfused into it."

In one of his compositions, Don Giovanni Torlonia addresses these lines to the Roman lady Teresa Gnoli:

And of Germanic concepts, take subject to your new rhymes after the free, majestic flight.

Don Giovanni is one of the few Roman aristocrats who pursues science out of necessity. There are, however, some in Rome who are truly gifted and active, such as Don Michelangelo Caetani, Duke of Sermoneta, of the famous Boniface VIII lineage, and Don Baldassarre Buoncompagni, who is so well versed in the mathematical sciences. Given how little Roman society is conducive to these studies, one must add to the praise for these men the gratitude of their homeland. Torlonia, a man of great culture, worked tirelessly to restore to honour the fine letters that had long been neglected in Rome. It takes bravery to be a poet in Rome, especially among the elite. The times of Vittoria Colonna and Leo X have past, and the arcadian organisations have done everything in their power to devalue poetry and poets.
Even today, the Romans use the phrase "he is a poet" to describe a man who does not practise law or any other job and spends his days travelling and gathering flies to sell.
Don Juan is both a patron and a poet, and in today's Rome, being a patron is far more useful than being a poet. He comforts and helps the young school of Roman poets, who gather around him

as a free academy for mutual encouragement and emulation. - I name just the most creative, personal and autonomous minds: Fabio Nannarelli, Ignazio Ciampi, Paolo Emilio Castagnola, Giambattista Maccari, and the poetess Gnoli. Under the auspices of Torlonia, this school has established its own organ, which promises to play an important role in Roman literature. It is known as "La Strenna Romana." Strenna is the Italian name for Musenalmanach. This Strenna was first published on January 1, 1858, by Torlonia and Castagnola. It contained various poems and prose, as well as a fragment of Nicola della Tuccia's Cronaca di Viterbo, printed by Ciampi. This mix of lyric poems and historical writings is not to be commended, and I express to my friends in Rome my desire to see the poetic portion separated and published in its own volume as soon as possible. After all, the lack of newspapers explains this promiscuity, which reflects the character of ancient Roman academies, where scientific discourse alternated with literary conversations.

The fact that the Strenna Romana is published in Florence, at Le Monnier, rather than in Rome, is a symptom of the literary situation in Rome.

-all the poets of Rome to this famous Florentine publishing firm. I begin with Don Giovanni Torlonia's poems (Poesie, Florence, 1856), a 66-page booklet that is the smallest of all those we will discuss. Its hallmarks are beautiful and pure language, poetic and melodic sentiment, and a propensity toward ideal nature. Torlonia's Muse is influenced by German lyricism; many of his songs are variations on German texts or imitations of German poems. If the audacity of the German metaphor could be rendered by the austere and rigid Italian language, he would have happily translated Heine and Lenau. This is extremely difficult, and I recall an attempt I made with an Italian poet to translate Lenau's songs into Italian. What was natural and simple in free German became inflated and artificial when it was introduced into this language. According to Lenau, "the spring launches the lodole, its singing rockets, into the air, and this beautiful boldness does not at all shock our German imagination: but how would an audience of Italians stop laughing if this poetic phrase was recited in their own language?"

Torlonia translated Espero from Lenau's Vergangenheit, among other works.

Oh, how melancholy is Hesperus' effulgence, when it sparkles languidly Among the dying day!
The little clouds, which resemble pale flowers, appear to weave a wreath for the dying day.
The human heart groans, but its delights remain, and the mute avello descends with the waning day.

Torlonia's verses are lovely, but they do not fully express the thought, despite the fact that these Lenau verses were among the most likely to be translated into Italian. This translation, on the other hand, exemplifies Don Juan's grace and ease with verse. He also made an excellent replica of Lenau's Painter of Flowers, Heine's song I Love a Flower, and Gothe's Miraculous Little Flower. It appears that his botanical studies in the Agro Romano influenced him to write flower poetry, since we can find several good poems on Agro Romano flowers in the Strenna. Because of the many flower refrains that are sung especially by the people, this type of poetry has a popular character among the Italians. Torlonia also has a good imitation of Geibel's Poet and Nature, as well as a lovely poem called Racconto, which he based on an English ballad.

The flowers of our German romanticism can also be found in this Roman poem. The tramontana appears to have brought their seeds from the lush slopes of Swabia to the dark remains of the Capitol and the Caesars' palace. These Rome-German opera relations, while less important than those with the German Empire, are quite interesting. As Torlonia has already stated, the seeds of German poetic literature have the potential to resurrect all of Italian lyricism.

It is true that an oleander tree will only produce oleander flowers and a linden tree will produce linden flowers, and grafting one onto the other would be futile; it is also true that the Italian genius is fundamentally different from the German genius, and thus its lyricism, which reflects the soul of the people; but Don Juan only intends that Germany could render Italy a service of literary culture, especially given the rapprochement that is taking place.

Fabio Nannarelli (Poesie, Le Monnier, 1853 and 1856) is a poet of uncommon ingenuity who, like the entire young Roman poetic school, has a noble spirit, passionate about truth, which he seeks in poetry and in life, without a trace of levity or frivolity. Nannarelli knows German literature, he is a fan of Schiller and Lenau, on whom he has produced a monograph; he has profound German components in him, and his Muse has a fully Germanic flavour. His primary tone is melancholy, serious, and passionate. There is a breath of death in his poetry, which appears to have come from the Pyramid of Caius Cestius, in whose shadow lay the shadows of Jung and Schelley, great introspective lyric geniuses so unique in the land of Rome. The inadequacy of an ill-ordered existence, which Romans feel more than an Englishman or a German, drives Nannarelli to seek solitude and to feel the cult of pain, which is not entirely free of sentimentality in him. Feeling the gulf that separates aspiration from reality, he turns to nature, like a German, to the consoling and healing nature, for which he strives to reach a philosophical contemplation of universal harmony. Tiedge's tagline:

Seek Hope, Faith and Peace, and fall weeping into the arms of Nature

which he has used as an epigraph to one of his poems, as well as passages from Schiller and Shakespeare's Hamlet,-indicates the exact direction of his artistic mind, which wanders into an incorporeal world of dreams, stripping suffering of its humanity and relegating it to the hazy domain of shadows. This is expressed clearly in the poem A Voice and the Poet. The voice exclaims:-What are you thinking so deeply, O poet? Crown thy brow with love's wreath!

-The Poet:-Love more was a dream, it withered like roses. Voice:-Turn then to Nature! Turn to Science, O Poet:-The soul trembles before the light of truth, and cannot grasp it.-Voice:-What remains for you then? -Poet:-The joy of tears and the peace of the grave.

-To this Scepsi leads; nature, in whose arms the poet seeks solace, becomes a sighing phantom for him, making him long for death. The sentimentality of a Jacopo Ortis is forgivable up to a certain point, because it consciously rests on the pain for a national unhappiness, and expresses a strong patriotic sentiment; but the annihilation of himself and the denial of all healthy work, are not tolerable, if they sway vaguely as simple lyrical matter.

The romantic cult of pain seems to snake like a disease through literature; yet, we do not often find it among the Romans. And they should beware of it; otherwise we might still see Werther's spirit wandering around the Colosseum in the moonlight, with Förster's guide under his arm. Even for a modern Roman, knowledge and work are always present between the Sorrow and the Mystery of the Grave. Travailler sans raisonner-says the philosopher Martino to the great philosopher Pangloss, c'est le seul moyen de rendre la vie supportable; and if the Romans allow themselves to be seduced by a sentimentalism that does not concern their nationality, we can rightly remind them: Cela est bien dit, Romains, mais il faut cultiver votre jardin.

The poet, meanwhile, by the force of his nature, happily rises above these periods of nervous exhaustion into the shining realm of the Beautiful, and intones his earthly sorrow to the eternal laws of the Universe. Vignanello is his most beautiful poem, to which Terenzio Mamiani would not have objected.

He is in the enchanting countryside of Viterbo, near Mount Cimino and, in contemplation of the great flourishing nature, he draws pure and sonorous notes from his lyre. The first part of this long poem, Venus and Sirius, is a happy variation on philosophical and natural themes: as he, admiring, contemplates those two vivid stars, he imagines that the first one says to him: Love! and the second: Think! Thus he expresses the two forces that fill and govern the moral world, and through which intellect and matter express themselves in harmony.

This pantheistic melancholy, which arises from a sense of resigned peace and from a soul that has merged and poured itself into the great divinity of nature, where the eternal love is most openly revealed, is good and beneficial.

He is content whenever the poet abandons the hazy and uncertain to sing of reality. Happy is the elegy To a Child, composed in the presence of a child playing; and very beautiful and profoundly human is the sigh: the path of life is strewn with roses at first, then with roses and thorns, and finally with only thorns! Another no less happy poem is: La viola dell'addio (The Farewell Violet), a maiden's lament over the violet her lover gave her before leaving for war. Its purity and intimate character are reminiscent of Chamisso.

Nannarelli also attempted a poem in loose verse from his youth: Guglielmo. In it, he tells the storey of an unhappy love, which he claims to have taken faithfully from the truth. Guglielmo, forced for political reasons to seek asylum in the workshop of a bronze sculptor, falls in love with the artist's daughter; he makes a beautiful bronze image of her; indeed, we find him intent on this work, which is very successful. The author does not keep the promise made in this good beginning, as the action does not unfold properly, nor does it reach a logical conclusion. That a young man unrequitedly loves a girl may be an unhappiness for him, but it is not yet a tragedy. We can only pity his weakness if he commits suicide, as long as this disaster is not based on a well-constructed, clear-cut tragic plot. But if he, inflamed with fury, stabs himself in the hall where his beloved is about to be married, and before the onlookers, and before her terrified self, we must confess that he did not really love the maiden, nor was he worthy of being loved by her. Such examples of violent but savage passion occur in life, but remain outside the realm of poetry. Although not lacking in some merit, this attempt shows us that our author does not have the qualities of a tragedy or epic poet; instead, he has, and to a high degree, those of the lyricist: fantastic impetus, imagination, warmth of feeling, reflective strength and a soul nourished by study and meditation, which does not content itself with sonorous phrases. This beautiful genius can be a true ornament of Rome, if it knows how to beware of misguidance, and resolutely turn to the true source of poetry, far from the mists of incorporeal abstraction, to feeling and life.

Ignazio Ciampi is a more serene poet with a romantic bent. He enjoys the catchy and simple tune, such as his Fata Morgana. Ciampi has a vivid imagination, a beautiful language, and lovely imagery. In the near future, an expanded edition of his poems will contain many good things; the one I have in front of me contains only a small portion of his lyrical production, notable for its Russian imitations. The Russian language, absolutely barbaric for a Roman, is not known at all in Rome, and Ciampi had a friend translate Puschkin's songs into Italian prose, to show his compatriots how even under a bearskin a poetic heart can beat. Even this fact, which was unheard of in Rome until a few years ago, demonstrates the spread of all European literatures. Rome is, during the winter, an inn of all nations; foreigners bring all languages and introduce all literatures to it; no wonder, then, if in Rome one begins to notice the influence of what is not national. This may broaden the horizon; however, not all nations can have a useful and beneficial influence, and none is more alien to the Italian character than Russia. Ciampi's endeavours are therefore to be considered merely as a literary curiosity; and he would be more benevolent to his homeland if he were to present, in an Italian guise, the foreign poets who have the closest relationship to Italy, or who have absolute classical value. He, moreover, handles the octave very well, and could therefore happily translate the Childe Harold.

Ciampi repeatedly showed his skill in romances in stanza. He wrote two verse novellas, Serena and Stella, the first in three cantos and the second in five. That one is a Tuscan legend, this one a Norman saga; both are absolutely romantic, with love stories, adventures and fantastic scenes. The style is easy and fluent: the descriptions, especially in Stella, are warm and vivid. But our generation has lost interest in this fantastic and chivalrous genre; instead, we want reality and the characters' deep psychology. The Italians, moreover, have little aptitude for romances and ballads, and do not admire the Venetian Carrer too much either. Ciampi has taken an uncertain genre that partakes of two natures, whereas he should have deliberately turned to prose novels, describing, for example, Roman life; thus he would have exploited a genre that is completely neglected in Italy.

Teresa Gnoli, from Rome, whose poems adorn the Poetic Almanac, possesses a true poetic talent, a deep and thoughtful feeling that is expressed in beautiful forms. Her Muse is patriotic, and among men, she brings her contribution to national civilisation in the name of her country's women. Women's literature is plentiful and very important in England, Germany, France and America, but in Italy it is still very limited. In Europe, the masculine spirit appears to be willing to leave the field to women in terms of poetic production and share it with them in the novel; for the time being, none of this is visible in Italy. Strange as this may seem, it is also true that in no other country are women, as here, lovers of family tranquillity and enemies of fame and publicity. Their education system is still largely that of the cloister, and they have very limited ideas about society and the state.

Because of the poetic cult of woman, which we see in Dante and Petrarch, there were female figures in the romantic and violent Middle Ages that the poets of Italy called their muses and inspirers; they imagined their woman to be the mystical sun that lit the flame of their genius. Later, women themselves began to make verse, and it was in Rome that the most famous poetess, and perhaps the liveliest Roman poetic genius of all time, arose. Recently, we had women improvisers in Rome, but art had nothing to do with them.

It would not be possible to compare the poems of the new poetess from Rome with the songs of Vittoria Colonna, all the more so because the young Ms Gnoli did not want to follow any model, but to open up her own personal path and that path she followed without hesitation. And she has succeeded. She often looks to the past, and one of her best poems is precisely: the Meeting of Beatrice and Laura in Paradise, where she delightfully evokes the two shadows, who affectionately amuse each other, soul sisters, and then fade like two stars

Nova tracing way
Of light and harmony.

Also beautiful and effective is a poem about the catacombs of Rome, about this strange domain of shadows and the past, the child of History and Death. Dante's descriptions of Inferno do not produce a more horrific impression than these lengthy dark passages strewn with bones, empty niches, sarcophagi, primitive Byzantine paintings and obscure, menacing inscriptions; here, too, Dante would have needed a guide like Virgil. Now, the Virgil of this underworld is De Rossi, the learned epigraphist; and, re-reading Gnoli's verses, I recall with pleasure the excursion I made to the catacombs with the poetess, the Neapolitan improviser Giannina Milli, and De Rossi who guided us. Hierusalem civitas et ornamentum martyrum Domini is the motto of the poem, taken from a 3rd century inscription.

Gnoli immediately follows the Night of the Catacombs with Homer's Hymn to the Sun, and frees us from the chill of the catacombs with contemplation of the Source of all light and all intellect. A religious spirit speaks in these songs; and it truly seems that Gnoli excels especially in great contemplative lyricism. She attempted, with less luck, the poetic drama with Torquato Tasso in Sorrento. But this melodramatic genre was no longer tolerated; Pastor Fido and Aminta no longer make any impression on us either. Melodrama can still have artistic value and content when it is treated with measured dramatic skill and the highest lyrical delicacy, like Calderon's Echo and Narcissus; but except for Tasso's introductory chorus in Sorrento, which is very good, the rest is reduced to a puerile game, and the figure of the great poet, who has disguised himself as a shepherd and lives among shepherds, who neither understand nor respect him, seems to us to be no more than a puppet, and the whole piece provides further proof of the incomplete and vain sentiment of this mannerist art.

Paolo Emilio Castagnola and Giambattista Maccari are two poets who have sister Muses. We find in them, too, the inevitable complaint of present miseries; Leopardi's disconsolate sadness, for which all but grief is in vain, has also touched them, but barely, like a whiff of musk that has crept into the robes of two healthy men who have passed through a dead man's house. Basically, they have two fresh and vibrant natures, and, instead of their anguish, would joyfully sing the great misfortune of their motherland, if they did not dread emigration. Both have a just and exact sense of reality and history.

In his romance, Emellina, Castagnola sang about Corradino's tragic end, Astura's betrayal, and his death. Emellina is the name of a young girl, the daughter of Frangipane, who falls in love with Corradino at first sight and tries in vain to save him while living in a lonely castle between the sky, the sea, and the woods. The subject is good, but the verses are not always good. The octave is not treated nobly enough, and oscillates between the elevated style and the popular tone of the chronicle; the characters are undefined and romantic. The farewell song of Emellina, who laments her fate from the top of the sinister tower, is valuable for its lyrical beauty.

If Castagnola occasionally attempts political singing, Giambattista Maccari expresses his thoughts more frequently and clearly. The political Muse finds occasion in Rome, more than once a year, to be heard: that is, when the fabulous Christmas in Rome is celebrated, for the anniversary of Tasso's death, and for the distribution of prizes in the Academies of the representative arts. There is no poet in Rome who, in such circumstances, does not boldly send greetings to his homeland, and once, with regard to a poem of this kind on the foundation of Rome, the sale of Torlonia's verses, in which politics did not enter at all, was forbidden. Maccari, too, therefore wrote verses for these occasions. His In the Birth of Rome is full of power. He addresses the Romans: 'O citizens, who have left behind you glorious and sublime ruins, listen now to my lament, arising from sincere sorrow, at seeing you wearing only pompous robes with haughty frowns, while you banish from you the knowledge that you despise as a vain thing.

And to the Roman ladies he says: O women who only offer yourselves to those who are rich in land and fine vessels, and think only of preparing vain things for your children: beware! Ignorance envelops them and suffocates them: what will be their future?

Also energetic and moving are Maccari's sonnets, composed on the occasion of the distribution of prizes to artists. "Italy, your proud monuments are no more than mute and useless stones: revive your spirit, and do not listen to the fool who consoles you with the memory of your great past'!

What does it profit you, degenerate nephews, To be proud of your ancestral glory, If you are made unknown to all the world!

Lonely and virulently noble voices amid the ruins of Rome! Let the Roman Epigoni thank the poet!

Maccari turns to the present, and from the ruins and palaces he moves on to the huts of the poor. Already in Castagnola we find popular stornelli, but in Maccari they are more numerous. He wrote ballads that describe life in the Roman countryside, such as the Venditrice di fragole (Strawberry seller), who descends from the mountains to the city with her elegant basket full of fruit. The refrain of this ballad is as follows:

The montanina came to town. Who Wants to Buy the Alpine Strawberry?

Other subjects of Maccari's poetry include the 'Pastorella' (shepherds), the 'Boscaiuola' (shepherds), who carries on her head the weight of wood gathered on the mountains, the 'Mietitore' (reaper), and the 'Cicoriara' (cicoriara); the latter two are the subject of idylls, the latter especially beautiful and graceful. These 'cicoriara', having picked their salad in the fields, come to sell it in Rome, clothed in a typical country attire, at the Pantheon or Piazza Navona. In these descriptions Maccari shows a very happy poetic temperament, and one feels that his Muse has breathed the fresh airs of the fields! And it is precisely in reality and nature that Italian poetry must seek renewal: this is what Rome's poets must understand. In this regard, I must express my delight at a small collection of popular songs published by the Strenna Romana under the title: Saggio di canti popolari di Roma, Sabina, Marittima e Campagna. The publishers owe a great deal to the efforts of Signor Visconti, who in 1830, for the first time, put his hand to a collection of this sort (Saggio di canti popolari della provincia di Marittima e Campagna). The current collection is modest but valuable. It contains flower refrains from the Roman Campagna, Sabine quatrains, and ten-verse stanzas from the Maritime and Latin Campagna.

The refrains are beautiful wild flowers, fresh and fragrant, grown on the plain or in the mountains. There is maybe no flower that the people here have not put as a sign of something. The man of the fields happily applies to a flower a statement or a thought, encased in a refrain, whether it for a rose, or for a narcissus, or for a daisy, or for a violet. Each bloom inspires him with a tiny sonnet, presented in three dream-filled verses. This flower language is passed down from generation to generation, altering and enriching itself through time. The whole of Italy has this soft flavour; refrains roam across the fields with the labourers and occasionally the same ones are sung in the Maremma, in Corsica, in the Campagna of Rome. But the genuine home of these ritornelli appears to be Tuscany, Italy's garden, possibly the happiest and most inventive region in the country. These refrains are very simply constructed. The first verse, which is usually very short, contains the name of a flower; the other two, which are endecasyllables, express the thought, so that the last verse rhymes with the flower's name, and the middle one usually ends with an assonance:

I bless the rose's flower; this is the fate of precious things; it is purchased with tears and returned in sorrow.

A refrain without a flower:

I see the sea when I glance out the window. All the boats I see approaching My true love does not wish to return.

This final picturesque stornello, as the Tuscans say, appears in Tigri's collection of popular Tuscan songs, but with an unpleasant variant: veggo 'l mare, invece che vedo mare. Tigri gathered 425 of them, many of which are truly poetic treasures. Many of them use the phrase m'affaccio alla finestra (I look out the window), as in this one, which is a tad pretentious:

I see night as I glance out the window; With my tears I soak the sheets; O fountain of beauty, good night!

I transcribe here a Sicilian refrain from Etna: Sciuri

> d'aranciu;
>> All the beddi di ssu munnu C'un capiddu di tia non ci canciu.

Aside from these little poems, the Roman Maremma's popular ten-verse poems are also worth mentioning. Such poems are known as 'rispetti' in Tuscany, however they are usually just eight verses long and constitute a stanza. Sometimes they have a greater number of verses. In Rome, I know just those of ten verses with crossed rhymes, with the last two rhymed. These stanzas include moral statements, proverbs, and popular serenades and love songs.

They are typically unsophisticated, but effective and full of poetry. For the last two decades, the study of popular songs has been widespread in Italy; several collections have been produced; most recently, Oreste Marcoaldi's collection of Umbrian, Ligurian, Picenian, Piedmontese, and Roman songs (Genoa, 1855) is notable; Tigri's Canti popolari Toscani (Florence, Barbèra e Bianchi, 1856) is a true treasure trove of poetry; and finally (Catania, 1857). Sardinia lags behind, despite the fact that it must hold a vast amount of rich resources. The poet Salvatore Viale is responsible for Little Corsica's collection of exquisite songs.

I complete my news about the poets of Rome, whose great endeavours and good triumphs I have gladly followed for many years, as a guest, sending them my friend's fraternal greetings and well wishes, over the Alps, on the banks of the Tiber... We are all indeed, as the classic Roman hymn goes, so many branches of a single stem, so many flames of a single fire o![10]

171

AVIGNON. (1860).

* * *

T here is an indelible prestige in this name of Provence, and this district, irradiated by the most beautiful sun, renowned for its beautiful singing, rich in vineyards and olive groves, irrigated by a great river, animated by a thousand memories of ancient times, still exerts a real fascination over the inhabitants of the northern countries. The romantic reflection of the troubadours' songs hangs over it like the glory of a happy sunset; for that era of Middle Ages poetry is tragically linked to the annihilation of the Albigensians, those brave heretics, those heroes of thought who bloodied Provençal poetry, the freedom of the city republics of southern France, the social civilisation of those lands. That was one of the high points in the history of the Middle Ages; the contrasts of that era, always strong and pronounced, were even more so in that time of liberty and despotism, of poetic love, voluptuousness, and inquisition, of flowers, feasts and the smoking pyres of Giraldo of Borneil and Peter of Castelnau; of Bertran of Bornio and St. Dominic. Add to this the attraction of a melodious, noble language, which was gradually disappearing altogether; of the oldest of the Roman languages, in which people wrote and poetised before Italian rose to literary status; of the Langue d'Oc or Occitania, from which the three main languages of the Latin race, Italian, Spanish and French, originated almost through geographical contact.

There is no province in France where one can go without feeling the same way. Except that the train is too fast, and that strange district, with its reddish rocks, ruined castles, gloomy and melancholy towns, laughing banks of its rivers, orange groves, and vineyards, passes no less quickly before the traveller than the historical memories evoked by the appearance of those regions, Boson of Arles, Raymond of Toulouse, Simon and Amaury of Monfort, the Counts of Beana and Oranges, Innocent III, Charles of Anjou

After all, Provence does not have the appearance of a paradise; in many places, it is comparable to the deserts of Arabia. The districts are stony, sun-baked, often strange, melancholy, and gloomily austere. When I saw this arid region, I understood how it could have been the scene of fanatical and religious wars; how on this sunburnt land a passionate race of men should grow, how the most varied passions, asceticism, enthusiasm, boldness of philosophical concepts, love of liberty, should reign here as in Calabria.

The curse of the terrible crusades against the Albigensians, Huguenots, the Cévennes wars, and Ludwig XIV's dragoon conversions still lives here. One could almost say that the deserted cities, the castles rising in ruins on top of the cliffs, still seem to speak of those times, like the bloody saturnalia of the last revolution; and they certainly do not lament the fall of feudal tyranny. Except that it is not only the ruined castles that bear this severe and melancholy imprint; villages and towns built from a reddish-yellow rock that, if seen among the thin foliage of the mulberry and olive trees, appears to be on fire. Not even in the wildest mountains of the Papal States, in the Volsci Mountains, in Sabina, not even in Corsica, have I seen such melancholic villages. They are mostly built in a haphazard manner, without order; the houses, made of small, rough stones, with sharp roofs, are small, almost hut-like; here and there you can see a window without a flap, closed only by wooden shutters; sometimes the whole wall has only a window and a small door. The streets are small, narrow, obscure, winding; they hardly deserve the name, because, either scattered here and there in no particular order, or piled one on top of the other, they do not lend themselves to the formation of regular streets, and seem rather to be in the winding turns of a stream bed, than in streets open to the interchangeable communication of men.

In most cases, a destroyed castle towers above each settlement, almost as a testament to the violent Middle Ages. There are few signs, traces of fine arts; the churches themselves are more than modest, and of entirely primitive architecture. The life that is lived there seems alien to civilisation, it generally bears the imprint of wildness and misery. Indeed, why would the fairly well-off peasants of today, who no longer have to fear the arbitrary or abusive actions of the barons, the incursions of soldiers of fortune, or the surprises of the satellites of the inquisition, continue to hide out in those miserable hovels, sad remnants of the Middle Ages? The habit is certainly, if not always sweet, then also quite tenacious, and the inhabitants of southern Italy are more stubborn than others in their customs, particularly in the arid and mountainous regions, in themselves rebellious to agrarian progress, and inertia and filth are unfortunately characteristic qualities of the districts.

I'm referring about the small villages of Provence, not the major towns used to civilization and social life, but which appear melancholy, decadent, and dirty. So is Donzères, Mondragone with its black castle, Palud Mornas with its bloody memories, Piolenc (strange, bizarre, sonorous names), and Orange, which brings to mind the history of Burgundy, the Netherlands, England, and even Prussia; once the seat of princes, from whom the House of Orange derived, but now a small town with a gloomy appearance, notable for some Roman and mediaeval antiquities.

The countryside is deafeningly quiet; a few peasants intent on working the land can be seen here and there, and despite the proximity of two major commercial cities, Lyon and Marseilles, there is little sign of industrial and commercial activity. Even the railway stations are generally empty of passengers; at each station, however, priests with their breviaries, nuns with their rosaries and large crosses are waiting. In a nutshell, this is not a French territory; the individuals with the sun-tanned, black-haired visage are not French; they are Roman priests or a mixed population of Ligurians, Celts, Burgundians, Visigoths, Romans, and even Massiliot Greeks, all of whom colonised these regions.

The banks here and there of the Rhone, with their warm colours, the wonderful look of them in many areas, as at the picturesque Roche de Glun, arouse the imagination, and the deeper one goes into the south, the more beautiful and original the land appears to him.

In the vicinity of Mornas When I first saw the olive trees, they appeared to be foreign vegetation. Despite the town of Orange's closeness, I noticed no lemons or oranges. Near Sorga, one comes across the famous Stream of the Same Name, which flows down from the romantic Valchiusa Mountains, where Petrarch wrote the beautiful Laura. Avignon, on the river Rhone, is nearby, and from there, the Palace of the Popes dominates the entire neighbourhood, one of the most remarkable monuments left from the Middle Ages, huge, with a solemn appearance; it is reminiscent in some respects of those in Egypt.

Avignon is neither vast nor lovely, but it is diverse in look and unique. It had eighty thousand inhabitants under the Popes' reign; today, the population of the ruined capital of the department of Valchiusa is thirty-seven thousand. It is a soulless monument, like so many other cities in Italy that have lost their historical life. The air there is imbued with legends and history, but not, as in much of Italy, with lovely and poetic traditions; everything here is austere. There is fanaticism, baronial overbearance, and clerical absolutism; civil life, the breath of democracy, the harmonious contrasts of active life, and the genius of civilisation are absent. The shadow of its mediaeval cyclopean castle stretches over the entire city, and one could argue that it oppresses it, preventing it from rising again; looking from that Avignon, one involuntarily thinks of a legitimist fallen into low fortune, on whose worn velvet robe there are still vestiges of gold embroidery.

When I walked on the truly terrible pavement of these dark and twisty alleyways, I felt as if I were still in Anagni, where more than once the popes held court and where the ruins of Boniface VIII's palace still stand. That city is as dilapidated, empty, dusty, ugly, as Avignon is. It was in Anagni that Boniface VIII was startled and treated in the most dishonourable manner by William of Nogaret, sent by King Philip the Fair of France. A few years later, the same King Philip took the papacy, deprived of its power and reduced to his will, into the French captivity, or, as it was called, the captivity of Babylon, fixing its seat there in Avignon. And these historical reminiscences, these relations between the two cities, made me think more and more about Anagni, of which I had deep recollections.

The magnificent city walls, the work of the Popes, with their square towers, battlements, and gates; the high and wide cliff (Rocher des Doms) with the cathedral and its immense palace; the grey-looking city, from which rise a few ancient towers; the Rhone that laps the walls; the picturesque remains of the bridge of St. Benezet; the suspension bridge leading to the island on the Rhone; the bizarre aspect of Villeneuve-les-Avignon on the other side Benezet; the suspension bridge leading to the Rhone island; on the other bank, the strange look of Villeneuve-les-Avignon with its towers and castle; these are the main features that first appear in Avignon.

The city's position, while not very picturesque, does have some worth; for the majestic river lends the city and its surroundings a sense of grandeur and majesty. The horizon is vast and beautiful, and I was surprised, despite my recent memories of Italy, when I climbed the long and wide steps leading up to the Rocher des Doms from the Rhone bank. I could see a completely southern-facing countryside, cultivated with olive groves and plantations of mulberry trees, madder, and vines, crossed by the Rhone, the Sorga, and the Duranza, irrigated by numerous canals, and populated by numerous villages. A bright and tranquil sky spans across that hilly terrain. On the right bank of the Rhone, arid and yellow-hued like the rocks of Sicily, one can see the shores of Villeneuve, Fort St. Andrew, Chateau-neuf-des Papes, the olive-grove mountains of Valchiusa, further on the high Bentoux, the blue Luberon, the peaks of the Dauphiné and Provence Alps, and finally the mountains of the Languedoc. All of these mountains lack the exquisite shapes of the Italian Alps, but they stand in a southern atmosphere and under a southern sky, announcing the wonderful country's vicinity. When the Italian and Roman cardinals (who were usually there at the court of the French Popes) cast their eyes over these fields of Provence, they could to a certain extent find there a recall of the beauty of Italy and a memory of the grandeur panorama of Rome. The cardinals and French popes who were linked to these areas by their love of their country might then cheerfully cast their eyes onto them and urge the Italians to comfort themselves with superb Burgundy wine and beautiful, black-eyed Avignonese ladies, a pleasure they never despised.

The vegetation of the Rocher des Domes is all southern. On the terraces, leanders, laurel, vines, broom and pines grow and bloom there, and I also saw some aloe plants, although these Italian plants were small, tisical, like exotic plants. One could see that the soil was not yet one in which they could take their full development. Thinking on the splendour of Italy's vegetation, it seemed to me that the Popes attempted to introduce Roman flora into Babylon's captivity. No matter how hot the weather is in Avignon, orange and lemon trees do not grow in the open air, and I did not notice the laurels, cypresses, and pines that grow so majestically in Rome. Moreover, the land of Avignon is productive, producing excellent wine and oil, figs, almonds and madder above all, in vast amounts.

A large bronze statue, which stands on the esplanade of the Rocher des Doms, refers to the cultivation of the latter plant.

I moved towards that one, used to seeing the statue of the city's patron saint on the squares of cathedrals in Italy, to see which was the protector of Avignon, and found written on the pedestal: Les Vauclusions reconaissants a Jean Althem, introducteur de la garance, 1846. In front of the cathedral of Avignon, in the vicinity of the French Vatican, stands not the statue of a pope, nor of a martyr, nor of a bishop, but that of a simple citizen, who introduced into Provence, not the Inquisition, but a little plant that makes the country rich, dyeing the trousers of six hundred thousand Frenchmen red. And this verified that I was not in Anagni, but in a bustling industrial city in France, somewhere between Lyon and Marseille. John Althen, however, was not an Avignonese, but a Persian. He arrived in this city in 1756 and died in Caumont in 1774.

When I reached that height, there was no air; despite the fact that it was October, the sun shone brightly on the bare rocks. However, the northerly wind, or mistral as it is known here, is frequently felt with force, and the town is particularly vulnerable to it; hence the old proverb.:

> Avenio ventosa, sine vento venenosa, cum vento fastidiosa.

However, I would make a correction to the last verse, saying: *Cum et sine vento fastidiosa.* This proverb reminded me of the one from *Tivoli: Tivoli of ill comfort, or it blows wind, or it rains, or it sounds dead.*

The name *Rocher des Doms* is derived from *Domnis* or *Dominis*, and the cathedral is also called *Our Lady of Doms*. The cliff on which it rests rises 138 feet above sea level and 81 feet above Avignon. There stood the old acropolis, and there have stood the major monuments of its history over the ages. In this regard, Avignon is similar to several cities in Latium and Etruria, which had an ancient fortress at their highest point and a temple next to it, both during paganism and during the Christian era; for the cathedrals and bishop's palaces, fortified and with their towers, were generally built with materials taken from pagan temples.

Before I introduce my reader to the famous Palace of the Popes, I'd like to look at the history of this city and its environs from this Capitol of Avignon, because what language can the stones and walls of a famous location speak if one is unaware of its historical life?

Avignon's origins are unknown; it almost probably predates G.C. The Greeks termed it Avenion, and the Romans Avenio; it is unclear if this was done by eliminating the names A vento, Ab avibus, Avineis, or another word. The city was definitely the capital of the Cavarians or Celts who colonised this region of Gaul, and later, as an emporium on the Rhone, the Massilots took up residence there. Avignon was a Roman colony with the right of Latin city at the time, and it belonged to the Gallic province of Vienna in the Dauphiné, together with Geneva, Grenoble, Valencia, Orange, Carpentras, Arles, and Marseille. All of these cities thrived during the first emperors, and there were several Roman architectural monuments in them. None remain in Avignon, although there are a few in the surrounding area, including Orange, Carpentras, Cavaillon, and Arles. It may be true, as the most recent Avignon writers claim, that those monuments were destroyed by the Burgundians, Goths, Franks, and Arabs; but, considering the colossal walls of the Popes' palace, it seemed to me likely that, like many churches and palaces in Rome, they must have concealed more than one Roman monument within them.

Provence, the last of Gaul's Roman provinces to become Roman in language and customs, flourishing in Latin civilisation, and wealthy in schools and academies, was briefly occupied by the Visigoths, then by the Burgundians, before becoming a Frankish province under Clovis. Except that all Germanic races were always despised by the Latin-speaking Provençals, and even after the Franks became French, southern France on both sides of the Rhone to the foothills of the Pyrenees was almost completely isolated from the rest of the country by language, national sentiment, customs, and habits. Southern France was vehemently opposed to the Merovingian, then Carolingian dynasties; those provinces desired to establish their own state, and thus their contacts with the Saracens, sworn enemies of the Franks. After defeating the Muslims in Tours, Charles Martel drove them out of Provence, captured Avignon, which had opened its gates to the unbelievers, and set it on fire. As a result, Provence fell under the dominion of the Franks.

Meanwhile, following the fall of the Carolingians, the Provençals withdrew from the French monarchy, electing Count Boson as their national king in Vienna (879), and thus the kingdom of Provence was founded, also known as Cisiuranic Burgundy because it included many parts of ancient Burgundy, Provence, the Dauphiné, a section of Savoy, Nice, Lyon, Bress, and part of Freiburg. Transiuran Burgundy remained independent until 933, when the two kingdoms merged to form the new kingdom of Arles. Rudolf III, the last king of this, named the kings of Germany as his heirs in 1032, and they held political dominance over those regions, now French, and even longer over Switzerland.

Provence was thus incorporated into the kingdom of Burgundy, although its national counts remained to control it as vassals of the kingdom and the empire. They settled in Arles about the year 900 and ended up decreasing their hereditary lordship almost independently, while national counts also developed in Languedoc, where they founded the famous line of Count Raymond of Toulouse.

Avignon belonged to the kingdom of Arles, but in addition to the Counts of Provence, the Counts of Toulouse, and the Counts of Forcalquier had rights over the city for a long time before becoming the dominion of the popes; a strange and absurd combination that only feudalism and its intricate system of public law can explain.

In the adventurous period when municipal liberties began to emerge and flourish, Avignon, like Marseilles and Arles, gained autonomy and was governed by consuls and podestà in the manner of the Italian republics. In 1137, Emperor Barbarossa validated the statutes of Avignon, and the prosperous city was given the title of imperial republic.

It was soon engulfed in the great upheaval, the great uprising known after the Albigensians.

Enfranchisement, emancipation of thought, went hand in hand with bourgeoisie enfranchisement, and the cities of Southern France, where municipal sentiments had been maintained since Greek and Roman times, ardently raised the banner of the Albigensians and Raymond of Toulouse in order to achieve full independence. The fatal crusades, first prohibited by Innocent III, then by Honorius against the Albigensians, had the goal of annihilating the freedom of those cities, damaging their prosperity, and having their ethnicity absorbed by France.

Simon de Monfort conquered Languedoc, the lovely property of the Counts of Toulouse, and Rome, which at the time gave countries as if the Pope were the ruler of the world, confirmed him in possession of these regions. Except that when Ramon and his son returned from exile in Genoa, they were met with transport by the republics of Avignon and Marseilles, and the battle was rekindled more furiously than ever. At the siege of Toulouse, a stone thrown by a woman's hand struck Simon de Monfort in the head, and the Albigensians won a brief victory.

They were defeated by the sword of Ludovic VIII, which Honorius III had given to him. Raymond was obliged to make peace, handing over several of his lands to the French crown and numerous rights over Avignon and the Venetian countryside to the Roman church. During the fight against the Albigensians, Rome won the first claim to a new seigniory in France, specifically Venasque and Carpentras; nevertheless, this cession was merely a commitment, and the Church was eventually forced to surrender those cities to the Counts of Toulouse. He never forgot his rights, however, and as early as 1273, the King of France declared an absolute and permanent cession to the Popes of the Venosine area.

After being forced to surrender by Louis VIII in 1226, Avignon was once again subject to the counts of Toulouse and Provence. However, by the terms of the Treaty of Paris, Raymond was forced to give his daughter and heir Joan to the king's brother, Alfonso of Poitiers. The illustrious lineage of the Counts of Toulouse died extinct with the death of the former in 1249, and its lands fell to France. A similar fate befell the lineage of the Counts of Provence; the last of them, Raymond Berengar, married his daughter Beatrice to Alfonso, brother of Charles of Anjou, later conqueror of Naples and executioner of Corradin, and so Provence fell into the hands of the French crown in 1245.

The two brothers attempted to stake their claim to Avignon and other places. The terrified republics sought assistance from the powerful Emperor Frederick II, their high lord, but vain; they were forced to surrender to the cruel conqueror. Avignon surrendered on May 10, 1251, and with it its republican order and flourishing municipal civilisation, which was to be succeeded sixty years later by another exotic and curial civilisation, established by the Popes in that same Provence, which their predecessors had put to fire and sword through legates, extinguishing the splendid civilisation of southern France, the brilliant science of Arles, Toulouse, and Nimes.

Avignon was reserved for the monarchs of Naples, who also held the titles of Counts of Provence and Forcalquier. Then, at the same palace of the Popes, I shall describe how the Roman Church was able to take this city from the crown of Naples.

The dark castle, with its vast, colossal towers, black, gigantic walls interrupted by a few irregular Gothic windows, moats, portcullises, and underground dungeons, creates a gloomy but also dangerous atmosphere. Overall, the castle is an unsightly structure, a mix of fortress and convent, palace and prison, created without a plan or design: a sort of labyrinth. Although the mass has a certain majesty, this papal fortress in France, isolated from the papacy's history and with no relation to the rest of the country's monuments, exudes a careless, pettiness when one thinks of the Vatican. A fortification sits nearby, but it is the mausoleum of a Roman emperor; the brilliance of the arts has softened its bulk, and the beauties of the classical world gleam in its enormous rooms. In Avignon, the little church Notre Dame des Doms, close to the castle, corresponds to St Peter's, near to the Vatican. This transitory residence thus represents the papacy's fate and decay during its stay in France; it was a prison for the popes, and its baronial castle harkens back to the age of feudalism, when the supreme hierarch of Christendom was no more than a vassal of France and did not blush to bear the feudal titles of Count Venosino and of Avignon.

The story of seven Popes brings the castle to life, but it is insufficient to fill such huge halls and inhabit its walls; after the Popes departed the palace, it did not hold as much interest as many other baronial castles.

The arms of Avignon, a city supported by two eagles, and three golden papal keys can be seen on the main entrance door; upon entering, one finds deserted courtyards, very high walls, eternal staircases, long corridors like monasteries, gothic chapels now closed, large halls now partitioned off, rooms in towers, underground vortices, a veritable Daedalus' labyrinth that makes one dizzy. Drums beat, soldiers guffaw, and huge rows of mattresses and lengthy lines of French soldiers can be seen in the magnificent apartments that originally belonged to Clement VI. After the revolution of 1790 drove the papal legates from Avignon, the palace was quickly reduced to the use of barracks, where it still is. It has retained its appearance despite being brutally devastated by soldiers during the revolution and the restoration of 1815. The valuable frescoes in the chapels and other rooms were completely destroyed, and only a few vestiges of beautiful paintings from Giotto's school may be seen.

These now-silent walls witnessed seventy years of papal history during one of Europe's most remarkable epochs, when the light of science was beginning to shine brilliantly again.

Clement V, Archbishop of Bordeaux and cunning fox in priestly garb, was the first Pope of Avignon. After secret discussions with Philip the Fair, he was elected and confirmed, and had himself crowned in Lyons against the will of the cardinals; he forced them to come to France, to follow him to Avignon, where he took up residence in 1309. The city was then owned by Charles II, King of Naples, and the Pope was his guest; because there was no papal house there, Clement went to remain in the Dominicans' monastery. He slavishly submitted to the French despot's desires, cruelly crushing the Templar order. As he lay dying, the Grand Master of the Templars, James Molay, called the Pope and King of France to the court of God, and his prophecy came true not long after: Clement died in Roquemaure in 1314. He enriched his nephews, but left only the memory of a sleazy miser, as described by two famous and illustrious Florentines, one a historian and the other a pious bishop.

After his death, his successor, a Provençal by origin and bishop of the city at the same time, remained to live at Avignon. John XXII boasted that he might reduce it to a Holy See seigniory and connect it with the Venetian countryside and Carpentras. The fate of Rome was rewritten in small Avignon; the Popes, who had gradually gained temporal control there, aspired to become lords of Avignon as soon as they built their home there. The energetic elderly guy resolved to establish himself in a foreign palace under the control of the King of France. This new home was to be a stronghold with ditches and turrets, and the Rocher des Doms, which overlooked the Rhone, was ideal for this.

The castle of Avignon was founded by John XXII, and the biggest tower, known as the Trouillas, comes from his reign. The stunned residents of Avignon could not grasp what doom had been set for their hometown as they watched this structure rise before their eyes. John moved into his castle, and it was from there that he unleashed the thunderbolts of his excommunications, which also struck Lodovico il Bavaro; it was there that he received the penitent antipope Pietro di Corbara, and it was there that he imprisoned him till his death. John XXII died at the age of ninety in 1334. At his death, twenty-five million gold scudi were discovered in his coffers, eighteen million in cash and seven million in pottery and precious stones.

Such was the wealth of the popes during their exile in Babylon, at a period when the Church was in full insurrection and all provinces were wrecked.

James Fournier, the third Pope of Avignon, assumed the name Benedict XII. He replaced the able John XXII, the friend of kings, with the noble purpose of cleaning the papal court of nepotism and the Church of a thousand abuses. The papal palace was then subjected to a stringent all-monastic discipline. Except that Benedict XII, on whom the Romans had so much hoped, remained deaf to their petitions and repeated requests to return the seat of the papacy to Rome. The French faction was vehemently opposed; the king pushed the pope to remain in Avignon, for which Petrarch heaped the harshest reproaches on him.

In keeping with his nature, Benedict XII transformed John XXII's residence into an impregnable fortress, even giving it the look of a monastery; his worldly successors could no longer remove this character from the edifice.

Clement VI was a man of spirit, education, and worldliness, a perfect gentleman of the family of Beaufort, a friend of Petrarch, a lover of the fine arts, poetry, and science; he summoned the Muses to his sensual Court of Avignon. The city known as Sodom, or the second Babylon, by the Italians, flourished at the time and shined with a transient brightness; in such a little stage, the Court of Popes and cardinals could not extend; and those French Popes were no more Provençal barons than inhabitants of little Avignon. While this flourished, Rome had degenerated into a village. Abandoned by the popes, whom it had ejected so many times from its walls, it now longed for their return, and when they did not chose to return, it abandoned itself, the everlasting city, to one of history's most unusual accomplishments. It was the Cola di Rienzo era.

Cola was among the legates sent to Clement VI by the Romans to persuade him to return to Rome. Petrarch first encountered him at Avignon. Among the emissaries was Stefano Colonna, the head of Rome's first family and a friend of Petrarch's, who had no idea that in a few years the young notary would murder his sons and grandsons.

Petrarch, Madonna Laura, and the lovely image of the last Roman tribune pop up before one's eyes today as one wanders through the wretched rooms of the Avignon castle, illuminating the misery that reigns within those walls. Except for Napoleon's red-coated soldiers, who had just returned from the bloody battlefields of Magenta and Solferino and were preparing to leave in garrison in that same papal Rome, which is now in far worse shape than it was during Cola di Rienzo's reign; those soldiers were constantly coming between me and the images of the past. They knew nothing about Petrarch, Dame Laura, Cola di Rienzo, or Joan of Naples; they did know, however, that these walls had housed popes and could think that even now, a pope was in some way a prisoner of France, and that he may be brought to Avignon. Yes, several factors compelled me to connect the time of the Avignon exile with the present in that Popes' fortress.

Thus, it was within these walls, at the beginning of 1344, that Cola di Rienzo delivered a speech to Clement.

VI. The occasion was magnificent, worthy of a Demosthenes or a Cicero; the youthful orator had expended all his energies in persuading the Pope and that noble assembly, while gaining immortal reputation for himself. He portrayed a realistic picture of Rome's sorrow, emphasising the cruelty and arrogance of the lords in particular. This was the source of his demise. The Colonna family, notably Cardinal Giovanni, warned the Pope against the bold demagogue, and Cola stayed in Avignon for some time in terrible health, mocked by cardinals and grandees. Clement VI was then forced to recall him to Rome as a notary of the Municipal Chamber. From that point on, he embarked on a fantastic career in Rome, aiming not only to restore the city to its former glory, but also to establish Italy's unity.

The huge tribune resurfaced at Avignon in the same palace. The first act of his magnificent play had taken place in Rome. He arrived in 1351 as a prisoner from Prague, given by Emperor Charles VI, and all the people were moved to see the remarkable man who had done such extraordinary things in Rome. Cola was carried to the palace and imprisoned there, where he was given scant nourishment; he was tried in front of the entire world, not just Avignon. The prestige of his name, of his exploits, was tremendous; the classical majesty of Rome enveloped the one-of-a-kind nephew who had dared to put on the toga and present himself as tribune of the people he had enchanted with a Roman spectacle. Petrarch wrote epistles to the Romans, pleading with them to try to save his miserable companion through an embassy. Meanwhile, Cola was tied up, fantasising, in a castle tower, possibly in the dreadful Trouillas that still stands. Actually, it is unknown where he was imprisoned, but tradition refers to that tower as his prison. His confinement, however, became less severe; food was sent to him from the Pope's table, and he immersed himself in the assiduous reading of Titus

Livius, in which he found a description of the ancient greatness of the Romans, and in which he could see the image of his deeds as well as the fate that awaited him. He stayed there until August 1353, when Clement VI's successor not only allowed him to return to Rome, but also appointed him as his vicar. The weird whim of fate allowed the previously fallen tribune to rise again in splendour; they were his hundred days in Rome, before he was stabbed by a sword at the foot of the Capitol.

I asked if there was any memory of this strange man's existence in the palace, and the caretaker showed me a portrait of Cola that he kept in his room. This oil picture depicted him in a senator's suit, with his hair in black curls and his head covered by a crimson cap. His huge and expressive head, noble face, and lack of a beard exhibited the broad, fat physiognomy that Cola is supposed to have had in his final years. His aquiline nose and Roman profile suggested vigour, and his gaze was serene and authoritative. I read beneath the portrait: Nicolas Calabrini dit De Rienzi, tyrant of Rome in 1347. To be honest, this painting lacked credibility and belonged without a doubt to the period when the Jesuit Cerceau produced the useless work Conjuration de Nicolas Gabrini dit De Rienzi, tyran de Rome, which was discovered in Amsterdam in 1734.

Another historical figure from the time of Rienzi and Petrarch looms over the Avignon palace: Joan I, Queen of Naples and Lady of Avignon and Provence, who was accused of murdering her husband and acquitted by the Pontiff. As heir to the throne, she had been betrothed to the young prince Andrew of Hungary by her ancestor Robert I from childhood. This king died on January 19, 1343, after establishing a regency council for Joan's minority. The princess, a sixteen-year-old girl, did not lavish attention on her consort, whose rude manners and ineptitude were most likely not exaggerated by Neapolitan historians. The Neapolitan nobles grumbled over the arrogance of the Hungarians who surrounded the fledgling court; they determined to get rid of Andrea, especially since Clement VI had already published the bull prescribing the minor Andrea's early coronation.

Joan was in Aversa with the king and his consort on September 18, 1345. Andrea was called out of his flats during the night on the pretext of receiving important dispatches, and as soon as the unhappy young man appeared on the balcony, he was seized by masked men, who threw a noose around his neck and hurled him into the garden, where his corpse was discovered hanging on a rope the next morning. The people were moved, and the queen fled to Naples, where she shut herself up in her palace; the public accused her of murdering her husband, or at the very least of being complicit in his murder. Trials and executions were carried out on Joan's orders as well as those of the papal legate, who arrived quickly from Avignon.

Meanwhile, Ludwig of Hungary, the slain's brother, assembled an army to march on Naples and avenge Andrew's killing, which he completely accomplished. Joan, who was youthful, attractive, sensual, like Mary Stuart later in life, and intellectual to the point where she was supposed to have inherited her great ancestor's superb wit, had no idea how to escape the looming peril that confronted her. She married Ludovico of Taranto, her cousin, for whom she had a great attachment even before her husband died. Meanwhile, the world heard the king of Hungary's allegations and protests of Joan's innocence; opinions were divided.

Ludovico and Giovanna's envoys appeared in Rome, before Cola di Rienzo, and the queen knelt herself before the tribune of the people, then master of Rome and in the splendour of his might, pleading her innocence with modest and fawning epistles accompanied by lavish gifts. To avoid the fury of the impending Hungarian, she set out in January 1348 for Provence, her property, with her new husband, and presented herself in Avignon to Clement VI, feudal ruler of Naples and initiator of the trial begun against her, who was both her judge and her lord.

The Pope assigned her to Villeneuve, on the opposite side of the Rhone; he certified her second marriage, which did not comply with canonical norms, and had the trial ordered, then invited her to appear before the cardinals and lords of Provence in his own palace. Joan delivered a Latin oration in her defence before the assembly with such zeal, calm, and confidence that everyone was taken aback. Her appearance as an accused, as an exile, the memory of her great ancestor Robert, the Church's illustrious guardian, and, most importantly, her youth, beauty, and elegance affected everyone, and the young queen was cleared of the charge of uxoricide.

Was the cardinals' decision sufficient to exonerate her before her conscience? Was she actually as innocent as they claimed? Some Neapolitan historians condemn her, while others acquit her, and the imposing sentence of Italy's most renowned historian points to her as an accomplice, at the very least, in the misdeed. Dessa was aware of the unlawful scheme but did not resist it, as Mary Stuart did later, following Darnley's death.

Joan made plans to return to Naples and reclaim her kingdom. She needed troops and money, so she sold Avignon to the Pope on June 8, 1348, for the pittance of eighty thousand gold scudi. Strict implications were formed from this circumstance; there is no proof to back them up, but the suspicion is simple to explain. The murder of a monarch and the acquittal of a queen accused of extinguishing him were the events that brought Avignon under the control of the popes. Joan reclaimed the kingdom of Naples, which she ruled wisely and prudently for many years in the midst of unceasing conflict. When Ludwig of Taranto died, she married James of Aragon, and after his death, she married Otto of Braunschweig. She was later captured by Charles III of Durazzo, her kinsman and mortal enemy, and this pretender to the throne ordered his scoundrels to execute her in the same manner as her first husband. In 1382, Joan of Naples was strangled in the castle of Muro, Apulia.

While the walls of the palace of Avignon reminded this bloody chapter in the history of the kingdom of Naples, my thoughts paused to ponder the kingdom's current state, whose unclear and anxious destiny draws the attention of the entire continent. I imagined the young King Francis imprisoned within the walls of Gaeta, heir to his fathers' errors and faults, fleeing from his capital, abandoned by his people, besieged by Italian troops in his last fortress, threatened by the King of Piedmont, who seeks to dethrone his kinsman, raising the ancient flag of Cola di Rienzo, the flag of Italian unity, with Rome as capital. The cannon fire from Gaeta is the final spark of a dictatorship that could no longer exist.

As a result, as we have seen, Avignon had become the property of the Holy See, and Clement VI did not waste time in taking possession of it, much to his delight, because he felt no less a lord there than he did in Venasca and Carpentras. Before the advent of the revolution that seemed to be breaking out in Rome from day to day, that stretch of Provençal country must have appeared to the Popes as a true haven and a refuge inaccessible to storms, at a time when the Church was gradually losing its possessions in Italy. Whereas they had been constantly forced from Rome by insurrection, and their survival there had become increasingly dangerous, they had peace and serenity at Avignon, and the seventy years of exile in Babylon were for a long time the Papacy's only peaceful years. It's no surprise that the Popes were hesitant to leave Avignon.

If the Roman Church currently owned land beyond the Alps, it is not implausible that Pius IX, in a situation reminiscent of Cola di Rienzo's, would seek sanctuary there rather than remaining in Rome under the doubtful protection of France.

Clement expanded and improved his predecessors' palace. He built there a magnificent chapel, or rather a Gothic cathedral, vastly superior in size and architectural splendour to the

Vatican's Sistine Chapel. He filled it, as well as other rooms in the castle, with exquisite fresco paintings by Italian painters. All of these paintings were destroyed; the chapel, which was separated onto two floors and various chambers, was converted into barracks, and the Gothic arches embedded in the walls and vestiges of valuable frescoes, unquestionably of the Giotto school, can be seen with agony.

Clement VI died on December 6, 1352, following a pontificate of more than ten years and a life of pleasure and splendour. He had gathered the flower of southern France in Avignon and introduced luxury to his court; feasts followed feasts in the halls of his palace, packed with beautiful ladies, knights, poets, painters, and intellectuals. He lavished his nephews, favourites, Church dignitaries, and the treasures accumulated from his predecessor's avarice. He was the most brilliant of the popes stationed in Avignon, and the dismal castle he ruled over was comparable to the Vatican under the reigns of Sixtus IV, Julius II, and Leo X.

After him, three popes remained in France; the last of these put an end to the untimely exile, restoring the seat of the supreme pontiff to the eternal city.

Innocent VI was the polar opposite of Clement VI in that he banned all luxury from the court in Avignon, sent Cola di Rienzo back to Rome, and accompanied him with Cardinal Egidio Alvarez Albornoz, one of the Church's most accomplished politicians and captains. In fact, he succeeded in restoring the lost provinces to the inheritance of St. Peter's better than General Lamoricière did in our time. Rome surrendered to that vivacious Spaniard and returned to the pope. On September 12, 1362, Innocent VI died in Avignon.

Urban V replaced him (1363-1370). He could thank his predecessors for ensuring that Avignon was fortified, for it would have fallen into the hands of the armed bands that were looting Italy and the south of France at the time. They besieged the city, and the pope was forced to pay a large sum of money to have them removed. Petrarch, now an elderly man, then persuaded Urban to forsake France and return to Rome, which had peacefully reverted to its former glory. The Romans had summoned him with an embassy, and in 1367 he returned to the barren city, except that in 1370 he abandoned Rome and Italy, which had become deserted, and the entreaties of Saint Bridget, who predicted that he would die if he returned to Avignon, did not aid him. And, as fate would have it, the prophecy came true, as Innocent died in December, shortly after returning to France. He had finished the papal palace, including the seventh tower, known as the Tower of Angels. Trouillas, St John's, the Estrapade, St Lawrence, the Bell, and the Gache were the names of the other six.

Gregory XI, his successor, was the last pope to visit Avignon. Shaken by the prayers of the Romans, Peter of Aragon, and the holy women Bridget and Catherine of Siena, the latter of whom even came to Avignon for this purpose, he left Provence forever on September 13, 1376, accompanied by all but six cardinals, who preferred to continue living in their pleasant villas on the Rhone.

The popes' palace lost all interest beyond this point, as it remained vacant after their return to Rome. However, two antipopes remained there during the schism: Clement VII and Benedict XIII, the latter of whom was besieged.

Avignon and the Venetian countryside were administered by cardinal legates beginning in 1409; however, the Italians, mostly always nephews, remained in Rome and were represented by deputy legates. The last was Filippo Casoni; the French republic forced him out of Avignon for good with the papal power, and this city was tormented by awful scenes of bloodshed on the night of October 16-17, 1791, under Jourdan, Duprat, and Jouve. The area where the unlucky victims were bathed in blood by those horrible animals may still be seen in the Trouillas tower. It was only logical that animosity, which had been focused for so long on papal dominance, should offer an excuse for these atrocities: the people spoke of the inquisition's underground prisons in the castle, of awful mysteries completed during the legates' authority. In the 15th century, during the terrible age of the Borgias, a deputy legate invited the most distinguished citizens of Avignon to a party in the papal palace, then closed the doors of the rooms and, after setting fire to the flats, burned his guests alive to avenge a nephew murdered by a betrayed husband.

When one visits Avignon, under the impression of such atrocities committed by the revolution, under the still fresh memory of the Royalist assassination of Marshal Brune on 2 August 1815, when one sees that uncouth and fanatical population, one feels a strong desire to leave that city as soon as possible. Nowadays, the people of Avignon are still considered superstitious, uncouth, angry, and ignorant, and it is probable that this province would once again become the site of heinous excesses.

However, I do not want to be ungrateful to such a wonderful place, so I will remain a little longer. It remains for us to visit the ancient cathedral, St Peter's of Avignon, because the one in Rome was able to envy this modest, black, and nondescript church as a usurper of its secular rights for a good seventy years. Meanwhile, the popes were reduced to a modest chapel in this corner of the world, removing the symbols of worship and the actions of Church history from the view of Christendom.

Saint Martha, sister of Lazarus, is supposed to have founded Nôtre-Dame des Doms after landing in the Camargue, introducing Christianity to Provence, and constructing the first church in Avignon on the ruins of a Hercules temple. The origin of Notre-Dame is unknown, and its claim to have been erected by Charlemagne is debatable; the only certainty is that it is a very ancient church, as evidenced by its main entryway, which is in a fully Roman style and flanked by two ancient Corinthian columns. The vandalism of the revolution, which destroyed other churches in the city, did not spare this one. The so-called Charlemagne Chapel remains, much to the delight of antiquities enthusiasts, but the monuments of successive popes, valuable remnants of Gothic beauty in the 14th century, were tragically lost. The tombs of Benedict XII and John XXII, in Gothic style, with exquisite sculptures and the figure of the pontiff laying on a sarcophagus, were restored. Some parts of Cardinal de Armagnac's tomb can be found in a niche; in the Sancta-Sanctorum, you can view the tombstone of Luigi Balbo Bertone of Crillon, called the Bravo and Arrigo's companion.

IV died at Avignon in 1615, and a bronze statue of him sits on Place de l'Horloge.

This is the city's most attractive piazza, located just a short distance from the Popes' Palace. It is bordered by several gorgeous structures, including the fine theatre and the modern municipal palace, both in the French Risorgimento style and preceded by a courtyard packed with columns. The custodian, who gave me a tour of the palace, told me with dignity that Louis Napoleon had honoured it with his visit on his way to Algiers, that the staircase had been carpeted, and the entire neighbourhood had been furnished with magnificent style. The Emperor was received with considerable pomp and circumstance; nonetheless, the legitimist party remains numerous in Provence, despite its lessened income. Meanwhile, Napoleon can relax for a while; he has the landowners and working classes all to himself; his praise is heard everywhere: he has quelled the movement, restored order, and brought enormous advantage to these wine-producing territories through trade contracts. Furthermore, our predominance! ... These are the words that one hears at every turn.

However, it must be stated that visiting this city is really exhausting. Its streets, where a few palaces in the Risorgimento style, a few antique and odd buildings, with arcades and courtyards that draw attention to themselves, are dark; the mood here is melancholy and conjures up painful memories.

How much more beautiful are the tiny towns of Tuscany, Prato, Pistoia, Siena, and Arezzo, where one encounters art marvels at every turn, memories of municipal freedom, and an ancient and wonderful civilisation?

I've seen practically all of the churches in Avignon; there isn't one that can be termed truly beautiful, and almost all of them bear remnants of the revolutionary era's damage. One Sunday, I attended St Didier's, a Gothic-style church, which was packed with women shrouded in white, kneeling and singing litanies. It was a picture full of soul and life; in that devoted recall, in the harmonies of those chants, I seemed to recognise Rome's long-standing impact on Avignon. It was a painting of a thoroughly Roman character, except that the plaza around the church, covered by big trees, had no Roman or southern feel to it at all, and instead reminded me of the country churches of my beloved homeland.

The mob of devout only gave me a cursory glimpse over a bas-relief known as images du roi René; for these sculptures are credited to the good king, and it is hard to estimate how many statues and paintings he is the author of in Provence.

Not far from St. Didier lies the church of St. Agricola, the town's patron saint, who is called in all public calamities, notably in times of drought. This church was built in the 10th century and later expanded; its Gothic façade, with enormous crenellated towers, is original, and the simplicity of the ogival style, even in the interior, indicates its antiquity.

The chapel of the Penitents Noirs de la Miséricorde is also noteworthy. It houses Guillarmin's famous ivory crucifix, a piece from 1659, and the nun who shows it narrates the history of the artist's nephew, condemned to death and spared by the intervention of that Christ.

I would have gladly visited the Dominicans' church and convent as a remembrance of a historical event, the struggle against the Albigensians, but those magnificent structures were completely destroyed by revolutionary rage. The first Pope of Avignon stayed in that now-destroyed abbey, and it was there that John XXII named Thomas Aquinas, the greatest philosopher of the Middle Ages, a saint in the presence of King of Naples. Among his most prized treasures was the magnificent parchment codex of the saint's Summa, which he bequeathed to the monastery library on the express condition that it be chained to the wall. The revolution arrived and released it, and now the treasured volume, covered in generations of dust, lives free or dies in the city library. Catherine of Siena, a nun of the same order, wrote to the Pope in that convent, pleading with him to return to Rome. That monastery had been built not long before, in the year 1330, and its courtyard was gorgeous, far superior to that of St Trophimus at Arles. Everything was destroyed by the Sanculots, including the tombs of twenty-four cardinals buried in the abbey. The partly ruined church was later turned to a gun factory.

A visit to the Avignon museum is recommended to acquire a sense of the revolution's vandalism in Provence. It's housed in a large 18th-century palace. After the well-deserving Doctor Calvet established this museum in 1810, treasures of the fine arts were housed here from churches, monasteries, feudal castles, and palaces not only in Avignon, but also in the surrounding area. All stages of the Middle Ages are represented, up to the time of the French revival, the rénaissance; and I was all the more interested in contemplating this collection of Middle Ages antiquities in southern France, because I had visited the German museum in Nuremberg a few months earlier, an institution destined for great development and deserving of Germany's support.

The museum at Avignon, on the other hand, pales in contrast to the one in Nuremberg, particularly in terms of the classical period, and, despite being organised into various divisions, it only covers one period of civilisation. Numerous sculptures may be seen in the Middle Ages gallery, and one can trace the evolution of plastic art from ancient Christian sarcophagi to the remnants of the mausoleums of the cardinals of Brancas and Lagrange, Count Raymond de Beaufort, and Marshal de la Palice.

Almost every city in the south of France contributed to the collection of classical antiquities; on the whole, however, it is poor and contains no valuable pieces; all the more so given that nearly all of those cities have their own museums. However, one examines with curiosity everything discovered in this region of France from the time of the Romans and the Greeks. There are various Greek inscriptions as well as Roman inscriptions. A remarkable collection of little bronzes and a rich medal collection from all provinces and ages of France should also be mentioned. In the same building lies the civic library, which houses about 60,000 books. It has a number of excellent publications on the history of southern France, although manuscripts and authentic documents are limited. The acts of the papacy during its stay in Avignon were, as is well known, long ago transferred to the Vatican's secret archives. Portraits of important figures from the department of Valchiusa, including the Duke of Mahon, the courageous Crillon, John de Althens, Cardinal Maury, the painter Mignard, Doctor Calvet, and portraits of Petrarch and Madonna Laura from a later period, can be found in a room of the library.

There is a gallery of paintings on the second floor, which is rather significant for Avignon; there are a few good old Italian, Flemish, and German paintings of worth, but many French ones, mainly by Mignard and the five Vernets, whose family hailed from this city. Furthermore, it should be noted that Avignon has produced no great talent; indeed, none of the famous, correctly or erroneously, Provence poets were born on the banks of the Rhone or the Durance. It was required for a foreigner to arrive from Arezzo in order to give those counties lyrical reputation, and Avignon offered him a lovely woman as the topic of his harmonious poetry, just as Crotone or Taranto offered Zeusis their girls as models. Florence, which can claim of Dante and Beatrice at the same time, was far more daring.

And so, farewell, Avignon's cathedrals, palaces, museums, and minor antiques! How tired are these photographs, monuments, and artefacts of a bygone era? How relaxing the enjoyment in the gorgeous Rhone valley at the city's foot! The glorious Provençal sun illuminates the green islands of the river, darkens the hill of Villeneuve, and invites the traveller to stroll in the shade of agitated poplars and plane-trees, to listen to the bellowing of the mighty waters, and to contemplate the large transport boats darting with the swiftness of an arrow under the bridge arches! The view of the wide Rhone with its two islands and the singular banks of the Languedoc from the Ouille gate in Avignon is indeed beautiful; however, it did not erase from my mind the image of the Vistula, the great river that unwinds its deep waters under the gigantic arches of the railway bridge near Dirschau, nor the image of the Nogat flowing calmly at the foot of the ancient and beautiful Mariemburg. The Knights of the Teutonic Order's Middle Ages fortress looms far more picturesquely there than the Popes' palace in Avignon.

The river divides Villeneuve from the town, as well as Provence from Languedoc. The two banks are connected by bridges; one, of Roman construction, has only four massive, highly picturesque arches that reach from the bank above the river and then stop. Above them, a little chapel stands alone and fantastically staring at the waters. The saintly guy who built the bridge itself is claimed to have lived there, and the tale about that structure is the only one of a benign and poetic kind that I have encountered in Avignon.

Little Benezet was shepherding his destitute mother's sheep in the Vivarais mountains when an eclipse plunged the slopes and valleys into darkness on September 13, 1177. "Benezet, listen to me, for I am Jesus Christ!" exclaimed the voice. "Where are you, O Lord, and what do you ask of me?"-"Do not be afraid, let your sheep graze, go down to the Rhone and build a bridge over it."-"Lord, I do not know where the Rhone is; I am a poor boy, I have only three pennies in my pocket, how do you want me to build a bridge over that river?" The voice replied: "Do as I have told you, for I know where and how you must build the bridge. The little shepherd came down from the mountain weeping, left his flock and met a pilgrim walking on his staff who said to him: "My son Benezet, follow me to the place where you must build the bridge. When they arrived at the river and the boy saw the water, wide, swift and deep, he began to weep more bitterly, but the pilgrim consoled him and told him to get into a boat, go down to Avignon, present himself to the bishop and carry out the task that had been entrusted to him. Benedict did so, and when he found the Bishop preaching in the cathedral, he said to him frankly and casually: "Bishop! The Lord has sent me here to build a bridge over the Rhone. The bold boy was quickly arrested and brought before the vicar. He repeated his mission to the judge, who, pointing to a large boulder in the courtyard, told him with a smile that he would fulfil his mission if he could lift the huge stone. The boy quickly lifted it, placed it on his shoulders and carried it to the banks of the Rhone to the applause of the people, who cried out for a miracle. Within moments, five thousand gold shields had been collected and the construction of the bridge was underway.

The magnificent legend about the ancient bridge of Avignon is as follows: the wonderful work was completed in 1188, but Catalan gangs began to damage it in 1395, and after that, time and the wrath of the waves reduced it to the state of ruin in which it exists today.

To get to Villeneuve, there are now two other bridges, one in iron and the other in wood, which connect the two islands in the river, the Ville de Piot and the Barthelasse. Villeneuve-les-Avignons is a picturesque village. It is said that in ancient times it was the site of Stathmos or Statuma, the commercial centre of the Massilians. The present village dates back to 1226; it was founded by the monks of St Andrew and enlarged and fortified by Philip the Fair. It served almost as a forward port for France on the Rhône and remained so until the Kings of Naples and the Popes of Avignon were masters of Provence. A beautiful tower, commonly known as the Tower of Philippe the Fair, still stands a short distance from the river. Its position, facing the Pont St Benedict, which may have been used for defence, is beautiful, and the tree-shaded walk to it is very pleasant, with a view of the river and the imposing mass of the Popes' Palace. The village, on the other hand, is grey, deserted, melancholy and even poor, although there are some madder dyeworks and a few spinning mills. Only a few churches and a few crumbling palaces can be seen here and there, reminiscent of the bygone days of feudalism.

While Avignon can brag about the man who introduced madder cultivation to Provence, Villeneuve can brag about the man who imported tobacco into France in 1560, presenting the first leaves to Queen Catherine de' Medici. I have not seen a bronze monument of John Nicot, France's ambassador to the court of Portugal, in Villeneuve, and one should be made for him, holding a large snuff box and a long havana cigar in his mouth. Furthermore, French cigars do not do John Nicot justice because they are of inferior quality.

There are only a few things worth seeing in Villeneuve: the tomb of Innocent VI, a gothic monument in the manner of a tabernacle, in the hospital church, which was originally part of the majestic Carthusian monastery there, now completely ruined. That has been restored, and the statue of the lying Pope has been replaced. The fort, St Andrew's, is located on the high Andaon hill and is still in good condition. It is reached through a big gate, and a chapel can be seen on the plateau of the hill, enclosed by walls. There is a lovely view of the Provence panorama from there, comparable to the one from the Rocher des doms, except that from here you can also see Avignon and its castle. The effect is beautiful when the setting sun colours the massive walls of this one pink or purple. This is a fitting site to bid farewell to this ancient Avignon, lighted by the setting sun.

I took a wistful glance over the Provence landscape, which I also wished to see. I was surrounded by Provençals, and their archaic speech evoked a thousand recollections of their history and culture in me. That language is dying; all efforts to restore it by poets, the most prominent of whom is Mistral, are worth nothing more than prolonging its artificial literary existence. I, too, wish I could intone the hopeful lyrics intended by a live poet to his friend Mistral, but I fear they convey little more than wishful thinking..

> Prouvenço, o pais dei troubaire Lou gai-sabé reverdira: Deja milo novèu cantaire Dison lou béu tems que viendra Lou mounde vèi la reinessènço: Lei Troubadour van reflouri... O moun païs, bello Prouvènço, Toun dous parla pòu pas mouri.

RAVENNA. (1863).

＊ ＊ ＊

S ince August of 1863, a railway line has connected Castel Bolognese and Ravenna. The travel takes only four hours from Bologna to Bagnacavallo, passing through Imola, Lugo, and Bagnacavallo. This is why one of the most fascinating towns of antiquity and the Middle Ages, relegated until recently to a seclusion, difficult to access, and half-dead, has suddenly found itself thrust into the centre of world life.

In their monuments, almost all Italian cities depict the two great epochs of the country's history: Roman antiquity and the Christian Middle Ages. Only Ravenna survives as a relic of the transition between these two epochs, and it is unparalleled in this regard.

Ravenna, in reality, experienced the fall of the Roman Empire, the initial foundation of the Germanic kingdom on the ashes of Caesar's dominion, the sixty years of Ostrogoth domination, and the two centuries of Byzantine oppression, and maintains inappreciable memories of them.

When contemplating these monuments from the 5th and 6th centuries, the traveller who arrives in Ravenna for the first time feels impressions comparable only to those aroused by the ruins of Pompeii; and, indeed, Ravenna is the Pompeii of the Gothic and Byzantine era.

When one considers the centuries of savagery and devastation that the buildings have endured, their near-perfect preservation appears to be a marvel. It can be explained in part by the fact that the Lombards were unable to seize Ravenna from the Byzantine exarchs. King Liutprand did not enter the city until 727 or 728, at a time when civilization had softened the invaders' norms greatly. Neither Liutprand nor his second successor to the Lombard throne, Astulf, damaged Ravenna's monuments;

only the suburb of Classe appears to have been destroyed by Liutprand.

Ravenna remained the centre of Byzantine administration in Italy for a long time, while Rome, which had fallen into tremendous decadence, was controlled as a mere provincial city. Ravenna took advantage of its advantageous location and the concern of the Byzantine emperors, who considered it to be the most valuable jewel in their territories in Italy for a long time.

The patriarchs or archbishops of Ravenna disputed the Pope's claim to the city's population after the fall of the Lombard state and exarchate, citing the privileges granted to him by Pepin's donations. They consolidated their control over Romagna, took over the succession of the exarchs, and, supported by the emperors' privileges, repelled the Holy See's attempts for a long time, preserving their authority over Ravenna.

The memory of the tragic events of the Roman decadence and barbarian invasion, the times of Stilicho, Alaric, Attila, and Genseric, the great figure of Theodoric, the gigantic struggles that ended the Goths' dominance and immortalised the names of Totila, Belisarius, Theia, and Narses; finally, the almost mystical darkness of the Byzantine exarchs, barely illuminated from time to time by a few faint glimmers from

How will the city that witnessed so many events appear to us? It will undoubtedly appear much more melancholy and dreary than the old Bologna. However, the hilarious contrast that reality nearly always affixes to the vision that the imagination makes of things remains.

The disappointment is enormous. A hundred other cities in Italy, even small defended villages lost in the mountains, are more vivid reminders of the past and provide a more historical and colossal look of the ancient Byzantine and Gothic metropolis at first glance.

Only gradually, as one wanders around the city, can one sense the breath of the past hovering over us. But then the impression becomes more powerful than everywhere, comparable only in intensity to what one feels in Rome, despite the fact that it is of a different character. The monuments of the Eternal City animate the soul of virtually the entire universal history; those of Ravenna belong to a little era, but the impact they leave is stronger than anywhere.

Ravenna's streets are deafeningly quiet; the residences are new and, for the most part, small; the streets are wide and straight; and the city is built on flat land. There was a strong remembrance everywhere. On the squares, one may observe strange mediaeval columns with images of saints; elsewhere, a statue of a pope who benefitted the city, contemplative and engrossed in his meditations. There is little evidence of the palaces that depict the great Guelph era with such beauty in other towns. Only a ruined tower can be seen from time to time. Churches, on the other hand, abound. Some have been restored, while others have retained their ancient Gothic character. They are often of tiny proportions, and none have the towering majesty of the cathedrals of Pisa, Siena, or Orvieto. They are said to have been put to sleep by an enchanter and have been preserved in this form till the present day; they give Ravenna a mysterious and poetic quality.

Surprisingly, no Roman relics can be found in Ravenna. Classe and Caesarea's suburbs, once important and full of large structures, have been swallowed up by the marshes, and there is little evidence of their presence remains. Ravenna was originally the Roman emperors' Avignon. When Honorius relocated his residence from Rome to Ravenna in 404, fearing an invasion by the Goths, he reinforced the fortifications and erected a palace. What was the location of this structure? It is impossible to determine nowadays, despite the fact that guidebooks do not hesitate to pinpoint the specific location. In 1762, Antonio Zirardini, an erudite jurist and archaeologist of renown in

Ravenna, published an excellent treatise on the antiquities of his homeland: Degli edifici profani di Ravenna.

His study is still the greatest on the subject, yet it only offers a sliver of light on Ravenna's roots.

It was in this palace that Honorius learned of Alaric's capture of Rome, and it was also where he died in August 423. He was, nevertheless, buried near to St Peter's in Rome. For us, the oldest historical landmark in Ravenna is the mausoleum of Honorius' sister, Galla Placidia, one of the most amazing female individuals of that age, whose fate is inextricably linked to the fortunes of the spiralling Roman Empire. At the age of twenty-one, the daughter of the great Theodosius was living in the Caesars' palace in Rome when Alaric arrived, besieged, took, and ravaged the city. Galla Placidia, who had been taken prisoner by him, had to accompany him to Calabria. Shortly after, the emperor's daughter and sister were forced to marry Ataulfo, Alaric's successor, in Narbonne. She later accompanied her husband to Spain, where she became a widow, lost her son Theodosius, and was sent back to Ravenna to her brother Honorius after suffering unworthy insults. He forced her to marry the commander Constantius, with whom she had two children, Valentinian and Honoria, as soon as she arrived. When Constantius died, her brother expelled Galla Placidia from Ravenna and deported her to Byzantium. After Honorius' death, she returned to Rome, escorted by a Greek fleet, and installed her young son Valentinian III on the throne of the West, exercising power for many years as the young prince's guardian, amidst constant difficulties and calamities, and finally ending her troubled existence in Rome, at the age of 61, in 450. The final descendent of the great Theodosius' imperial race died with her son Valentinian III, who was killed five years later.

The tragedy of Theodosius' familial annihilation parallels the Roman Empire's suffering, and the mausoleum of Galla Placidia looks to us now as the tomb of Caesar's supremacy. Entering this modest and dismal sepulchre, decorated with marvellous mosaics, one experiences a sense of historical remembrance that not even Augustus' mausoleum or Hadrian's Roman tomb can arouse. The poor princess desired to be buried in Ravenna, which she adored and had delighted in enriching with countless churches, rather than in Rome, where she was tied by such bitter memories. She had a tomb made and dedicated it to Saints Nazaro and Celso as an expiatory chapel.

When one compares this monument of Rome's final imperial family to the grandiose mausoleums of the first emperors, one can plainly see how different the times were. Everything is imbued with a Christian ethos; its shape is a Latin cross, fifty-five Roman palms long and forty-four wide. The chapel is topped by a mosaic-covered dome, as are the niches and vaults; half-light enters through small windows. The mausoleum contains five sarcophagi: two little ones put into the side wall of the entrance and three huge ones placed in the three recesses formed by the cross's arms. The largest of the urns, seven feet high and quite basic, can be found in the main niche, right opposite the entrance. Honorius' sister is undoubtedly buried there. According to legend, she remained in the sarcophagus for generations, sat on a throne of cypress wood and dressed in her imperial robes. According to more recent historians, the body did not decay until 1577. It is also reported that children placed a lit candle into the sarcophagus openings, causing the walls to catch fire, reducing Placidia to ashes.

What characters are contained within the other sarcophagi? It is impossible to say with certainty. The two larger ones most likely contain the remains of General Constantius and his daughter, the tragic princess Honoria, who, after a life of wild emotions, came to spend the last years of her life in a Ravenna monastery, engaged to the horrible Attila. The belief that Honorius' body was also discovered in one of these sarcophagi is incorrect, as this emperor died at Ravenna but was buried in the imperial mausoleum in Rome, near St. Peter's.

The mosaics of Galla Placidia's mausoleum are notable for their antiquity; they date from before 450 and are the oldest produced by Christian art. In addition to the skillfully constructed arabesques, they display individual figures of prophets and evangelists, as well as the image of Christ in two locations. The attractive, youthful, and beardless physiognomy of the Saviour is striking here, as it is in all the old churches of Ravenna. This image of Christ relates to the ideal that people established throughout the early days of Christianity. It wasn't until later that the Saviour's face was portrayed in the traditional, dark, and melancholy Byzantine style. Ravenna exemplifies the fallacy of such an appellation. Byzantine mosaic masters, notably those of Justinian's reign, were forced to work in Ravenna more than any other city in Italy. Even in the mosaics of San Vitale, which were created some 100 years after those of Galla Placidia's mausoleum, we see the same juvenile form of the Saviour figure, far apart from the so-called Byzantine tradition and rather closer to the primordial ideal typified by the catacomb paintings. The strange thing is that the second type, with an almost demonic expression, can already be found on the triumphal arch of St Paul's in Rome, which was also decorated with mosaics by order of Galla Placidia during the reign of Pope Leo I (440-462), as the inscription proves even today: Piacidiae pia mens operis decus... The Saviour is represented in half-length, in superhuman proportions, with a dismal look that evokes horror. There were no Byzantine painters in Rome at the time; the mosaicists were still from the antique school that had decorated the Baths. As a result, the stern and terrifying Christ image is a Roman, not a Byzantine, conception.

Galla Placidia founded many additional churches in Ravenna. They reflect this unusual woman's highly religious and melancholy personality, who dedicated the latter years of her life to religious reflections and pious contemplation of the past.

And, unlike that miserable Honorius, who, as they say, only lamented the loss of his favourite chick 'Rome' at the capture of Rome, Placidia's unfortunate and complicated existence strikes us with sympathy and great regret.

After visiting his monument, one can proceed to Theodoric's, which relates to the second era of Ravenna's history and one of Italy's most remarkable times.

Odoacer, the Germanic leader who ended the Western Roman Empire and declared himself the first king of Italy in 476, reigned wisely and strongly in Ravenna when he was assaulted by Theodoric. For three years, he fought valiantly; ultimately forced to surrender, he was slaughtered in his palace by the victor's command, despite the terms of the capitulation.

Theodoric ruled Italy from Ravenna, which had been united as a kingdom for the last time under the dominion of the Goths. He constructed a splendid palace there. If he had ever lived in this edifice, one may conclude that the palace of the West's final rulers had already perished in the storm of the barbarian invasion. However, ancient writers who dealt with Theodoric's palace pointed out that he did not inaugurate the structure built for him, which in the parlance of the time meant that he did not dwell there. If this is right, it perfectly describes the fate of the Ostrogoths, who never managed to establish a permanent foothold in Italy. As a result, the Ostrogoth monarch most likely continued to stay in the old imperial house while constructing the other, of which some fragments remain.

They can be viewed on the main route that connects Porta Serrata and Porta Nuova, passing through Ravenna from end to end. There is a high brick wall with a big niche and eight little Roman arches on top. The gates are similarly shaped like Roman arches. These remains, in their current state, provide a glimpse of the coming Middle Ages, which are distinguished by the demise of the grandiose Roman architectural concept. This diminution in size can also be seen in Ravenna's monuments. Indeed, it would be rash to deduce from the tiny size of the ruins of Ravenna's Gothic palace that the structure as a whole was neither luxurious nor majestic. According to ancient chroniclers, Theodoric brought rare marbles and columns from Rome and Constantinople, and he especially used the rich fragments of the demolished 'Pincio' palace. This is remarkable because Ravenna must have been a wealth of exquisite materials. According to legend, Theodoric's home was flanked by porticoes and ornamented on the interior with magnificent mosaics.

Theodoric's equestrian statue in gilded bronze stood in front of the palace façade. The beauty of this painting significantly captivated the spirit of his contemporaries as well as Charlemagne, a lousy art connoisseur in truth. If Theodoric's death stopped him from settling in his completed house, his successors did. Following that, the exarchs settled there, while the ancient palace of the emperors experienced the destiny of Rome's imperial homes, namely, progressive deterioration. The same fate befell Theodoric's palace, which survived only two centuries. With Pope Hadrian I's permission, Charlemagne sacked it and removed marble and mosaics from it to build his famed church and residence in Aix-la-Chapelle. He also transported Theodoric's statue across the Alps. However, Zirardini, using old texts, claims that the palace of the Goth kings was still mentioned in the 11th and even 12th centuries, and that very major remains of it had therefore been preserved intact, at least until that time. A whole neighbourhood of Ravenna was named 'Theodoric's palace,' and even today, the name of the great ruler of the Goths is retained, and the traveller can see it, not without astonishment, written on the street corners.

The rest of the wall, as indicated above, was unquestionably part of Theodoric's palace. The tradition of the area where this structure stood could not be lost in Ravenna. Furthermore, a piece of mosaic, thankfully survived in Sant'Apollinare Nuovo, showing the palace's façade, reproduces an architectural style comparable to that of the wall I described. A papal legate had a porphyry urn put into this wall in 1654, and because it had been discovered near Theodoric's tomb, he reasoned that it had contained the ashes of the great king of the Goths, as plainly declared in the inscription still visible today.

The Goth king died on August 30, 526, in utter defiance of the Churches of Rome and Byzantium; he was buried in the mausoleum he had erected for himself and his family near the city's entrance. This iconic sepulchre, a testament to the Goths' dominance in Italy and a link between two periods of art history, has been kept to this day in much the same way as Galla Placidia's mausoleum. Most of Rome's great tombs have been totally demolished, such as Augustus', or transformed into castles and rendered unrecognisable, such as Hadrian and Cecilia Metella's; Theodoric's monument, on the other hand, has withstood the test of time, at least in its fundamental components. The arches that undoubtedly ringed the upper floor terraces have vanished, but neither the stone buttresses nor the massive monolithic dome that topped the great barbarian king's last dwelling have been destroyed by the centuries. Because the railroad passes close by, approximately a hundred metres distant, this monument is the first sight that strikes the traveller as soon as he arrives in Ravenna. It is set among vineyards and gardens. An avenue of trees leads to it, and the tall grass that covers it demonstrates how few visitors there are. This untamed seclusion and lovely flora complement the tastes of the Germanic hero, who, like all his people, was in love with fresh nature.

While the pious Placidia, who lived in Byzantium for a long time, was buried in a nearly subterranean chapel adorned with mosaics and sacred images, Theodoric, the Goth ruler, desired a funeral fit for a northern barbarian commander and a Roman Caesar. The grandiose simplicity of the monument, for which the giants appear to have been the only ones capable of raising the roof of rock, fits well with the memory of the ancient Dietrich von Bern, the hero of the Nibelungen; on the other hand, the Roman character of the building as a whole evokes the memory of a Germanic already almost transformed by civilisation. The last asylum was well adapted for the sovereign buddy of the literary Cassiodorus, for the successor, as well as the emulous, of the emperors of the Eternal City.

An arched door on the lower floor leads to a vaulted hall in the shape of a Latin cross; on the upper floor, a square door leads to the hall, which has the dome as a ceiling. The two stone staircases that lead to the top floor were not finished until 1780. There is no longer a sarcophagus in the two empty halls, and no inscription identifies the last resting place of the great monarch and his successors. Nobody knows when or when the burial urns vanished or where they were moved. The only tale holds that Theodoric's porphyry coffin stood at the top of the structure, above the dome; however, this must be a mistake, as the sarcophagus should have stayed in the spacious niche on the upper floor, opposite the entrance door. According to another version, Theodoric's sarcophagus was found at the church of Santa Prassede in Rome. More likely, when Belisarius seized Ravenna, the Greeks and Isaurians plundered the interior of the mausoleum in retaliation and scattered the ashes of the valiant Goth leader far away; and if the sarcophagus was not destroyed at the time, one of the exarchs probably had it transported to Byzantium as a trophy. In any event, Charlemagne did not discover it in Ravenna, or he would have had it transferred to Aix-la-Chapelle, where he might have bowed.

When Theodoric built his tomb, he undoubtedly believed that his entire dynasty would be laid to rest there; nevertheless, he was duped. His home would shortly be destroyed in a rapid and horrible cataclysm, and the entire Goth empire would be swept away by the same storm. When one stands in the middle of the tomb, between the barren walls, looking for evidence of the dead, for whom it was to serve as an asylum, one is reminded of this sudden disaster. Amalasunta, Theodoric's noble and brilliant daughter, buried her son Atalaric there in 534, the last scion of her father's line, who had been murdered in his youth by Italian excesses. Amalasunta was strangled on an island in Lake Bolsena shortly after, and her body was reportedly returned to Ravenna. Theodotus, her spouse and, most likely, her killer, whose neck was slashed in 536 while escaping from Rome to Ravenna, found no rest in Theodoric's mausoleum, nor did the unfortunate Matavintha, daughter of Amalasunta, whom Vitiges, Theodotus' successor, had persuaded to take him as a husband. She, like Vitiges, died in jail in Byzantium or another Eastern city. None of the final Ostrogoth rulers left any mortal remains in Ravenna. Totila was buried in the Apennines and Teia, near Vesuvius, on the battlefield where he fought like a Homeric hero.

When the German visitor is alone in that vegetation desert and examines Theodoric's grave, he feels the enormous air of history passing over him and a deep, melancholy affection for his homeland. The ghosts of that glorious century hover about the austere monument of the Ostrogoth monarch, in which Homer's Greek epic seems to blend with the German epic of the Nibelungen. The mind conjures up images of Belisarius, Narses, Totila, Theia, Theodoric and Amalasunta, Cassiodorus, Procopius, Boethius, Justinian, and a plethora of other Goth and Greek figures who played their parts in one of the most magnificent dramas in the chaos of nationalities and civilisations that blurred and fought on the eve of the Middle Ages. The triumphal arch of Constantine marks the border between paganism and Christianity in Rome; in Ravenna, the monument of Theodoric is the link between the ancient world and the Germanic-Roman Middle Ages, as well as the tomb of art, literature, science, and civilisation, generally protected by Theodoric and his daughter but condemned to disappear after them, for centuries and centuries, in the thick darkness of barbarism. Every day, the tomb's foundations sink deeper into the muddy subsoil. If I'm not mistaken, a well-meaning pope, Gregory XVI, attempted to divert the stagnant waters via a walled canal, but his endeavour failed. I discovered a true bog at the driest season of the year, which I imagine will engulf the lowest floor of the monument in autumn. Worst of all, the upper floor's cutting stones are coming away here and there. Count Alessandro Cappi, a Ravenna preservationist, complained bitterly to me about the monument's state of neglect, for which nothing has been done for many years; and here I can only join him in pleading with the Italians to take action as soon as possible to save this important document from further deterioration. Who recalls Cassiodorus, the last Roman to serve to the great Theodoric? When the accusation of the Goths destroying ancient civilisation was placed before him, he yelled out, "Gothorum laus est civilitas custodita!" This is a goal that should motivate modern Italians; if they have a historical right to Theodoric's tomb, we Germans have a moral attachment to him. As a result, we maintain the mausoleum of the great Goth monarch with the piety that recollections of one's magnificent past normally inspire. Thank God, we no longer live in a time when the most magnificent masterpieces of art and history were abandoned with indifference to rot and ruin.

At the end of 539, the great Belisarius triumphantly entered the hitherto impregnable city of Ravenna and took up residence in Theodoric's abandoned residence. As a result, fate reserved the honour of finishing the horrible war conducted against the Goths for his emulous emulous in courage and grandeur, the eunuch Narses. Justinian made this patrician general and administrator of his Italian provinces, and Narses established himself in Theodoric's palace, while Ravenna remained the capital of Italy.

The most notable church in Ravenna is San Vitale, which is located near the Galla Placidia tomb. Begun in the final year of Theodoric's reign and continued during the Goth war, it remained unfinished when Belisarius entered the city. Finally, in 547, Archbishop Maximian consecrated the church at the same time as Totila besieged Rome for the second time, and Belisarius triumphantly defended it. San Vitale was thus built contemporaneously with the destruction of the Goths and honoured Constantinople's success. Simultaneously, Justinian created the great St Sophia monument in his capital, the image of which is reflected in the form of St Vitale. This Byzantine basilica displays the purest kind of construction and artwork of the Justinian period, of which very few authentic monuments remain, even in Constantinople, except from St Sophia. This is especially true given the abundance and quality of mosaics in Justinian's Byzantine basilicas, the most of which have already vanished.

San Vitale is an octagonal structure with a dome. The church is supported by internal columns, and a half-height gallery of arches surrounds it. The dome was previously covered in mosaics, but these have gradually deteriorated, whereas the presbytery's famous mosaics have been maintained in their entirety. The structure was so well-built that the work has lasted for 1300 years without requiring any significant repairs: a very significant fact in the history of mosaics. The San Vitale covers appear to be from two independent epochs, presumably separated by a century. The most recent mosaics can be found in the top presbytery. The representations of Christ and the apostles are already quite similar to what is known as the Byzantine type. Christ had a beard and long blond hair. On contrast, the Saviour appears with a younger face in the tribune; he is seated between two angels, on the globe of the world, and delivers the crown to the martyr Vitale, while St. Ecclesius, the basilica's founder, hands him the building design. Christ wears a halo with a cross and a dark cloak that is all one colour. The expression of this juvenile physiognomy has an archaic grace and ideal purity that I do not recall seeing in any other mosaic. Along with the religious figures, the artist dared to represent contemporaneous profane pictures of Emperor Justinian and his courtiers in the same tribune. I'm not aware of any other examples, as the renowned Lateran mosaic in Rome showing Charlemagne was primarily designed for a dining room. On the right wall of the tribune, Justinian stands, his head wrapped by a halo, demonstrating that this symbol did not yet have the doctrinal importance afterwards given to it. He has an offering in his hand; a gold star shines on his plain, dark robe; his feet are shod in Byzantine purple coturni; his head is youthful, a regular oval, his physique strong and lean. The emperor wears a moustache, whereas the troops who surround him, armed with spears and shields carrying the monogram of Christ, are beardless. Saint Maximian, flanked by two clerics, advances towards Justinian on the opposite side of the artwork. One could argue that he voluntarily abdicated the halo out of respect for the imperial majesty, which also claimed the supreme pontificate; he does not, in fact, wear this attribute, which is a characteristic of Byzantine dogma and reflects the inaccessible nature and divine prestige of imperial power. Furthermore, we know that the halo was derived from depictions of Apollo and that it already ringed the heads of Roman emperors honoured in apotheosis.

We see the emperor's bride, Theodora, opposite, on the left wall of the tribune, once a prostitute in Byzantium and famous for the shameless skill with which she reproduced the most impudent scenes on stage, later empress of East and West; she is also reproduced with the halo of Christ on her head, in a sanctuary, surrounded by saints! Knowing the extraordinary stories recounted about this woman by Procopius, Belisarius' historian and the last of the classical writers of antiquity, and recalling how he stigmatised Justinian's character in his Storia secreta, one is absolutely astounded to encounter such a picture in a hallowed church painting. Of course, we would not want to be without them for this reason, as they are invaluable to history. And, because art of the time was still capable of portraying resemblances, it can be accepted that these imperial figures were not the product of fancy and were very close to the original.

Theodora is shown as a young, gorgeous, imposing woman with an imperial bearing. She wears the beautiful Byzantine diadem, and her sacred mantle is elaborately embroidered with gold needlework and precious stones in the oriental manner. She, like Justinian, is holding a vase in her hand as an offering. The ladies of the court, like their mistress, are arrayed in brocade draped in the antique style, in rich and various colours, at her sides. Their hairstyles are stunning, eerily similar to those of Roman women during the Flavii and Antonines. It would be foolish to expect to locate true portraits in these figures, which resemble each other; nevertheless such female types, belonging to the most brilliant, luxurious, and sophisticated age of Byzantium's court, cannot be ignored. Without ever exaggerating, the artist has given them a character of great grandeur. Their physiognomy has an equal expression of solemnity and gravity, and therefore, despite their profane nature, the holiness of the location is not disturbed. When one looks at those magnificent mosaics, one cannot not but notice how close to antiquity Byzantine art, of which they are an emanation, was. There is no trace of that exalted religious vision, the adversary of all human joy, nor of that austere monastic style that has become, for some reason, known as Byzantine.

As beautiful as the mosaics in Rome's cathedrals are, they only date from the sixth century and cannot compare to the artistic and historical importance of those in San Vitale. The Church of the Twelve Apostles was built in Rome while the basilica of Ravenna was being completed, or at most ten years later, under the administration of Narses. Unfortunately, nothing of the mosaics that ornamented it survives now. Only the mosaics of the ancient basilica of Saints Cosmas and Damian, constructed by Pope Felix IV on the Roman Forum, have survived (524-530). Their style is vibrant and unique, yet it falls short of the artistic excellence of the Ravenna mosaics.

I was delighted to discover Roman mosaicists in S. Vitale, who had been engaged on restoring the mosaics for many years, during the reign of the papal rule. Once upon a time, after this art had vanished from Rome, artists from Byzantium or the legendary Montecassino school were brought in. But things changed in the 13th century, when Roman art received a new impetus under Innocent III and Honorius III. The craft of mosaics has flourished on the banks of the Tiber from then until now, with only minor breaks.

The artisans I met in Ravenna, a father and son, belonged to a family that had been practising this art for several generations, similar to the Cosmati family who resided in Rome in the 13th century. Ribel, one of the mosaicists, was cleaning and fixing the damaged areas of a tribune side mosaic with a newly found chemical substance, which allows the blackened mosaics to restore its original splendour. The mosaicist's test on one of the figures was so successful that the image, revitalised and revived, sparkled with the most vibrant colours. All of San Vitale's paintings will eventually undergo the same procedure, and only then will we be able to completely appreciate their primordial beauty.

Those artists gave me a gift that I couldn't find in photo albums: a business card portrait of Justinian. They had discovered an image of this emperor in specific pieces of mosaic that had originally graced the inner wall beneath St Apollinaris' gate, and had cleaned and photographed it. Justinian was portrayed in a half-length bust, as he was at San Vitale. His face was similar to the one in the basilica, but broader and slightly effeminate.

He wore the same sacred robe, which was fastened to his shoulder by a diamond clasp; his diadem was studded with two rows of precious stones, like on coins. A round, purple-red aura surrounded his face, sprinkled with white, pearl-like specks. The figure stood up against a gold background, and the name Justinian could be read in Roman characters beneath it. In a nutshell, a fascinating portrait.

The splendid basilica of St Apollinaris was completed practically simultaneously with San Vitale.

The exterior, like that of the other Ravenna basilicas, is uninspiring. The bell tower on its side has a unique shape that appears to be unique to Ravenna, where there are numerous more examples. These barbaric-looking tunnels are round and of ordinary height, built of rough brick, without armour or other ornamentation, and pierced by small arched windows that are divided into two portions by a small column. I assume they are 8th or 9th century structures rather than 6th century structures. The interior of the church is divided into three chambers, each with twenty-four columns of Greek marble and, like most of Ravenna's basilicas, a majestic simplicity. What separates these churches from Roman structures of the same era is their peaceful grace and apparent attachment to earthly powers. One can also perceive that they are the free creation of a vibrant era, realising an ideal that has passed into type with its own uniqueness. Although the old city, which was in ruins at the time, could have provided an abundant harvest of ancient columns, the builders of St Apollinaris refused to use them. Their uniform columns and capitals, which are considerably more difficult to create, are original works, not copies of prior monuments. This is in contrast to Rome, where they habitually integrated as many materials as possible obtained from ancient buildings to make a new basilica, destroying heterogeneous columns and even caps.

Beautiful mosaics adorn the central hall of Sant'Apollinare. If the mosaics of San Vitale are notable for the historical figures whose portraits they show, those of Sant'Apollinare are notable for their depiction of Ravenna monuments at the period. The city of Ravenna, with the cathedral of San Vitale, many other monuments, and the palace of Theodoric, may be seen on the right wall of the central room, bright with fresh colours.

On the pediment of the monument, in gold letters, is written a name that could only belong to Theodoric's house, Palatium. This is followed by twenty-five representations of saints, each carrying a crown and separated by palms. A Christ clad in black attire and seated on a throne stands at the end of the array, surrounded by angels.

A symmetrical arrangement on the left wall displays a procession of youthful saints, magi worship, and building reproduction. The Virgin sits on the throne, a lovely and delicate figure with her head encircled by the nuns' veil. The Magi's barbarian origins are visible in their short brocade cloaks, vivid colours, and full attire. The holy women are covered in expensive Byzantine textiles and white veils and wear Greek diadems on their hair, devoid of personality and uniform even in the contours of their features. These clear, delicately shaded images separate themselves from older-style saint figures found in Roman basilicas, for example, St Paul's and other churches, most notably on the triumphal arch and side panels of the tribunes. The tradition of ancient art can be found in those of St Apollinaris. There is no trace of the neighbouring barbarism in them; the monotony of the forms does not tyre the eye, but rather imparts a solemn tranquilly to the entire, enlivened by the delicacy of the shapes and the richness of the costumes.

At the end of the mosaic, we see the now-destroyed suburb of Classe, which corresponds to the representation of Ravenna on the opposite wall. It is a fortified castle with crenellated turrets that front the azure sea, which is dotted with vessels with white sails. It has an exceptional overall effect.

There is no other church in Ravenna that can compete with the majestic grandeur and felicitous proportions of Sant'Apollinare. It does, however, retain a number of historic and noteworthy basilicas, which I shall only mention. Theodoric had numerous Arian churches built there, including the Holy Spirit, which still stands, and Santa Maria in Cosmedino: I will not stop there, just as I will not discuss other older monuments from Galla Placidia's period, such as San Giovanni Evangelista, Sant'Agata, and San Francesco. Only the city's cathedral needs a thorough examination because it was once the seat of the patriarchs, who were once quite powerful, but were fully restored in the 18th century. This cathedral was the oldest of Ravenna's churches, dating back to Archbishop Urso, from whom it gained its name, and was only slightly later than the Roman churches of St Peter and St Paul and St John Lateran. It was once a basilica with five naves supported by fifty-six columns. Scenes from Ravenna's past were portrayed in vast numbers on its walls. All of this has now vanished, and whatever the appeal of some components of the new structure, nothing about it piques our curiosity.

Today, the archbishop's palace's most valuable treasure is its archives. The parchment collection, which contained nearly 25,000 documents, and the papyrus collection, which dated back to the 5th century, could have been considered an inexhaustible mine of documents before parts of these two collections were transported to the Vatican, while others were destroyed and dispersed.

The former baptistery of San Giovanni in Fonte, a short distance from the cathedral, is also credited to Archbishop Urso. This unusual octagonal structure is made up of two rows of superimposed Roman arches with a very old aspect, and it is topped by a dome fully covered in mosaics depicting Christ's baptism and the twelve apostles.

Outside the city, two historic basilicas can be found: Santa Maria in Porto and Sant'Apollinare in Classe. The latter is without a doubt Ravenna's most gorgeous church. Let us go there. As is widely known, the sea formerly pushed to within a short distance of the city, and because of this proximity, as well as the waterways and lagoons, Ravenna enjoyed security and commercial importance comparable to those that would later build Venice's fortune. And, like Venice, Ravenna, which dates back to fantastic times, was initially built in part on islands.

The Emperor Augustus, enamoured with Ravenna's remarkable geographical situation, decided to hide the Adriatic fleet there, giving rise to the suburbs of Caesar and Classe, the latter named after the naval base itself. For many years, Ravenna held the commercial monopoly in the East; nevertheless, the silting up of its port and political conditions resulted in its demise, all to the profit of Venice.

Since then, the Adriatic has receded seven miles from the city and is no longer visible. Only the damp wind that blows from the open sea and passes above the coastal trees exposes the water's vicinity. The actual location of the historic harbour is no longer known. The only reminders of the docks and arsenals are the names of a church near the city walls, Santa Maria in Porto, and the square of Sant'Apollinare in Classe.

To go to the basilica in Classe, one must travel around three kilometres north-east. After crossing Ponte Nuovo, above the Ronco River, you can see the historic church with its circular, solemn bell tower to one side two kilometres away, in utter solitude. A large swampy plain with a stern and melancholy appearance surrounds you, broken here and there by rice fields. The famous and massive Pineta can be seen on the sea's edge, resembling a dark green belt. The distant, bluish peaks of the Apennines rise up on the horizon to the west.

Julian Argentario, who erected most of Ravenna's basilicas at the period, built St Apollinaris in 535. Patriarch Maximian, who also constructed San Vitale, consecrated the church in 549. Only the front half of the square portico that surrounds it survives, which now serves as the vestibule; this is designated by the term Ardica in all Ravenna's historic churches (derived from Narte). The interior of the basilica is stunning, with grand and simple proportions. The naves are separated by twenty-four magnificent columns of Greek marble, cut specifically for this monument and ornamented with matching capitals. The raftered roof has no adornment, according to ancient custom. The atmosphere of antiquity pervades the entire monument, and this feeling is emphasised by the sight of a lengthy row of sarcophagi in the aisle walls. Except at Arles, I have never seen such a vast number of sarcophagi erected in isolation within churches. The sight of those at St Apollinaris quickly brought back memories of the old Provençal city's famous tomb-covered boulevard.

Ravenna's burial urns differ significantly from Roman sarcophagi from the Christian era. Rome has a huge number of highly fascinating ones, some dating from the second period of the Middle Ages; they may be found in the Vatican Grottoes, the St John Lateran Museum, and in churches here and there. Many early Christian tombs are also sculpted in relief with religious topics. The Ravenna funerary urns, on the other hand, date from the Gothic-Byzantine and even the Barbarian eras and are nearly always enormous sarcophagi composed of yellowish white Greek marble with no ornamentation other than Christian symbols and a plain inscription. None of them, in my judgement, are marked by pagan antiquity, as several papal tombs in Rome are. They were all executed for their original purpose in Ravenna. Their grandiose and unique features leave a lasting impression; one could argue that such sarcophagi, with their high and huge vaults, were used to bury Gothic heroes rather than patriarchs.

Sculpture appears to have faded out in Ravenna before the reign of Galla Placidia, as it is only found alive in its direct link with building. In those semi-barbaric ages, the art of replicating figures was totally centred in mosaic work, producing a rich and precious blooming there. These sarcophagi were previously placed beneath the church's exterior portico in accordance with Christian custom. From the fifth to the eighth centuries, they housed the bodies of the city's patriarchs. At Rome, the walls of the naves were covered with a row of portraits representing the long sequence of archbishops of Ravenna, similar to what was done in the church of St Paul Outside the Walls; however, this decoration is modern. Just as the list of Popes begins with St Peter, the list of Metropolitans of Ravenna begins with the missionary Apollinaris, the archbishopric's founder. According to Roman tradition, the patron and hierarchical head of Ravenna was appointed bishop by St Peter in Rome; he was thus a disciple of the prince of the apostles. However, he long claimed supremacy over the Christian world against St Peter; or, to be more exact, his successors, the bishops of Ravenna, rejected Rome's primacy for several centuries. The temporal wealth of St Apollinaris were also substantial, as the archbishops owned holdings all throughout the world, including Sicily and the East. As I previously stated, after the fall of the Longobard kingdom, they stood for a brief period as lords of the Exarchate, opposing the claims of the popes.

In the 11th century, the Patriarch of Ravenna was still so wealthy and powerful that the Emperor Henry IV found his strongest backing in him during his conflict with Gregory VII and Countess Matilda. The emperor elected to raise the city's archbishop, Vilbert, to the status of anti-pope, under the name Clement III; however, this act signalled the end of Ravenna's splendour.

Several Germans were promoted by the Emperor to the status of archbishops of Ravenna and provided with significant privileges for this title during a time when the Empire was prospering.

During Otto III's reign, the city also saw some of its metropolitans accede to the papal throne, including the iron John X and the legendary Gilbert or Sylvester II. Around the same period, two renowned saints, Romuald and Peter Damian, shone a bright light on Ravenna's Church. And so, the history of the archbishops is intertwined with the history of the Roman church and the Italian Middle Ages up to the 12th and 13th centuries. Agnello da Ravenna wrote the first effort at a work on this topic in the middle of the seventh century. The Liber pontificalis carries the imprint of that still barbaric time, but its antiquity makes it of immense value, and the countless rich historical information it includes gives it an inestimable price, while its childlike naivety surrounds it with a certain grace.

After Charlemagne, until the period of the Hohenstaufen, very few German emperors missed to visit Ravenna, either on their way to Rome or during their campaigns in Italy: the itineraries show this:

During their protracted fights with the cities and the popes, the emperors had a strong foothold on the peninsula thanks to the capital of the ancient exarchate.

The emperors refused to recognise the Holy See's property titles on Ravenna. Romagna and the exarchate were recognised as Empire provinces and administered by imperial counts since the Ottons. Rudolph of the Habsburgs was the first to formally abandon, in favour of the Holy See, the Empire's claims over those regions throughout antiquity. The Ottonians had a great fondness for Ravenna, and Otto I, above all, visited it five times, in 967, 968, 970, 971, and 972. This prince, the most powerful of the German rulers who extended their dominance over Italy, regarded the Pope so little as Ravenna's master that he had a new residence built near the city walls. The actual site of this imperial house is unknown; what is definite is that neither Caesar nor Classe had yet vanished at the time.

Otto II stayed at Ravenna twice and Otto III stayed there three times. This youthful prince declared the first of the German popes, his cousin Bruno, who eventually placed the imperial crown on his own head as Gregory V. Otto III adored Ravenna and its saints with the fervour that defined his personality. There he elevated his lord, the famous Gerbert, from the episcopal throne to papal rank. Otto III returned from Ravenna a few years later, this time as a refugee, driven out by the Romans, and resided for a few weeks in the monastery of Classe, in the cell of the famous Romuald, under the monk's uniform and amidst penance procedures.

This occurrence is remembered on the walls of the basilica, in current lettering and of ecclesiastical construction.

"Otto III, Emperor of Germany, King of the Romans, came barefoot from the city of Rome to Mount Gargano, spent forty days as a penitent in this cloister and in this basilica, expiated his crimes under the cilice and with voluntary mortifications, giving an august example of humility and, Emperor, illustrated this temple and his repentance o"[11].

The famous convent of San Romualdo was not suppressed until Napoleon I's reign. Its damaged houses exist near the basilica, surrounded by fern and olive tree shrubs. Only one of the monks remains, wandering melancholy in the church over which he is custodian. The original basilica is in ruins, as is the bell tower next to it, which resembles a lighthouse rather than a bell tower. The solitude of the old monument is infinite, and the sight of the lonely countryside that surrounds it is both heartbreaking and breathtaking. I observed the vast marshy area during a hurricane that rumbled far above the invisibly blue Adriatic and obscured the sky with dark clouds. The sunken ruins, the old basilica and the immortal memories it evokes, the deserted road that crosses the countryside towards Cesena, the gloomy pine forest that stretches as far as the eye can see and whose gigantic tops lie calm and majestic like great palm trees; on the other side, through the lightning-filled atmosphere, the towers of the ancient city: all this silent, melancholy, and dead ensemble, without a chirp of birds, without a human profile, contributes to throwing the soul into a deep and unspeakable emotion.

The melancholy banks of the Ronco still bear witness to another historical event, one of the most dreadful fights that has bled Italian land, a fight so gallant that Theodoric and Odoacer both applauded the heroism of the soldiers. The army of Louis XII, King of France, commanded by the young Gaston de Foix, attacked the joined armies of the Spanish and the belligerent Pope Julius II, who were heading to the rescue of General Marco Antonio Colonna, who was imprisoned in Ravenna. The French claimed victory, but at the cost of their great and gallant general's life.

The battle featured the most distinguished captains of the day, those who would go on to distinguish themselves during Charles V's glorious century, Spaniards, French, Italians, and Germans, the flower of the aristocracy. Ariosto, a brilliant poet, was imprisoned in the camp of the Duke of Ferrara, and he was later to be Pope Leo X, then legate.

Nothing could have stopped Gaston de Foix from conquering Rome and Pope Julius II if he had survived his triumph. But the good fortune that so often belonged to the Holy See brought about a positive shift; the victorious French were defeated and compelled to depart Italy.

Donato Cesi, the papal administrator of Romagna who eventually became a cardinal, erected the commemorative column that may still be seen today on the battlefield, on the banks of the Ronco. Inscriptions carved on medallions of poor quality recount the historic event.

Unfortunately, I was unable to see the well-known pine forest known as Pineta. The forest appears to be from ancient times.

It is reported that materials for the harbour's casting were extracted from it as early as Roman times. When Theodoric besieged Odoacer at Ravenna, the Gothic army camped here. The majority of it is made up of thickets of various vegetation, among which stand tall trunks of pine trees. The fruits of these trees include hazelnuts, which are shaped like almonds and are widely traded in Ravenna. Every year, it is believed that ten thousand staia of this fruit are shipped away. The people of Ravenna have described the wild and deserted interior of their pine forest, the thickets where hunters hunt wild boar, and the parts where the forest advances all the way to the coast and dies on the shores of picturesque gulfs washed by the sea. The forest spans about twenty-four kilometres along the Adriatic, from Cervia to the mouth of the Po, known as Spina or Spinetrium. It has a maximum width of three miles.

We investigated Ravenna's monuments in chronological sequence rather than topographic order, and we only dealt with a few of them, those that best characterised their era. We discovered that almost no palaces or churches date from the Great Guelph era. In the absence of magnificent monuments, the residents of Ravenna proudly display a little funeral chapel in a back alley, which they would not trade for the most beautiful cathedral in the world. There lies buried, with Galla Placidia and Theodoric, Italy's greatest intellect, hero and victim of the Guelph-Ghibelline conflict, to whom he constructed an imperishable monument.

Even if Ravenna's only attraction was Dante's tomb, and his only glory was that he provided the Poet with the last sanctuary, this would be enough to save his name from oblivion.

Dante travelled from Verona to Ravenna in 1320, homeless and in terrible poverty. According to Boccaccio, at the time, a great nobleman named Guido da Polenta was the master of Ravenna, a historic and important city in Romagna. He was well-versed in the liberal sciences, and he admired men of valour, especially those whose education elevated them above others. When he learned that Dante, whose renown had long before him, was in Romagna, in agony and discouragement, he resolved to offer him sanctuary and rescue him from his grave circumstances without being asked. Dante spent some time at Ravenna under the benign care of this noble lord after he had given up hope of returning to Florence.

There he taught a number of students the art of poetry, particularly in the common language, which, according to Boccaccio, he was able to raise to the level of the Greek Homer and the Latin Virgil for their own tongue.

Guido da Polenta was the nephew of the lovely Francesca, who was married to Giovanni Malatesta da Verrucchio, podestà of Rimini, and whose memory is immortalised in Dante's epic, when the Polenta family became mistress of the city in 1275. The Lord of Ravenna did not misinterpret the words in which Francesca da Rimini's shadow appears among the shadows damned to eternal damnation.

Dante died in Ravenna, under the protection of Guido.

The Polenta palace has vanished without a trace, and all that remains of their reign is the poet's tomb. Apart from this remembrance, nothing revives their name except a plaque embedded in the wall of St. Francis Church, which depicts a man clothed in a Friars Minor cassock and has the inscription: "MCCCLXXXVI die XIV Mensis Martii occubuit Magnificus Dominus Hostasius de Polenta ante diem felix obiens. Cujus anima exigent pace."

Dante's impassioned soul's battles, the passions that so violently fired his work and imprinted him with such an unparalleled identity, had all calmed down by the time the great poet came to conclude his days in Ravenna. His final years were dedicated to devout and noble meditations, to the Contemplative Life.

He wrote his Psalms of Penance and his Creed there. He appeared to have changed himself into a penitent, much like Emperor Otto III, who had put on his habit and hidden himself away to pray in St Apollinaris' cell after seeing his control over Rome erode. When he realised his end was near (he died on September 14, 1321), he requested to be buried in the Franciscan garb. This is why the Friars Minor regarded him one of their own; it should also be noted that in his poetry, he depicted himself girded with the rope of this order.

Guido da Polenta had the poet interred in a marble sarcophagus in the Friars Minor convent. A grandiose memorial commemorating him was proposed, however the project was never completed. The grave was forgotten during the disturbances that killed the Polenta family. Only the sacred responsibility, which had long been forgotten, was remembered in 1482. The Polenta family had been evicted. Ravenna was administered by praetors of the strong Republic after being ceded to Venice. Bernardo Bembo, father of the great cardinal, was one of the latter who took up Guido da Polenta's initiative and had a splendid mausoleum built for the poet in 1482. This is the one we see today, but it was altered by Pope's legates in the 17th and 18th centuries. In fact, under the papacy of Julius II, who also linked Bologna to the authority of St. Peter, the Venetians submitted Ravenna to the Holy See in 1509.

Dante's tomb is built in the Renaissance style and is shaped like a little temple with a dome on top. The interior features bas-reliefs and inscriptions. Virgil, Brunetto Latini, Can Grande della Scala, and Guido da Polenta are represented by four medallions. The marble sarcophagus faces the entrance door, and over it is the relief medallion of the Poet.

The famous inscription he wrote is as follows::

Jura monarchiae superos Phlegetonta lacusque Lustrando cecini
voluerunt fata quousque: Sed quia pars cessit melioribus hospita

castris, Autoremque suum petiit felicior astris, Hic claudor Dantes patriis extorris ab oris Quem genuit parvi Florentia mater amoris.

The tomb is constantly shut. Count Alessandro Cappi, who accompanied me on a visit to the mausoleum, told me that he had seen Lord Byron, who was then in love with Countess Guiccioli, in Ravenna when he was younger. My guide told me that Lord Byron never passed within sight of the monument, even from afar, without showing himself respectfully, and I recall the lovely lines he dedicated to Dante's grave.

And it is, in fact, a sanctuary that no man of elevated soul could approach without emotion, a place of pilgrimage and remembrance for all those capable of comprehending and admiring the Poet's creative genius, so powerful as to raise above storms and passions an eternal ideal of calm and sublime serenity.

Dante embodies what makes his homeland's history so remarkable, art and science blooming in the middle of the most dreadful civil strife.

In this and many other ways, the Florentine poet is the embodiment and representative of Italian talent at the end of the Middle Ages.

The seclusion in which Dante's tomb stands leaves an indelible image, and one must be grateful that the people of Ravenna refused to surrender their national treasure to the contrite Florentines. Dante thus continues his exile's destiny; he lies in the cell whose friendly shade sheltered his final days, in a monument to which the Most Serene Republic of Venice and the Holy See contributed. His grave rises from the sea, free and solitary like a sovereign's tomb, like the great Theodoric's mausoleum..

NOTES:

[1] I infer these speeches from the writing of a French officer who witnessed the scene.

[2] Evidently, Gregorovius' impartiality fails here. When the German historian was writing these lines, a denigrating campaign against the shining Hero of our Independence was taking shape, especially abroad. In France, for example, a liberal and a valuable writer, Maxime du Camp, was writing about Garibaldi at the same time and much worse. This, after all, was but the effect of the devious and concealed campaign of the enemies of our freedom. (*Ed.*).

[3] Levate, venerabiles fratres, in circuitu oculos vestros, et videbitis, ac una Nobiscum vehementer dolebitis abominationes pessimas, quibus nunc misera Italia praesertim funestatur... Datum Romae apud S. Petrum die 17 octobris anno 1867. Pont. Nost. A. XXII.

[4] Count Costantino Nigra, born in Villa Castelnovo, Ivrea, in 1828, and died in Rapallo on 1 July 1906, was one of the most illustrious personalities of our Risorgimento. Cavour had him as his secretary during his political trips to London and Paris, especially during the memorable Congress of 1856, where the great statesman put the question of Italian nationality clearly before the representatives of the powers. Nigra then remained at the Court of Napoleon III, and became the welcome interpreter of Cavour's ideas and King Victor Emmanuel II's intentions. He was Italy's minister plenipotentiary at the Court of France ever since Sédan and always cooperated greatly with the interests of our country and its unity. (*Ed.*).

[5]   This characteristic trait is recounted to us by the chaplain of the Zouaves, also a prisoner, who simply and faithfully described the Garibaldians' stay at Monte Rotondo in 'Prigionia del P. Vincenzo Vannutelli'. Episodes of Garibaldi's invasion of 1867. Historical notes extracted from his journal. Rome, Salviucci, 1869.

[6]   The narrative of the chaplain Vincenzo Vannutelli has been largely disavowed by trustworthy contemporaries and serene, impartial historians. Vannutelli had every interest, one understands, in highlighting Garibaldi and his valiant companions. Gregorovius, a historian usually so impartial and certain, can only be reproached for having paid too much heed to what was then being propagated in Urbe by the adversaries of Rome as the capital of Italy, and although he certainly did not accept as sacrosanct truth what the chaplain of the Zouaves had written. The following words prove this:

"The reader will have noticed that the Roman monk of 1867 describes the Garibaldini with the naivety with which Herodotus described the Scythians or Villani the Huns. When, still a prisoner, but escaped death and disguised, he was travelling on the Spoleto railway line, in a train full of Garibaldians returning to Umbria, on passing through a tunnel, as the train slowed down, he, looking around, thought: 'Here is an exact picture of hell. The uncertain light of the carriage, the underground race, the din of the train, the clamour of all these men dressed in red, everything contributes to making me believe I have plunged into the deepest of infernal abysses'.

[7]   "After the taking of Monterotondo, many made themselves, in the brocade of their priestly robes, the badges of an officer, presented themselves to their supposed subordinates and said: 'You see, I am a lieutenant, captain, and so on; to which was replied: 'I am a lieutenant, captain, and so on.

I stand with mocking applause, whistles and other high-pitched sounds they made by putting their fingers in their mouths'.

[8] Pantaleone defended his former comrade, who was to be shot. Even relatives, whom he had among the Garibaldians, spoke in his defence; other young men shielded him with their bodies against the furious men, who wanted to finish him off, and who were instigated by an emancipated countess, a certain Martini, who advised them to *pass him off*. The monk was set free, but interned in Perugia, from where he happily returned to Rome.

[9] The Roman marquis Capranica translated *The Albigensians* and *Savonarola* by Lenau; but these versions are still unpublished.

[10] Since the year 1858, in which I was writing these pages, many things have changed in Rome's literary circles. The sympathetic Giovanni Torlonia died on 9 November 1858 at the age of 27, leaving an irreparable void in the young school. Nannarelli was called to Milan as a professor at the Academy; the lawyer Ciampi happily carried out his faculties, and is now a successful author of comedies in verse. Recently, the Roman officer Muratori has also acquired a good reputation as a dramatic poet. (*Author's note*).

[11] Otto III. Rom. Imp. Germ. Ob Patrata Crimina Austeriori Disciplinae Sancti Romualdi Obtemperans Emenso Nudis Pedibus Ab Urbe Romana Ad Garganum Montem Itinere Basilicam Hanc Et Coenobium Classense XXXX Diebus Poenitens Inhabitavit Et Hic Cilicio Ac Voluntariis Castigationibus Peccata Sua Expians Augustum Dedit Humilitatis Exemplum Et Imperator Sibi Templum Hoc Et Poenitentiam Suam Nobilitavit Anno DCM.

ABOUT THE AUTHOR

Ferdinand Gregorovius

Gregorovius was the son of Wilhelmine Charlotte Dorothea Kausch and Ferdinand Timotheus Gregorovius, the Neidenburg District Justice Council. An older ancestor by the name of Grzegorzewski had migrated from Poland to Prussia. Over the course of their more than 300 years in Prussia, members of the Gregorovius family produced several judges, preachers, and painters. One of Ferdinand's well-known ancestors was Johann Adam  Gregorovius, who was born in Johannisburg, in the Gumbinnen district, in 1681.

Ferdinand Gregorovius was raised in Neidenburg, East Prussia (now Nidzica, Poland), and attended the University of KÃ¶nigsberg to study theology and philosophy. He joined the Corps Masovia, a student organization, in 1838. After spending several years as a teacher, Gregorovius moved to Italy in 1852 and stayed there for more than twenty years. In 1876, he became the first German to be named an honorary citizen of Rome. He has both a square and a roadway named after him. He ultimately made it back to Germany, where he passed away in Munich.

His two most famous works are the massive Die Geschichte der Stadt Rom im Mittelalter (History of Rome in the Middle Ages), a classic for Medieval and early Renaissance history, and Wanderjahre in Italien, his description of his foot adventures through Italy in the 1850s. In addition, he translated Italian authors into German, including Giovanni Melis, and authored biographies of Pope Alexander VI and Lucrezia Borgia, as well as books on Byzantine history and medieval Athens. Father John Hardon, a Jesuit, described S.J. Gregorovius as "a bitter enemy of the popes."

Printed in Great Britain
by Amazon